NIGHTMARELAND

NIGHTMARELAND

Travels at the Borders of
Sleep, Dreams, and Wakefulness

LEX "LONEHOOD" NOVER

A TARCHERPERIGEE BOOK

tarcher
perigee

An imprint of Penguin Random House LLC

penguinrandomhouse.com

Most TarcherPerigee books are available at special quantity discounts for bulk purchase for sales promotions, premiums, fund-raising, and educational needs. Special books or book excerpts also can be created to fit specific needs. For details, write: SpecialMarkets@penguinrandomhouse.com.

Library of Congress Cataloging-in-Publication Data

Names: Nover, Lex Lonehood, author.
Title: Nightmareland : travels at the borders of sleep, dreams, and wakefulness / Lex Lonehood Nover.
Description: New York : TarcherPerigee, an imprint of Penguin Random House, 2019. | Includes bibliographical references and index. | Summary: "From a Coast to Coast AM insider, a mind-expanding exploration of sleep disorders and unusual dream states—the scientific explanations and the paranormal possibilities"—Provided by publisher.
Identifiers: LCCN 2019021679 | ISBN 9780143132844 (trade paperback) | ISBN 9780525504726 (ebook)
Subjects: LCSH: Sleep disorders. | Dreams. | Parapsychology.
Classification: LCC RC547 .N68 2019 | DDC 154.6—dc23
LC record available at https://lccn.loc.gov/2019021679

p.   cm.

Printed in the United States of America

1   3   5   7   9   10   8   6   4   2

Book design by Lorie Pagnozzi

To the night sky:
Inky and black, dappled with stars,
mysterious as hell.

CONTENTS

INTRODUCTION

The mind is a curious cocktail. Though our consciousness is cordoned off into three basic states—deep sleep, REM (rapid eye movement), and waking—these "locations" have porous borders, inviting bleed-throughs and mixtures. Odd chimeras of experience during or adjacent to sleep and dreams hint at wider and hidden aspects of ourselves and the strange territory we may traverse, from the savage and frightening to the astounding and sublime.

The sleeping mind is a mysterious backdrop that science is just beginning to shed light on. Consider that it was only sixty-some years ago that researchers discovered REM, the rapid eye movement cycle that's correlated with dreams. More recently still, the state of sleep paralysis, known since antiquity and often associated with the supernatural, has been legitimized by scientific and medical researchers.

Before it became associated with disturbing dreams, the word *nightmare* was actually used to denote sleep paralysis, the uniquely petrifying combination of REM and wakefulness that is the launchpad for this book. Sleep paralysis, with one tentacle in the surreality of the dreamworld and the other in a frozen, yet wide-awake awareness of one's actual surroundings, rockets to a place where the paranormal, folklore, and science overlap, and then diverge. The incubus, the Old Hag, and vampiric demons are some of the "friends" we'll meet.

Our journey continues with the panoply of aberrant activity

called parasomnias. These include relatively benign behavior such as sleep talking, diet-busting sleep eating, and more potentially dangerous activities such as "did I or didn't I?" sexsomnia, as well as sleepwalking and sleep driving that can take the somnambulant out into the world. There's also REM sleep disorder, in which people seem to be acting out their dreams, thrashing their limbs, or sometimes punching the air or their unlucky bed partner. Even more alarming are the "Ambien zombies," who act out bizarre actions and sometimes crimes they have no memory of later.

It's estimated that in the United States around 8.4 million people sleepwalk each year. On rare occasions, something goes horribly wrong. Worldwide, around seventy people have been murdered by those claiming to be sleepwalking. We'll take an unflinching look at what happens when someone commits murder in their sleep. Even when a killer is able to show evidence they were sleepwalking, is their subconscious somehow liable?

Afraid of what you might do in your sleep? On the reverse end, if you try to go without it for long periods, your brain will insert REM hallucinations and microsleep intervals that can turn into waking nightmares for those behind the wheel on a long drive. Encompassing radio DJ stunts, consciousness explorers, torture victims, and people with the rare, fatal familial insomnia disorder, stretches of sleep deprivation delineate a remarkable if mostly harrowing road map of what happens when our shut-eye is shut down.

Beyond sleep paralysis, even "normal" nightmares can shake a person to the core. Who hasn't woken up in a sweat, relieved that yes, it was only a dream, yet still imprinted by the disturbing experience or even feeling a physical residue? Once, when my teeth turned inside out in a nightmare, my mouth hurt upon waking. Research has found what separates a nightmare from a mere bad dream is that a nightmare will wake you up either out of fear or to escape the scene. Steel yourself for a deep dive into extreme dreams and recurring nightmares, and, if we dare, facing our subconscious monsters head-on.

I'll introduce you to a slippery borderland where phantom images, faces, and phosphenes float unbidden through the mind's eye. In the hypnagogic state, tenuously perched between waking and sleep, a person may have heightened sensitivities to PSI and mediumistic communications with spirits and the dead. Synesthetic glimpses defy translation. Shamans enter this liminal realm like a gateway or portal, while artists such as Salvador Dali have culled some of their unforgettable surrealistic images from it.

We'll navigate the mental minefield, where it can be difficult to distinguish between REM-fed phantasms and external apparitions of torment. Some contend that behind the curtain of sleep and dreams, it's open season for attacks and interference by a grab bag of ghosts, poltergeists, and astral entities. But it's not only the spirit realm that can put its spectral hooks in us—people with strong psychic skills are said to be able to mentally attack others, particularly in the susceptible sleep state, sending out havoc-inducing thought-forms.

Do aliens represent other-dimensional beings, similar to astral entities that can occasionally intersect with our reality? A number of researchers have declared in a sort of "case closed" mind-set that most reports of alien abduction are simply misunderstood episodes of sleep paralysis. Yet the typical pattern of similar-looking Greys conducting repetitive examinations and experiments aboard UFOs doesn't really jibe with the unique entities or presences conjured during sleep paralysis. Peering into bedroom abductions and their proximity to sleep, we'll look for explanations of aliens in the shifting sands of consciousness and in the context of other paranormal phenomena.

Finally, we'll explore the fascinating world of lucid dreams, where the dreamer becomes consciously aware they're dreaming and can exert some control over a malleable environment. Another phenomenon, only verified by scientists in the last few decades, "awakened" dreaming offers a pathway to revolutionizing one's dreamworld, tapping into creativity, expanding self-knowledge, and evolving as a spiritual being . . . or just having a bunch of wild adventures and fantasy sex. And yet, in recent years, there've been whispers of the "dark side of lucid dreaming" generally not spoken of in the workshop circuit. For truly unbalanced individuals, lucid dreaming may trigger combustible consequences.

Thank you for letting me be your GPS as we wind our way through the darkly illuminating labyrinth I call Nightmareland, where the borderline is the destination.

—*Lex "Lonehood" Nover*
October 2018

CHAPTER ONE
SLEEP PARALYSIS

The year was 1999, and I was living in New York City, a bit jittery as the millennium beckoned. It was late at night, and I was listening to Art Bell on the radio, who at the time was the maestro of the strange and paranormal. But then, as it sometimes happens when listening to the radio in bed in the wee hours—I fell asleep.

Only I didn't fall asleep in the way I usually do. I had entered a quasi-dream state in which I was conscious of my physical surroundings and the live radio show, and yet a menacing being was materializing in full view. I was terrified but couldn't react. My body was completely frozen. I was watching a green-eyed blond man dangling from the ceiling, as though in a web. Stark naked, he seemed to loom over me with a murderous intent, as an innocuous commercial for shortwave radios played in my ear. The event seemed tortuously long but probably spanned less than a minute before the paralysis ended and the figure vanished.

I had encountered such a state once before, and so I recognized it as an episode of sleep paralysis (SP). But that earlier experience happened without a point of reference. It both alarmed and intrigued me. I searched for something that might help explain what had happened to me but couldn't find much. This was before the Internet. Even so, I learned that the event had a name and that I wasn't the only person who had experienced it.

It took me years to share my story, probably for fear people would think I was crazy. I first wrote about SP back in 2001. Since then, there's been a profusion of research, books, articles, and online forums on the topic. But even now, many people are still unfamiliar with this curious and terrifying state. Like me, those who have experienced it may be shy about telling others, ashamed or embarrassed.

It's surprising that SP remains in the shadows given that some 40 percent of the population will experience it at least once in their lives, with a much smaller percentage plagued by repeat episodes.[1] Reports of the phenomenon date back thousands of years. Galen, an influential physician of the second century AD, attributed it to indigestion, though the malady has been associated with a vast array of causes over the centuries, including carbon dioxide poisoning of the brain, an elongated uvula, and the consumption of West Indian alligator pears.[2]

Across cultures, a great deal of supernatural lore has accumulated in tales of the incubus and the Old Hag. The original Anglo-Saxon definition of *nightmare* comes from *nicht* (*night*) and *mara* (*incubus*). We'll delve into accounts of the incubus and succubus (female demon), along with other beings, a bit later, but for now, here's a look at the nuts and bolts of a typical SP occurrence:

- The person knows they are completely awake and not asleep and are typically supine.

- They have a realistic view of their room or environment, and their eyes may be open.

- Except for the eyes, the body is completely paralyzed.

- There is a sensed presence in the room, accompanied by an overwhelming feeling of fear and dread.

- A heavy pressure is felt on the chest, and there is difficulty in breathing.

Additionally, a variety of voices, sounds, and vibrations are sometimes reported as nonsensical language, buzzing, tingling, or even a kind of electrocution, along with floating or out-of-body sensations. Things get even creepier in cases when the "presence" takes form and starts to interact with the experiencer.

An experience of SP is recounted by "Ron" in David Hufford's seminal 1982 book *The Terror That Comes in the Night*. Ron describes an episode when he was living in a fraternity and had come home dead tired in the middle of the afternoon and decided to take a nap. He fell into a deep sleep lying on his back. A door slamming woke him up, but when he opened his eyes, no one was there. Ron could hear a stereo playing from a nearby room. "But the next thing I knew, I realized I couldn't move. . . . I was able to look around the room. And I started to feel (chest) pressure. . . . And it increased. . . . I just laid there."

Ron said an amorphous being suddenly emerged in his room. "This grayish, brownish murky presence was there. And it kind of swept down over the bed and I was terrified! I can't remember when I was this scared! . . . It was kind of like a surrealistic shape. . . . It was like nothing I had ever seen before. . . . I felt this pressing down all over me. . . . I couldn't breathe. I couldn't move." This undefined presence stood over him with a glare that he described as evil. He felt an enveloping pressure and struggled to get out from under it. Eventually, Ron was able to move his arm and the presence quickly dissipated. "But everything else just remained the same. The same stereo was playing next door."[3]

During an SP experience, the sensed apparition or hallucination can evolve from a shadowy form to an actual entity, at first seen from a distance. "Bad odors are frequently reported, which is striking as most dreams do not include this sense impression," remarks dream researcher Ryan Hurd, who adds that the intruder's (or intruders', in some cases) appearance is unique for each person, and accounts have included "demons, hairy monsters, disfigured people, hooded figures with gleaming red or yellow eyes, the Devil, witches, hags . . . [and] aliens."[4] If the SP victim is not able to end the paralysis, the entity may actually initiate physical contact, sitting on the person's chest or choking them, as well as making sexual advances.

Research professor and pharmacologist Ronald K. Siegel experienced an SP episode in which a gelatinous "succubus" climbed into his bed and straddled him, whispering in what sounded like backward spoken English from a mouth that stunk of tobacco. The intruder's hand felt cold and dead but "she" had him in a tight grip, squeezing him "like a soda straw" in a suffocating mix of sexual intoxication and terror. Siegel hypothesizes that hyperventilating during sleep paralysis reduces the brain's supply of oxygen, and this may contribute to the hallucinations as well as triggering a sexual response not unlike the practice of autoerotic asphyxiation.[5]

In his book *Dark Intrusions*, paranormal researcher Louis Proud, who frequently experiences sleep paralysis, describes a hideous being that seemed surprised to encounter him, as though it were seeing a human for the first time. "With its large wrinkly head, and glassy black eyes, the entity resembled some sort of troll. Still paralyzed, I lay there studying it for a moment. The entity looked startled, embarrassed even, for it must have assumed I was sound asleep." Then, Proud continued, it rose up in the air and in a manner of seconds began to shrink, as though it were being sucked down a tube.[6]

Not all intruders are humanoid. Prof. Chris French, the founder of Goldsmiths' Anomalistic Psychology Research Unit, relates the account of one of his students, Peter Moore, who used to be a frequent SP sufferer. One night, he awoke to find himself paralyzed and nearly unable to breathe. "He could see his bedroom and managed to tilt his head, only to see an evil-looking black cat sitting there hissing at him," French recalled. "But what was most terrifying about this vision was that the cat's white skull was inverted and dripping some sort of black goo. By a huge effort of will, he finally managed to break out of his paralysed state with the intention of attacking his visitor, only to find himself delivering a right hook to thin air."[7]

BATWINGS, ELVES, AND CRONES: SLEEP PARALYSIS AROUND THE WORLD

Before we plunge into the scientific and paranormal explanations, let's take a spin around the globe, in a kind of "Olympics parade" of sleep paralysis, to sample the cultural terms and interpretations applied in different locales.

Perhaps best known in North America is "Old Hag," an expression native to Newfoundland, where SP is not an uncommon occurrence. By saying "I had Old Hag last night," a Newfoundlander can quickly convey what otherwise might take ten or fifteen minutes to explain.[8] In his study of the phenomenon there, David Hufford notes that the locals sometimes referred to the victim of an attack as being "hag rid," which may represent part of the etymology of the word *haggard*. Regardless, Hufford writes, "the word 'haggard' has been as thoroughly laundered of its original supernatural connections as has the word 'nightmare.'"[9]

Called *kanashibari* ("bound by metal") in Japan, the phenomenon is depicted in folktales and manga as a magical power used by monks to immobilize people and animals, as well as in popular TV shows. "Almost all Japanese . . . know the word [*kanashibari*] for this usage. Some believe the phenomenon is caused by spiritual beings, some not," psychologist Kazuhiko Fukuda of Edogawa University told *The Atlantic*.[10]

On the island nation of Saint Lucia, and elsewhere in the Caribbean, an attack of the *kokma* is said to occur when someone is either just falling asleep or waking up. Islanders believe it's the spirit of a dead baby haunting the area that's attacking them, jumping on their chest, or clutching their throat.[11]

In the far north Arctic regions, native people speak of *agumangia* and *ukomiarik*, in which the paralyzed person feels a "soul" try to take possession of them.[12] Among the Inuit, the experience is closely linked to the spirit world and "the frightening manifestation of a shapeless, or faceless, presence."[13]

Dab tsog, an evil nightmare spirit, afflicts the Hmong of Laos.

Some Hmong refugees to the United States have died suddenly in their sleep, in what appears to be SP-related cardiac arrest. These cases of sudden unexplained nocturnal death syndrome (SUNDS) will be explored later in the chapter.

On the Hawaiian islands, the *Hauka'I po* ("Night Marchers") are conceived of as avenging spirit warriors from the ancient days. In a more auditory spin on SP, the heavy sound of their footsteps and drums strikes fear as they grow nearer because it's said that looking into the warriors' eyes will bring death.[14]

According to German lore, the Alp is a demonic being or elf that attacks and paralyzes people in their sleep, in what is called *Alpdrücke* ("elf pressure"). They are said to be able to enter one's sleeping chambers through the keyhole of a closed door.[15]

In Zanzibar, a *Popobawa* ("bat-wing") assault may involve someone waking up in the night to find themselves being "attacked by an amorphous or shape-shifting intruder which was most frequently described as 'pressing' or 'crushing' their chest and ribs," as described by social anthropologist Martin Walsh. Unfortunately, this led to a panic in 1995, when frenzied mobs killed or attacked strangers suspected of being manifestations of *Popobawa*.[16] A similar panic took place in Tanzania in 2007, when sex attacks were blamed on the bat demon. "Some men are staying awake or sleeping in groups outside their homes. Others are smearing themselves with pig's oil, believing this repels attacks," the BBC reported.[17]

The lovely sounding *Kikimora* is not so lovely to those in Slavic countries such as Poland and parts of Russia, where this female house spirit (said to grow from a dead fetus or stillborn child) disturbs both men and women during their sleep.[18]

In Brazilian folklore, the *Pisadeira* is described as "a crone with long fingernails who lurks on roofs at night and tramples on the chest of those who sleep on a full stomach with the belly up." The *Pisadeira* is believed to be a descendant of the Portuguese myth *Fradinho da Mão Furada* ("Little Hand-Hole Friar"), in which the Friar enters people's bedrooms "and places his 'heavy hand' upon their chest, preventing them from screaming."[19]

A DEMON FOR THE ARTS

While it's fascinating to observe how a shared neurobiological and/or paranormal phenomenon is understood through different cultural filters, SP has also been portrayed in major works of art and literature over the years, and more recently in films and documentaries. The most ubiquitous image is Henry Fuseli's 1781 oil painting *The Nightmare*. The painting, in which a demonic imp leers at the viewer while sitting atop the chest of a sleeping or unconscious woman (as a mysterious horse peers through a curtain), created a sensation during its first London exhibition in 1782. There even were rumors that Fuseli dined on raw pork to induce his nightmarish inspirations.[20] Art historian Dr. Noelle Paulson remarks that Fuseli's masterwork prefigures Sigmund Freud's psychoanalytic theories regarding dreams and the unconscious. Allegedly, Freud kept a reproduction of the painting on the wall of his home in Vienna.[21]

Mary Shelley, meanwhile, came up with the idea for *Frankenstein* while vacationing with a distinguished group that included Lord Byron, John Polidori, and her future husband, the poet Percy Bysshe Shelley. One weekend, they decided to write horror stories to combat the boredom from being kept inside by bad weather. But she drew a blank, and it was only after Mary had a "waking dream" akin to an SP experience, late one evening, that the idea for the horror classic came to her.[22]

Jason Jam portrays the unbridled terror of sleep
paralysis in his 2016 drawing *On the Ceiling*.

Not surprisingly, the master of melancholy and the macabre,
Edgar Allan Poe, incorporated the SP phenomenon in his work as
well. Here is an excerpt from his "The Fall of the House of Usher"
(1845):

Sleep came not near my couch—while the hours waned and waned away. I struggled to reason off the nervousness which had dominion over me. I endeavored to believe that much, if not all of what I felt, was due to the bewildering influence of the gloomy furniture of the room—of the dark and tattered draperies, which, tortured into motion by the breath of a rising tempest. . . . But my efforts were fruitless. An irrepressible tremor gradually pervaded my frame; and, at length, there sat upon my very heart an incubus of utterly causeless alarm. Shaking this off with a gasp and a struggle, I uplifted myself upon the pillows, and, peering earnestly within the intense darkness of the chamber, hearkened—I know not why, except that an instinctive spirit prompted me—to certain low and indefinite sounds which came, through the pauses of the storm, at long intervals, I knew not whence. Overpowered by an intense sentiment of horror, unaccountable yet unendurable, I threw on my clothes with haste (for I felt that I should sleep no more during the night).[23]

Other authors who've included descriptions or allusions to SP include Herman Melville, F. Scott Fitzgerald, and Ernest Hemingway. In a more commercial context, Prof. Shelley Adler writes about how in 1997, Reebok started marketing a women's running shoe called the Incubus, perhaps an indication of how far the word's original meaning had fallen off the radar. "More than 50,000 shoes were sold over the period of a year," she writes, "before someone realized that a demon that attacked women in their sleep was a poor choice of namesake for women's athletic apparel."[24]

A GLITCH IN THE SYSTEM

In the midtwentieth century, psychologists and psychiatrists applied psychoanalytic interpretations to hallucinatory sleep paralysis episodes and considered them to be indicators of a variety of mental health and neurological issues, including psychosis, epilepsy, and that Freudian chestnut, "repressed homosexuality." It wasn't until 1967 that psychiatrist Sim Liddon associated modern SP accounts with the folkloric tales and declared that "the experience of sleep paralysis has no specific psychological meaning in itself and that it might be interpreted by different patients in different ways."[25]

In the 1970s, Hufford's pioneering studies of Old Hag accounts in Newfoundland, along with the work of sociologist Robert Ness, reinforced the idea that generally healthy people were experiencing SP and that it wasn't that uncommon. This further eroded the associations of SP with psychopathology,[26] though people with narcolepsy and post-traumatic stress disorder (PTSD) may be prone to higher occurrences of it.[27] The paralysis that can be so disturbing actually stems from a natural part of the sleep cycle. During REM (the rapid eye movement phase of sleep that is associated with dreaming), the body is immobilized, aside from darting eye movements. The muscle atonia or paralysis serves the useful purpose of preventing people from moving around or acting out their dreams and is accomplished through the inhibition of motor neurons.[28]

REM sleep is sometimes called "paradoxical sleep," as the brain is highly activated in the dream state but the body is frozen. A sleeper typically goes through a set cycle, starting with three to four stages of non-REM sleep that move from lighter to deeper periods, followed by REM sleep. This cycle repeats through the night, usually four or five times. SP could be considered a kind of "out-of-sequence" REM state that occurs while the sleeper is partially conscious, either when first falling asleep or when just waking up. This glitch in the system carries paralysis into the waking state, along with a blending or superimposing of "hallucinatory" dream content into one's actual environment. This is often interpreted as a threatening "sensed presence," which kicks off the brain's fight-or-flight response.

University of Waterloo psychologist J. A. Cheyne, one of the world's leading experts on the phenomenon, suggests that the sense of presence and its associated terror during SP "are a result of activation of the amygdala. . . . In normal emergency fear reactions, the immediate sensing of danger is quickly confirmed or disconfirmed . . . but in the absence of exogenous [external] origins, attempts to analyze the source of fear will inevitably fail to produce corroboration. Hence the state of apprehensive suspicion that normally might last only milliseconds may last many seconds or even minutes during SP."[29]

With fight-or-flight options off the table, and coupled with the sensation of weight on the chest from not being able to breathe deeply due to the paralysis, the person is driven into a deepening feedback loop of fear. Are they inadvertently feeding their own living nightmare? I've noticed in regular dreams, when sometimes you're initially suspicious of a dream character, they can end up acting out your worst fears about them, so perhaps there's an element of the self-fulfilling prophecy taking place with the SP intruder.

FEAR AND LOATHING

The intense fear and dread evoked by some encounters are almost without parallel. One Korean War veteran who'd been in the battle-front for thirteen straight months said all that paled to a 1964 sleep paralysis episode: "Never, before or since, have I ever experienced the fear of that night."[30] Nineteenth-century sleep researcher Dr. Robert Macnish described how "the whole mind . . . is wrought up to a pitch of unutterable despair . . . and the wretched victim feels as if pent alive in his coffin, or overpowered by resistless and unmitigable pressure."

"At one moment," Dr. Macnish continued, a person may have "the consciousness of a malignant demon" at their side. "Then to shun the sight of so appalling an object, he will close his eyes, but still the fearful being makes its presence known; for its icy breath is felt diffusing itself over his visage, and he knows he is face to face with a fiend. Then, if he looks up, he beholds horrid eyes glaring upon him . . . Or he may have the idea of a monstrous hag squatted upon his breast—mute, motionless and malignant; an incarnation of the evil spirit—whose intolerable weight crushes the breath out of his body, and whose fixed, deadly, incessant stare petrifies him with horror and makes his very existence insufferable."[31]

SUNDS: SUDDEN UNEXPLAINED NOCTURNAL DEATH SYNDROME

SP can scare the hell out of you, but can it actually kill you? In the early 1980s, young male immigrants to the United States from Southeast Asia were dying mysteriously in their sleep at a rate higher than the combined top five causes of death for other American men in their age group.[32] Among the 117 or so deaths within a few years, the median age was just thirty-three, and all but one of the men were reportedly in good health. None had complained of illness before going to sleep. Relatives were sometimes awakened by the sound of gasping or moaning, but the sleeper would be dead within just a minute or two and unable to be revived.[33] Reading about these cases inspired director and writer Wes Craven to conjure the horror movie icon Freddy Krueger and the premise of the *Nightmare on Elm Street* series.

"I'd read an article in the *L.A. Times* about a family who had escaped the Killing Fields in Cambodia and managed to get to the U.S. Things were fine, and then suddenly the young son was having very disturbing nightmares," Craven told *Vulture* in 2014. "He told his parents he was afraid that if he slept, the thing chasing him would get him, so he tried to stay awake for days at a time. When he finally fell asleep, his parents thought this crisis was over. Then they heard screams in the middle of the night. By the time they got to him, he was dead. He died in the middle of a nightmare."[34]

While numerous medical studies around the time led to inconclusive results, Prof. Adler revisited the incidents decades later from a medical anthropology perspective, interviewing Hmong men and women (many from Laos) about their traditional belief system and sleep paralysis experiences. Though some of the Hmong had converted to Christianity since immigrating to the United States, they retained belief in the *dab tsog* (pronounced "da cho"), an evil nocturnal spirit that can smother or crush men and assault women in their sleep.

What Adler uncovered was that the Hmong believed they were more susceptible to such attacks if they didn't honor their ancestor spirits with various rituals that typically involve animal sacrifice. In their new homes in America, conducting these rituals had become more difficult and often fell by the wayside.

Not only were the Hmong under the stressful situation of adapting to a new country, as well as PTSD from the Vietnam War, but they were under the sway of powerful nocebo effects. Referring to nocebo as "the evil twin of placebo," Adler explains how "the phenomenon produces an unpleasant or harmful outcome as a consequence of a person's belief."[35] Fears of *dab tsog* were so great that some of the Hmong men would set their alarms to go off every twenty to thirty minutes to bring them out of sleep.[36] Further, "once you are visited by one of the *dab tsog* evil spirits . . . often they will come back to you, until you have the worst nightmare and probably die," one of the Laotian refugees told Adler.[37]

It was eventually revealed that many of the SUNDS victims had Brugada syndrome, a hidden genetic abnormality that causes a disruption of the heart's normal rhythm and is particularly prevalent in those of Asian descent. Adler deduced that what caused the deaths of the healthy young men was the treacherous combination of the nocebo effect from belief in the *dab tsog* and their cardiac vulnerability.

AN ASTRAL HYPOTHESIS

Consider a parallel track for understanding SP, running alongside the neurobiological explanation. Could low-level astral entities and spirits invisibly exist all around us? These astral spirits might nourish themselves on human energy, the way dust mites in our beds happily dine on our sloughed-off skin and hair. "The evidence seems to suggest," writes Louis Proud, "that all imperfect spirits are energy vampires to some extent,"[38] and human fear, in particular, is a prime source for their replenishment.

Further, Proud continues, many SP attacks take place either when a victim is staying in a haunted house, just after a "curse" has been placed on them, or after engaging in spirit communications such as the Ouija board. Such patterns suggest that at least some SP incidents are "directly related to the influence of spirits," he writes. We will discuss this further in Chapter 7.

If SP is a kind of trance state that may last for some duration, it could well be a direct portal into the spirit realm, as well as "the main means by which spirits, alien beings, and maybe even UFOs are able to enter and leave our dimension," Proud proposes, adding that the impinging spirit realm and its inhabitants may have a profound influence on our lives, one much greater than we can imagine or comprehend.[39]

INCUBUS AND INCUBATION

An incubus, derived from the Latin word *incubare*, refers to a demon that visits a person in their sleep, often sitting or exerting a heavy pressure on the sleeper. It's interesting that *incubus* and *incubate* share the same root meaning: to lie or sit on. While incubation is something creatures do to keep their developing eggs warm, in the dream context, we think of it as a technique wherein one "plants a seed" in their mind before going to sleep in order to get solutions to a question or problem. But in the ancient era, this was not an at-home practice but rather an elaborate ritual. People traveled great distances to Greek and Egyptian temples and elsewhere to receive divine dreams and healing from gods like Asclepius and Imhotep.

Descending to a "pit" or "earth-womb" of the temple for their incubatory sleep,[40] the dreamer sometimes slept on the skin or hide of a freshly sacrificed animal. The healing sanctuaries, British writer Sarah Janes notes, were a kind of "hospital for the spirit body" and "filled with living snakes" moving freely throughout the subterranean chambers. The slithering creatures served as sacred symbols of medicine and regeneration.[41] Inscriptions at places like the Temple of Asclepius at Epidaurus suggest that the "incubant" received a visitation while either dreaming or "in a strange state between sleep and waking."[42]

Many came to the "sleep temples" for sterility cures. Andromache of Epirus was said to visit Epidaurus and dreamed that the god raised her dress and touched her abdomen, and this led to the birth of a son. Another incubant, Andromeda of Chios, was visited by a god who appeared in the form of a snake that lay on her. She hit the fertility jackpot and bore five sons![43]

As the ancient pagan traditions fell away, notions of the incubus and succubus became diabolized in the Christian faith, and around the year 1400, it was declared that sexual relations with incubi (formerly thought to occur only against a person's will) could be entered into voluntarily by witches who sought out this kind of infernal congress,[44] paving the way for the three hundred-year-long tragedy of the witch hunts.

While initially there was some disagreement in Catholic doctrine as to whether an incubus could actually father a child, the esteemed theologian Thomas Aquinas worked out the mechanics of "demon lovers," and his reasoning was widely adopted by the Church. Prof. Walter Stephens outlines the Aquinas explanation: "To sire human children, a demon first becomes a succubus by constructing the body of a woman from air and vapors. The demon assumes or inhabits this body, using it to steal semen from a man by having sex with him. Then the demon transgenders itself, giving its virtual body male form and becoming an incubus. Having sex with a woman, the incubus injects the stolen semen into her."[45] Strange and sometimes powerful offspring were said to be the result of these "unholy" unions, including the legendary wizard Merlin (son of an incubus and a nun), Caesar, Alexander the Great, Plato, and even the entire population of the island of Cyprus.[46]

Perhaps the first woman burned to death for having sexual relations with the Devil was Angéle de la Barthe, a prosperous resident of Toulouse, France, whose worldly goods were confiscated in 1275 (even before there were laws on the books against congress with demons). She confessed under torture to having sex with an incubus every night for years. Their spawn was a "monster" with a wolf's head and a snakelike tail that she said lived off the flesh of dead babies. Her confession detailed how she murdered children and then dug up their bodies at remote church graveyards to feed to her child before it eventually ran away.[47] Some have called into question the story, as there are no records in Toulouse of her trial in that time period.[48] Still, it speaks to the gruesome climate that was to overtake Europe, and America to some degree, as demons became a legal "reality" and thousands of people were executed under the belief that they'd used powers of the Devil to bring misfortune and ill will to others.

To what extent is this related to SP? I would argue there's a connection. For the belief in demonic entities to become so widespread and intractable, it's possible such creatures were witnessed not only by the "witches" but by the Church canonists themselves, seeing with eyes wide open supernatural beings with evil intent while straitjacketed with sleep paralysis.

WITCHES, VAMPIRES, AND LORE

Many cultures around the world have blamed the occurrence of SP on demonic or witchlike entities. So it's not a surprise that "nocturnal oppression" occasionally came up as an accusation during the witch trials. In England's prosecution of Olive Barthram in 1599, one of her alleged victims testified that a shape-changing spirit sent by Barthram tormented her at night after entering via the chimney. It appeared as a "thick dark substance about a foot high," though on one late evening it solidified as a cat, first scraping on the walls, before "slavering" her with kisses and lying on her breast. Then "he pressed her so sore that she could not speak, at other times he held her hands that she could not stir, and restrained her voice that she could not answer."[49]

"An animal the length of a man had come into their bed and lain on him, being so heavy that he was unable to make the sign of the cross with his hand, but had to do it with his tongue," reported Mongin André during a witch trial in Lorraine, France. The "animal," André said, was none other than a neighbor named Jacquot Petit Jacquot, whom he'd seen enter through the keyhole of the door.[50] Heaviness on the chest also figured in a 1747 Hungarian trial, in which a wife found her husband frozen stiff, barely breathing. When he came out of it, he uttered "My Lord Jesus, help me! Oh! Fiery witches took me to Máramaros and they put six hundredweight of salt on me."[51]

Such examples indicate that the accusers' nightmare attacks were not only "powerful confirmation of their bewitchment, but also, through their hallucinatory experiences . . . conclusive proof of the identity of the witch," writes Owen Davies.[52]

According to the *Malleus Maleficarum* (The Witches' Hammer), the odious medieval treatise by Heinrich Kramer and Jacob Sprenger that became the handbook for witch persecutors, impotence and infertility were a frequent torment that witches placed upon couples, even causing a man's penis to be "bewitched away." Fornication between witches and the Devil or demons (the subject of frequent court testimony) seems to be clearly drawn from the SP/ incubus experience, "and the prevailing theological views of the time lent them the appearance of reality," psychoanalyst Ernest Jones suggests.[53] Of course, since many confessions were obtained under torture, a considerable number of these sexual encounters were likely fabricated.

Folkloric tales of such nocturnal creatures as the vampire and werewolf are steeped in the legacy of the incubus/succubus from ancient times to the present. In his research into Romanian superstitions, Heinrich von Wlislocki details how the "Nosferat" not only sucks the blood of slumbering victims but also "does mischief as an Incubus or Succubus." The undead being, he notes, has hardly been put under the earth "before it awakes to life and leaves its grave never to return. It visits people by night in the form of a black cat, a black dog, a beetle, a butterfly or even a simple straw.... It also appears in the form of a handsome youth or pretty girl while the victim lies half awake and submits unresistingly. It often happens that women are impregnated by the creature and bear children who can be recognized by their ugliness and by their having hair over the whole body.... The Nosferat appears to bridegrooms and brides and makes them impotent and sterile."[54]

One of the most ancient accounts of a vampire is that of Lilith, described in some texts as Adam's first wife. Called the "princess who presided over the Succubi" by the Dutch occultist Johann

Weyer, she drifted from Babylonian and Hebrew lore into medieval demonology.[55] Also called the Winged One and the Strangleress, Lilith is a night demon who erotically entangles men and women who sleep alone. "Attempts to suppress or deny her date from the sixth century BC,"[56] writes psychologist Barbara Black Koltuv, but like the raven, she returns evermore.

The ancient Greeks associated their horned god Pan with *ephialtes* (their name for sleep paralysis), and indeed many have encountered human/animal mixes in this state, as in this case reported by nineteenth-century German psychologist Paul Radestock: "Once in the early hours of the morning I saw appear before me at the foot of my bed a hideous small brute of barely human form. It seemed to be of medium height and to have a thin neck, spare figure, very dark eyes, and a narrow, wrinkled brow. . . . Furthermore, it had a goatsbeard, upright pointed ears—like Pan—dirty dry hair, dog's teeth, a pointed occiput, a projected chest, a humped back, withered hips, and wore dirty clothing. The phantom took hold of the edge of my bed, shook the bed with tremendous force, and said: 'You will not remain here much longer!' . . . I sprang out of bed, hurried to the cloister and threw myself down before the altar and remained there a long time, numbed by fear."[57]

DOORWAY TO THE BEYOND

For those who experience SP a few times in their lives, it's probably chalked up to peculiar happenstance. But to a small group of people, such as Proud, SP occurrences are far more frequent. An intriguing paper by J.-C. Terrillon & S. Marques Bonham profiles the experiences of those with recurrent SP, and many of these cases lead into even further-out-of-bounds territory, suggesting out-of-body experiences (OBEs), near-death experiences, and lucid dreaming:

> If no attempt is made to move, that is, if the fear is overcome or if it is mild, another complex of phenomena sets in: what seems to be a 'phantom body' slowly slips away from the physical body. There seems to be dissociation from the immobile physical body, and consciousness is perceived to reside within the phantom body. At that point, the immediate surroundings of the room may be 'seen,' sometimes vividly, by the phantom body, and a sensation of rising and/or floating, sometimes rolling is experienced. . . . The surroundings appear to the consciousness as they would while in the wake state, eventually with some odd modifications . . . or in another possible scenario, the phantom body may feel accelerated inside a 'tunnel' that seems to appear out of nowhere. . . . The whole process may be repeated several times in the course of one night, in what may be described as a complex of sequential or 'back to back' episodes.[58]

Comparing SP states to the kinds of OBEs that Robert Monroe has documented, Proud writes about how in some cases of SP, there is a kind of partial dislocation of the astral body from the physical body, and a dual awareness that can take place. "Assuming that the astral body leaves the physical body every time we fall asleep," he notes, "it would not be unreasonable to state that the only difference between an SP sufferer and a non-SP sufferer is that the former has some awareness of these astral experiences, these interactions with non-physical beings, and is able to remember them in the morning, while the latter has none."[59]

Intrepidly pondering this hall of mirrors, writer and lucid dreamer Lucy Gillis poses an interesting question from the perspective of an astral body traveler: what if the frightening sensations of SP are the "result of the sleeper himself experiencing difficulty in trying to get back into his body? For example, if the sleeper is jumping on his own chest in an attempt to wake, or get back into, his body, could it translate to the dreaming mind as something terrifying pressing on his chest?"[60]

Stephen LaBerge, a psychophysiologist who was one of the first to scientifically study lucid dreaming, believes SP can be used as a tool to enter into lucidity (becoming aware that you're dreaming while in the midst of a dream). "The next time you experience sleep paralysis simply remember to relax . . . you are on the threshold of REM sleep. You have, as it were, one foot in the dream state and one in the waking state. Just step over and you're in the world of lucid dreams," he writes.[61]

Psychologist Jorge Conesa-Sevilla, the author of *Wrestling with Ghosts*, has also talked about converting SP into a more positive state. "I have wrestled with several hairy beings in my own bedroom for nights at a time; been visited by many hags and beauties, been whispered to, shouted at, buzzed, electrified, boomed, and hurt; been touched, pinched, and caressed by phantoms unseen; cried empty screams without anyone hearing them; been assisted by friendly entities who taught me how to move from the paralysis into lucid dreams; meditated in lucid dreams, attaining sublime bliss; and 'flown' to places indescribable until flight itself is assumed to be an intrinsic right and property of the body-mind."[62]

BREAKING OUT OF PARALYSIS

"When someone is plagued by the incubus," wrote Rufus of Ephesus, "prescribe emetics and laxatives, put the patient on a light diet, purge the head by sneezing and gargling, and later rub in beaver oil and the like to prevent epilepsy."[63]

Even if you're running low on beaver oil in the medicine cabinet, you can take a number of actions to reduce the likelihood of sleep paralysis. One of them is simply to get more sleep, as there is evidence linking insomnia and erratic sleep schedules to SP. When the body is deprived of REM sleep, it can go into rebound mode, compensating with REM that might occur out of the normal cycle.[64]

Aside from the standard "live healthy" adages of the type your mother might espouse—get some exercise, eat a balanced diet, and don't drink alcohol or caffeine before bedtime—one of the leading bits of advice to repel SP is to not sleep on your back, as most SP reports come from people immobilized in this position. However, most sleepers don't start out on their back and may turn to a supine position during sleep, especially when they are entering or moving out of REM sleep.[65] People who frequently experience SP might benefit from what's called the "sleep ball" or "tennis ball" technique, which was developed as a remedy for sleep apnea. A tennis ball is tucked into a pocket sewn into the back of the pajamas, or in a sock pinned to the back of a shirt, and acts as a deterrent to sleeping on your back.[66]

Should you find yourself awake and paralyzed, you can sometimes break out of the hold by wriggling an extremity such as a toe or finger, though it might take all your concentration. Coughing or speaking aloud can also be useful in bursting the SP bubble, or having a sleeping partner shake you awake if it looks like you're struggling.[67]

Once one of the nefarious entities has materialized or made contact, what are your options? Ryan Hurd recommends tamping down your fear and confronting the being in a neutral or empathetic manner, mentally asking what it wants. This may transform the "autonomous other" into something less threatening, he says, while adding that one can't always count on this "spiritual laundromat" effect.[68]

Hurd should know—he's had regular bouts of SP since his youth. To convert some of these frightening incidents into "transcendent" journeys, he's made use of apotropaic magic—an ancient method for warding off malevolent forces. Different objects or amulets placed in strategic thresholds can be imbued with protective or transformative properties and function as liminal objects "traversing both the waking and dreamworld" versions of your room, he explains.[69]

COURTING THE HAG

If you're a horror writer or someone looking to hitchhike into a lucid dream or OBE state, you might choose to seek out SPs rather than avoid them. Ben Guarino writes of a daredevil online subculture gathering on message boards, wikis, and subreddits, comparing notes on how to dive into your worst nightmare. Now there's an extreme sport that Red Bull doesn't yet sponsor. In a kind of reverse engineering, the typical advice involves waking yourself up about halfway through your sleep cycle and then staying awake for thirty minutes. Then you lie on your back and try to stay absolutely still. If you eventually begin to feel a buzzing or vibration moving across your body, try to make a small motion with a finger or toe. If you can't do it, you have officially entered the sleep paralysis zone. Congratulations?

One army recruit posting on Reddit sought to use SP as a kind of combat training: "I know that the first time I see combat I'm either going to shit myself and shut down, or shit myself and power through it. . . . I want to start experimenting with controlling my fear and using it to motivate me. From what I've heard, SP . . . is one of the most psychologically terrifying experiences a kid from the suburbs can have. So if being dream-stabbed by a hallucinated spirit is the closest thing I can get to facing an insurgent who wants nothing more than to kill me and everything I hold dear then yes, shoot me, but I'll take two orders of SP with extra demon on the side."[70]

TURNING THE TABLES

And then there's Jimmy.

As I was finishing this chapter, I happened to mention to my good friend of twenty-five years that I was working on a book on sleep paralysis and related topics. Though I'd known of Jimmy's longtime fascination with the paranormal and the occult, he suddenly "came out" to me as having experienced frequent SP, and proceeded to relate a litany of bizarre and menacing attacks he'd experienced from the age of eleven onward. In addition to the garden-variety Old Hags that pressed down on his chest, there were menacing rubbery doll-like creatures and Lovecraftian reptilians, as cold as ice.

Things reached a crescendo when he was in medical school and sleeping on the fly. He tried various New Age methods of reasoning or engaging with his tormentors, but nothing seemed to work. Finally, one night when a gargoyle-like hag descended upon him in his paralyzed state, he managed to shift into a lucid dream. As the hag pushed down on him, he experienced a moment of clarity. Instead of trying to get away, he did the opposite, pulling her closer. To the shock of the creature, he ripped into her chest, tearing out her heart and eating it. Not only did this savage shamanic exercise dispose of the hag, but the SP episodes began to subside. Physician, heal thyself, they say. But Jimmy came up with a trick they don't teach you in med school.

CHAPTER TWO

PARASOMNIAS

While sleep paralysis may be unsurpassed for sheer fright, it's merely one of a hornet's nest of conditions categorized as parasomnias. Defined as abnormal physical or emotional occurrences that accompany sleep, the term *parasomnia* combines Latin and Greek root words and was coined by French researcher Henri Roger in 1932.[1] The study of sleep itself dates back around 2,500 years when Greek luminaries like Aristotle and Hippocrates probably went without it, pondering and writing about the mysterious state.

Although it's understood that there are just three primary states of being—awake, REM dreaming, and deep sleep—each with their corresponding brain wave patterns, the parasomnias point toward a more porous mental model. When there's a hiccup in the system, the borders of these three states can bleed or blend into each other, creating hybrids. About seventy-five clinical sleep disorders run the gamut from benign or amusing to dangerous or violent. Up to one third of the population will be affected by one of them at some time during their lives, though many may go undiagnosed.[2]

Sleepwalking and sleep talking have been known throughout the ages. Shakespeare's somnambulant Lady Macbeth, for instance, with her "Out, damned spot" speech and imaginary bloodstains, is forever imprinted on our psyches. But a number of parasomnias are fairly recent discoveries, such as REM sleep behavior disorder. Conditions such as these aren't really new, it's just that they've recently been medically classified. Patients have come out of the shadows, learning that they aren't alone (often through the Internet), and medical treatment or intervention is possible.

Instead of counting sheep, try counting sleep clinics, which have multiplied across the United States in recent years. The first opened at Stanford University in 1970, and now the American Academy of Sleep Medicine accredits some 2,500 sleep centers—tech-equipped facilities designed to evaluate and treat disorders and staffed by board-certified sleep medicine physicians.[3] While it's no picnic having your head wired to a bunch of electrodes and sleeping in an observation room, at least compared to days of yore, help is at hand!

The lab diagnosis is accomplished through a polysomnogram, a kind of sleep polygraph test that includes an electroencephalogram (EEG) and measures a variety of physiological parameters during sleep.[4] The tests reveal which brain states are associated with a given parasomnia. My friend Timothy recently visited a sleep clinic in Toronto for possible sleep apnea and said he adjusted relatively quickly to sleeping with the attached electrodes, though the ambiance of the windowless room fell somewhere between a Ramada Inn and a jail cell.

One of the main revelations of the modern sleep lab era is that "the vast majority of those with extreme sleep disorders have psychological profiles that look no different from the rest of the population," writes pioneering psychiatrist Dr. Carlos Schenck of the Minnesota Regional Sleep Disorders Center, one of the first such centers in the United States. Previously, it was thought that those who exhibited strange or disturbing behaviors during their sleep cycle most likely had festering psychological problems.[5]

While there's some overlap in the conditions, in this chapter, we'll unravel some of the individual categories, some common, others less so.

THE SOMNAMBULANT SOCIETY

On a cold winter night in Minneapolis, a wife traced her husband's footprints in the snow, circling a three-block radius of their home. The prints, she realized, traversed their well-trod dog-walking path. The dog had stayed in his warm bed that night, but her husband was being wheeled away in a stretcher. Earlier, he'd awakened to wet sheets and pulled back the covers. What he discovered was far worse than bedwetting. Surrounded by melting snow, his toes were blackened with severe frostbite.[6] The man woke his wife, who called an ambulance. While he was sleepwalking, his brain had not processed the sensory input that would normally inform him that strolling barefoot in the snow was, perhaps, best left for the dog.

Colder climes are a particular threat for sleepwalkers, notes biologist H. Craig Heller of the Stanford Neurosciences Institute, who considers sleepwalking to be the scariest of all the sleep disorders. "Sleepwalking is more an extension of normal waking behavior, but you are not aware of what you are doing," he explained. People can sleepwalk out of the house and freeze to death. "In one case a child was found dead in the morning just curled up in a snowdrift immediately outside his house. Some apparent suicides may even be cases of sleepwalking," he added.[7]

Some sleepwalkers are at first thought to be attempting suicide. Such was the case when a London fire rescue team responded to an emergency call after a teenage girl was spotted on top of a 130-foot crane one summer night in 2005.[8] But the fifteen-year-old was not debating whether to jump; she was curled up sound asleep on the arm of the crane.

A firefighter who scaled the structure was baffled as to how to proceed, fearing that if he startled her, she might fall. He was able to find her mobile phone and call her relatives, who confirmed that she was a frequent sleepwalker. The relatives then rang the girl's phone, and this finally awakened her. She was rescued without further incident.

How the girl managed to climb out on the crane while asleep is mystifying, but Dr. Irshaad Ebrahim of the London Sleep Centre wasn't entirely surprised, as people lack the fear factor while in this state. "I treat people who have driven cars, ridden horses and even attempted to fly a helicopter while asleep," he remarked, adding that up to 10 percent of adolescents sleepwalk, so her age was a common factor.[9]

It's even more common in younger children, with up to 17 percent having episodes.[10] Sleepwalking is generally considered less of a concern for kids than adults,[11] because their nighttime jaunts are more often mellow and lethargic, whereas adults can make quick unexpected movements and act with urgency, as though they were in a hurry to accomplish something,[12] making them more prone to injury.

Few sleepwalkers have found themselves in a more nightmarish plight than seventy-seven-year-old James Currens, who awoke one night in 1998 nearly chest deep in water, his legs stuck in mud, with several alligators, some larger than three feet long, swarming around him in a swampy pond. The Palm Harbor, Florida, resident, known for his nocturnal wanderings, used his cane to bat away the gators, while his neighbors, hearing his cries, summoned the police. Currens escaped with only minor injuries.[13]

VILLAGE OF THE DAMNED

Sleepwalking typically arises out of the non-REM cycle of sleep during the first third of the night, in the deepest sleep stages, which are indicated by delta or slow-wave brain patterns. It is not usually associated with active dreaming, and sleepwalkers most often have no recollection the next morning of what they've done, or where they've gone, though adults tend to have more recall than children. Parents can be unnerved by the *Village of the Damned*–like blank expression of their sleepwalking child and the glassy-eyed stare that seems to "look right through them."[14]

Michael K. shared an intriguing memory with me from his childhood days in a split-level home in New Jersey. When his parents were going through a messy divorce, his mom let him stay up and watch Johnny Carson with her in the living room. On one evening, his younger twin sisters appeared at the top of the stairs. With fixed stares, the identical duo descended the stairs together, sleepwalking side-by-side, straight out of *The Shining*. While his mother had seen this before, Michael was thoroughly spooked.

Perhaps the twins' mirrored behavior is not that surprising given that sleepwalking tends to run in families and is possibly associated with a genetic marker in the HLA complex.[15] Sleep deprivation and medications like Ambien (which we'll cover a bit later) can also be precipitating factors.[16]

Longtime sleep researcher Rosalind Cartwright reported on the brain imaging of a male sleepwalker, which was unusual to achieve in a lab setting. It revealed a "mixed in-between state" with his body active, along with emotional arousal, yet "the higher mental processes of judgment, rational thought, self-reflection, and memory were still asleep."[17]

The idea that sleepwalkers can perform complicated maneuvers such as driving may seem inexplicable, but not to Caltech neuroscientist Christof Koch, who argues in his paper "The Zombie Within" that much of human behavior is automated by an army of unconscious sensory-motor agents. "Zombie agents control your eyes, hands, feet, and posture, and rapidly transduce sensory input into stereotypical motor output. They might even trigger aggressive or sexual behavior when getting a whiff of the right stuff. All, however, bypass consciousness. This is the zombie in you."[18]

Sleepwalkers can be difficult to wake, but it's a myth that arousing them will "scare them to death," writes Dr. Schenck. This belief can be traced back to ancient or indigenous cultures, who thought a person's soul left their body during sleep, and that if a sleepwalker was awakened, the soul could be lost.[19] Still, it's important not to startle them, as they can turn aggressive or even violent in rare instances.[20] Indeed, murders and heinous crimes have been committed by people who were allegedly in this state, which we'll review in the next chapter. In most cases, it's best to gently wake them and guide them back to bed to prevent injury.[21]

Injury in sleepwalking is more likely to occur in an unfamiliar place such as a hotel. One hotel in Sydney even banned sleepwalkers' conventions because of the damage conventioneers had previously wrought. Still, it's possible to injure yourself at home, as one teenager who sleepwalked out of the kitchen door found out.

Unfortunately, the family home was an RV, which was zooming down a San Diego highway at the time.[22]

A GRAVEYARD CHAT

One of Dr. Schenck's patients was a woman named Jan, who'd been plagued by sleepwalking since childhood. During her episodes, family members characterized her as being in a zombie-like state, with bulging eyes. Flipping around the paradigm of a parent spooked by their sleepwalking child, one night Jan's ten-year-old daughter slept in her room and woke to see her mother sitting on the edge of the bed. She had pulled up the shade and was looking out the window, which faced a cemetery across the road.

Jan seemed to be talking to the graveyard residents, asking "who fed them, what they ate, and if they ever got lonely." She was having a conversation, asking a question and then waiting like she was getting answers, the daughter observed. One wonders if, like some mediums, she could really have been communicating with the departed. Still, not exactly the heart-to-heart a daughter might crave. Indeed, she never slept in Mom's room again.

Dr. Schenck found it unusual that Jan's sleepwalking episodes seemed to be associated with elaborate dreams, even though lab tests showed that her behaviors were emerging out of the non-REM cycle. He was able to successfully treat her with low dosages of Klonopin (clonazepam), a benzodiazepine medication that increases the arousal threshold (makes one less likely to have partial awakenings), and her disorder has been under control for many years now.[23] Klonopin is successful in treating some 80 percent of the parasomnias, Schenck has found.[24]

THE SLEEP RUNNER

John Mosedale was haunted by "sleep terrors" as a young boy but did not grow out of them as an adult. Sleep terrors (which we'll look at more in Chapter 5) generally don't involve dream narratives, but they did for Mosedale, along with sleepwalking, or rather sleep running. His mother said John frequently had dreams where she'd be awakened by his screaming. He thought someone was chasing him or trying to get him and he had to flee. "He always had a glazed look in his eye, like he wasn't really of this world at the time—he was somewhere else," she said. In one case, he jumped through a bedroom window, climbed down a tree, and ran through the neighborhood covered in blood.

Describing one of the episodes, Mosedale said he watched a glowing blue-white figure begin to descend through his bedroom ceiling, as he heard a narrator's voice telling him he had to get out of his room. "If you don't get out of the room before the body comes through," the voice declared, "you're dead." He took off running in a "freight train of fear."[25]

Mosedale, the pain still visible behind his clear blue eyes, came forward to publicize his experiences in the documentary *Sleep Runners*, helping to combat the shame and fear associated with certain sleep disorders. Though he was eventually successfully treated at the Minnesota sleep clinic, sadly, many of those plagued by parasomnias don't seek help for fear of being branded as crazy.

SLEEP TALKIN' MAN

"I'd rather peel off my skin and bathe my weeping raw flesh in a bath of vinegar than spend any time with you. But that's just my opinion. Don't take it personally."

Such was one of the many caustic zingers issued by Adam Lennard in his sleep, and documented by his wife, Karen, in her popular blog *Sleep Talkin' Man*. Karen, you see, was an insomniac, and her British husband's quippy utterances offered some hilarious late-night entertainment for her. Sometimes Karen would accidentally wake Adam because she was laughing so loud at what he said. "Everything Sleep Talkin' Man said was super sharp and perfect, whereas when he's awake, Adam is sometimes known to make those really lame dad jokes," she admitted to *U.S. News & World Report*.[26]

The recordings of Adam's sleep talk on the blog, delivered in his precise British cadence, have a kind of Lewis Carroll whimsy, even when he's spitting out expletives or gross-out metaphors:

"I'm sure you'll be thrilled and ecstatic at the thought of going out with me. But look at it from my point of view: Leeches attached to my testicles and a mass of flesh-eating caterpillars and ants over the rest of my body, gorging themselves on my flesh. A slow and ultimately painful death. So I hope you can see my point of view. It'll be a no to going out with you. Now run along and poison somebody else's life."[27]

When the *Sleep Talkin' Man* blog went viral, it led to a book and international media appearances as well as Adam's quips splattered across a vast array of merchandise including coffee mugs, T-shirts, and aprons. And yet, much to Karen's disappointment, after the birth of their daughter in 2013, Adam's sleep chatter stopped. They speculate that it may have arisen initially out of stress, as back in 2009 they were dealing with an appeals process to the Department of Homeland Security to obtain a visa to move to the United States.[28]

As with many parasomnias, the cause of sleep talking (also known as *somniloquy*) is murky, though it can be associated with sleep deprivation, stress, genetic predisposition, or PTSD. Up to 14 percent of the population is said to regularly speak or mumble something in their sleep, usually for just a short burst;[29] it's rare for such material to be the kind of bon mots and monologues tossed off by Adam Lennard.

Sleep talking can occur in both REM and non-REM phases, as well as during transitory partial awakenings. When somniloquy takes place during a dream, one theory posits it as a kind of "motor breakthrough," in which the ordinarily quiescent vocal ability is activated, and we speak aloud whatever our dream character is saying.[30] However, sleep speech has also been shown to occur irrespective of dream content in lab studies, like a reflex action without an attached story.[31]

It becomes a problem when the utterances are waking up or disturbing one's bed partner—not to mention if they call out the name of a previous lover. The meaning of sleep talk can be looked at in the same way as dream interpretation. In other words, what someone says is not necessarily meant to be taken at face value. It can be related to recent activities, past experiences or feelings, fantastical or nonsensical dream content, or some combination of these.

In an odd case, the sleep talk of one half of a couple triggered a confused arousal in the other. A wife's sleep chatter awoke her husband, and in a bewildered state, he started arguing with her, which escalated into a shouting match. A neighbor in their apartment complex, on the verge of calling the police, banged on their door. This caused one of them to snap out of their reverie and answer the door. They were both aghast, as they had no memory of shouting in the middle of the night, or that they'd even been talking.[32]

People can also lie or confabulate while asleep. One woman reveled in sexual exploits in her sleep speech, to the dismay of her male partner. Although she'd never had any of these torrid affairs, she had a hard time convincing him otherwise.[33]

Studies have shown some interesting differences between sleep talk and everyday speech. Sleep talkers can have more difficulty retrieving the correct word or be more likely to jumble a pronunciation and use neologisms (newly created words). In some ways, their speech resembles that of aphasic patients and schizophrenics in that sentences may be unconnected or incoherent.[34] Yet there are exceptions like Adam Lennard, when people can be more creative and eloquent than they are in their waking lives.

THE SURREAL SLEEP TALK OF DION MCGREGOR

Dion McGregor's amusingly twisted somniloquies were turned into the 1960s cult record *The Dream World of Dion McGregor (He Talks in His Sleep)*. In the early 1960s, McGregor was a struggling songwriter crashing on friends' couches in Manhattan, including those of the actor Carleton Carpenter and film director Peter de Rome (later anointed "The Grandfather of Gay Porn").

As McGregor loudly babbled into the night, Carpenter was annoyed, while de Rome tried to write down some of the outlandish orations. Eventually, McGregor moved in with Michael Barr, his songwriting partner (their song "Where Is the Wonder" was recorded by Barbra Streisand in 1964). Barr was so amazed by the sleep monologues that he set up a reel-to-reel recorder near the living room bed where McGregor slept.

When he played back the tape for his roommate the next morning, "this came as a revelation to Dion, who'd always been told he talked in his sleep, but had no idea his utterances were so elaborate, expansive, and strange," Steve Venright of Torpor Vigil Records recounted.[35]

Barr would go on to record hundreds of hours of McGregor's nocturnal narrations, and some of them were used for the Decca Records LP, which was released in tandem with a book published by Random House featuring printed versions of the monologues, with illustrations by Edward Gorey. To circumvent claims of an elaborate hoax, the publisher commissioned a psychiatrist to check up on McGregor, and as far as he was able to determine, the case was legit.[36]

While Barr was thrilled to bring the offbeat tales into the daylight, McGregor was somewhat embarrassed by the whole thing and told one interviewer "It's like being famous for wetting your bed."[37]

One of the curiosities of the recordings is that you often hear the sounds of street traffic, like loud horn honking. Of course, to an inveterate New Yorker's ears, that's the equivalent of crickets, and not enough to wake them up.

Whirl it around, whirl it around! Spin that Lazy Susan and everybody take what they want off it. Hurry! Hurry! Grab it! Grab it, grab it, grab it! We're playing food roulette! Food roulette! Yes, there's a poisoned éclair on there. We have a poisoned éclair on there, and somebody's going to get it! Now . . . Spin it, spin it, spin it, spin it! We don't *know* which one is the poisoned éclair! There are a hundred and thirty on there. Spin, spin, *spinnnnnn . . . spinnnn* the Lazy Susan!

—"FOOD ROULETTE" BY DION MCGREGOR;
TRANSCRIPTION BY STEVE VENRIGHT

In the preceding story, McGregor manically spews a black-humored account of hundreds of people standing in line to get a crack at "winning" a poison éclair from a giant spinning turntable. After all the participants have gotten their eclair, they bite into them simultaneously, and you hear McGregor happily chewing his. Suddenly, there's a horrible scream. Apparently McGregor himself was the "winner."

In another piece, "Our Town," McGregor reveals the secrets of a small town, including a mortician who was so proud of his work that

Dion McGregor, a one-of-a-kind somniloquist. Illustration by Kerry Zentner, 2013 (reference photo: portrait from *The Dream World of Dion McGregor*, Bernard Geis Associates, 1964).

he props up embalmed bodies in his storefront window, a beauty parlor that doubles as a bordello, and a dairy where the butter is made from yellow grease. In the surreal *"New York Times,"* he's sucked inside a magical copy of the paper of record. "I can walk through the pages, I can sit in the ads. . . . We are stuck here until somebody opens these sections and lets us out!"

Enjoyment of McGregor's stories may be somewhat of an acquired taste—writer Bill Hayes noted that "he sounds as if he were channeling Truman Capote on acid: flirtatious, slushy, disconnected from reality—the voice of self-*un*consciousness."[38] Instead of being asleep, could McGregor have been putting himself in a trance or self-hypnotic state, a kind of Edgar Cayce of the off-off-Broadway scene?

Venright was intrigued enough to put out new discs of the idiosyncratic recordings on his label in 2014. In some of the tracks, it's like he's addressing an invisible person, "and you become a character in the dream," Venright notes.[39]

Harvard Medical School psychologist Dr. Deirdre Barrett, known for her research into dreams and hypnosis, was also intrigued by the material and used Venright's vast selection of transcripts for an analysis. Surprisingly, she found the McGregor monologues to be less bizarre than the average dream, with more internal cohesion and fewer abrupt shifts in characters and scenes, though he scored as more aggressive and unkind as well as much friendlier than the typical dreamer.[40]

Another Harvard psychologist, Dr. Robert Stickgold, took a more skeptical view of the McGregor material, finding it unlikely there could be so much cohesion within a dream story. At one point, "he lists 16 items that people are supposed to go out and find in a scavenger hunt [including a Welsh shoelace, a dirty napkin used by

Garbo, and a wolf's dream] . . . I've never heard a dream report that can go on for six or seven minutes . . . just listing things without drifting off topic."[41]

"I'm not calling them dream reports," Barrett counters. "They seemed to be sleep-talking from a sort of atypical REM stage." She correlated the McGregor material with studies of sleep psychologist A. M. Arkin, who looked at some similar cases, including McGregor himself (he declared McGregor's sleep talking to be a "spectacular" example of "macrodissociative sleep-utterance"[42]). Arkin measured the brain activity of sleep talkers in his lab, and the ones who went on for longer periods "seemed to be talking in a sort of hybrid almost REM sleep, but showing a bit more waking signs in their EEG"[43]—a state midway between waking and sleeping.

Given McGregor's bewilderment over his "ability," Barrett doubts he was faking it. "If you had to pull a scam it would seem an unlikely one," she says, though she admits it's hard to decipher to what degree his strange tales emerged from his unique persona and what was due to the hybrid brain state.

She's excited about the advent of sleep talk apps, in which people can record and then post their nocturnal chatter on websites, perhaps paving the way for fascinating new somniloquists to emerge.[44] From what I observed on the SleepTalkRecorder.com site, that has not happened yet, though the mournful wailing of a UK woman "who wants to be a potato" has potential. McGregor eventually left New York for Oregon with a partner and reportedly ceased sleep talking. Alas, he passed away in 1994 and missed out on the resurgence of interest in him and the topic.

CATATHRENIA, ANYONE?

After I evacuated to a friend's place in Atlanta during Hurricane Irma, my host reported hearing odd sounds coming from the guest bedroom, a cross between groaning and talking. It was an odd feeling, as a newly crowned chronicler of peculiar sleep behavior, to have my own hidden parasomnia suddenly called out, like being caught with my hand in the cookie jar of the subconscious.

Later, back at home, perhaps because I was made aware of my "condition," I seemed to catch myself in the act of eliciting an unconscious groan, like a kind of train signal as I switched sleep states. Or was it just a dream?

Nocturnal groaning or catathrenia is thought to be unrelated to sleep talking, occurs on the exhalation, and isn't typically associated with mental anguish or breathing problems.[45] Yet which was I doing—sleep talking or sleep groaning? It was time to download the Sleep Talk Recorder app and hear the evidence for myself. The app nabbed a sample first time out. It was a few seconds long and occurred in the early stages of slumber; I would characterize the outburst as "babble," a kind of nonsensical mumbling of average volume. On another occasion, the app recorded a brief utterance that had a musical dint to it, somewhere between a hum and a phrase. Although my nocturnal vocals weren't actual words, they do seem to fall into the sleep-talking category, though I won't be giving Sleep Talkin' Man or Dion McGregor a run for the money anytime soon.

APPETITE FOR THE NIGHT

In April 2007, around midnight, Erwin suddenly appeared in the kitchen. His niece Barbara and I, sipping wine, glanced over from the living room of his Palm Springs condo. He proceeded to pull a bag of tortilla chips out of a kitchen cabinet and then pour them into the stainless steel sink. And then he began to munch on them.

"Did you want a plate for those chips, Uncle Erwin?" Barbara asked. Erwin, an old friend, was a fastidious fellow, so it was quite odd that he was eating out of the sink, even if it was clean enough to do so. He replied in a low, monosyllabic grunt.

We strolled over to the breakfast bar. "Erwin, are you . . . OK?" I inquired.

He issued another uncanny, short grunt.

There was a robotic, downcast look about him, and he seemed intent on devouring those corn chips. We recalled that about ninety minutes earlier he'd downed an Ambien, and it dawned on us—Erwin was sleep eating. Earlier, he'd told us that sometimes he would find empty ice cream pints the next morning and assumed he was eating them in his sleep. Once he even discovered open cans of partially eaten sardines used as bookmarks in expensive coffee table books.

Erwin is an articulate artist and attorney, so it was eerie and unnerving to see the zombification of my friend up close, even if there was an explanation. This seemed to be a lower-functioning subpersonality of the real Erwin, driven by only one purpose at that moment: MUST . . . EAT . . . CHIPS.

Sleep-related eating disorder (SRED) is thought to affect about 1 percent of the population,[46] and indeed the glassy-eyed look, mumbling speech, and single-minded intent are hallmarks of the condition.[47] Most cases arise from the NREM (deep sleep) state.[48] Nocturnal eaters may have some hazy recall of their foraging, which can occur up to five times in one night. One of the curiosities they report is that it's not associated with actual hunger but rather a compulsory drive to eat. Some even say "they will be unable to return to sleep unless they eat."[49] And it's generally the high-carbohydrate and sugary items that are the go-to choices—apparently, no one ever makes a healthy salad in their sleep.[50]

ONE CAT-FOOD SANDWICH TO GO

People can prepare and consume some bizarre things in this state— buttered cigarettes, anyone? "One of my patients used to eat salt sandwiches . . . Another preferred sugar sandwiches," Dr. Schenck writes. He also described a woman who'd endured twenty years of sleep eating. One night, she prepared a cat-food sandwich for herself but then decided not to eat it. It wasn't because she suddenly recognized the distasteful prospect of eating cat food—it was simply because "in her mind at the time, she was not inclined to eat a sandwich."[51]

In 2013, a British woman in her fifties, Lesley Cusack, came forward with her struggles: she consumes up to 2,500 calories a night in her sleep. "The worst things that I know I've eaten are emulsion paint, Vaseline, cough syrup, raw potatoes, and soap powder. The night I ate paint was the only time I've ever woken up. I can still remember standing in the kitchen touching my mouth and being very confused. It took me a while to work out what it was. It was thick and horrible."[52]

During a 2002 episode of his TV talk show, host Montel Williams revealed that he experienced sleep eating. Though he had no memory of it, he'd frequently find signs the next day. He no longer stocks raw meats in the fridge because "I wake up in the morning and there's a pack of chicken, and there's a bite missing out of it."[53]

Frenzied food prep can involve toasters, microwaves, and ovens, and often there's a sloppy residue left behind, as sleep eaters rarely clean up. The trail of crumbs might lead you to chocolate frosting on the pillow, or cherry pits and pork chop bones in the sheets, as in the case of a fifty-seven-year-old woman who began sleep eating in her teens.[54]

Nancy Weber dealt with the messes of her husband, such as peanut butter smeared on the refrigerator door and blobs of grape jelly under the kitchen table, but it wasn't until she discovered he'd left the gas burner on during one of his middle-of-the-night forays that she sought professional help.[55]

Weight gain is one of the most troubling consequences,[56] though injuries can also occur like black eyes from walking into a wall, hand cuts, and dental problems from gnawing on frozen food.[57] Guilt and self-loathing are also by-products. "It's quite disturbing for patients to think they have performed some complex behavior in their sleep and don't remember it," said Dr. Helene Emsellem, the medical director for the Center for Sleep and Wake Disorders in Maryland, adding that it can also be quite embarrassing, "which is one reason patients don't even tell their doctors about it."[58]

Though the physiological causes of SRED are not clear—there may be irregularities in hormones like leptin, which regulate appetite—once again the problem often runs in families, suggesting a genetic component.[59] In some cases, it can be triggered by stress, as well as being on a diet. "The theory is," said Katherine Morgado, an administrator of a New Jersey sleep clinic, "that if you're consciously denying yourself food, the unconscious brain is undermining you by satisfying that urge to eat at night."[60]

Aside from medication and hypnotherapy, people have tried a variety of methods to stop the automated eating—tying themselves to the bed, setting obstacle courses on the way to the kitchen, putting locks on the fridge or cabinets, or having someone lock them inside their bedroom. In one such instance, a woman broke the door frame trying to get out of her bedroom after her mother locked her in for the night.[61]

In an ingenious solution of pitting one malady against another, a therapist suggested that her patient, a woman with an intense snake phobia, place a rubber snake on her kitchen table every night. Although this largely put an end to the food raids, Dr. Schenck considers it a risky therapy, as such a sight might trigger a panic for someone in this vulnerable state.[62]

KICKING AND SCREAMING

In a grainy black-and-white video, a slumbering middle-aged man suddenly seems to awaken. He's slack-jawed, yet thrashing about in herky-jerky movements—the swinging electrodes attached to his head give him the air of a demonic marionette as he pounds his hand on the side of the bed and kicks his legs. While it could pass for an outtake from *Paranormal Activity*, it's actual footage of a patient with REM behavior disorder (RBD) from Dr. Schenck's Minnesota sleep clinic.

"Here are people," writes journalist Chip Brown, "in the midst of 'partial' arousals who spring from bed and rip off the electrodes glued to their heads, removing patches of their scalp as well; people who box the air, flail at imaginary snakes, twitch, jerk, groan . . . or rock and tremble like bobble-head dolls." Rational by day, "at night [they] find themselves locked in life-and-death struggles with intruders."[63]

Take the case of Martin.[64] In February 1983, his perplexing symptoms emerged—a combo of violent kicking and arm thrashing, as he slept next to his wife, Gertrude. This was accompanied by loud vocalizations. "Rarely was it words you could understand . . . I think the screaming was the most disturbing part to me. It was violent screaming, and it would wake me out of a sound sleep," Gertrude lamented.

Sometimes he'd hit or scratch her, but a few times things got truly horrifying. One night Martin dreamed he was on a fishing trip in Canada and a skunk had snuck into his tent (this had happened to him in real life). With his bare hands, he grabbed the wild critter, tugging at it and trying to expel it. Flash back to Gertrude, and Martin is savagely pulling her hair. If she hadn't managed to wake him, he might have torn it out. While most people with RBD generally keep their eyes closed,[65] in this mixed dream-awake state, Martin somehow interpreted her hair as the skunk's fur.

With sleep paralysis, you're awake but frozen as REM dream images seep into your waking reality. RBD is like the fun house mirror version of that. You're in a dream state, but normal muscle paralysis isn't functioning. So people can physically act out their dreams, though they generally stay in the bedroom rather than sleepwalk.

THE MINNESOTA DISEASE

The "patient zero" of RBD was a man named Donald Dorff, who showed up with a gash in his forehead at the Minnesota sleep clinic back in 1982, complaining of "violent moving nightmares."[66] His troublesome episodes involved violent sports or confrontations with strangers or animals in which he had to either fight or flee in order to survive. In one, he was in a motorcycle gang and got into a quarrel with another gang member as they rode their bikes down the highway. The gang member tried to ram Dorff's bike, so he started kicking the other vehicle away. Dorff's wife awoke to find he was "kicking the hell out of" her.

It took some detective work by Dr. Schenck and his associates to pinpoint what exactly was happening, as they'd never seen a case like this before. For a while, other sleep doctors even referred to it as "the Minnesota disease," until more cases started coming to the surface.

Like other parasomnias, RBD existed before, it just eluded medical diagnosis. A few centuries ago, Donald Dorff might have been considered possessed by demons; more recently in the Freudian era, his behavior would have been seen as misplaced aggression.

Many people with RBD are described as quite placid during their waking hours, so the Jekyll-Hyde transformation is all the more dramatic. That was the case with Mel Abel, a mild-mannered sixty-seven-year-old Minnesotan, who in his sleep spewed foul-mouthed rants, and once while trying to snap the neck of a deer, he woke up with his hands on his wife's head and chin. It's often the partners of people with RBD who suffer the most and seek clinical help.

In the 1960s, Dr. Michel Jouvet, a French sleep expert, and his colleagues were trying to find the part of the brain responsible for REM sleep. Using lab cats, they made lesions in areas of the brain stem called the *pons* and discovered that while the cats still went into REM after the surgery, they lost the atonia (muscle paralysis) associated with it. They "seemed to fight imaginary enemies or to play with an absent mouse, striking out with forelimbs, and manifesting fear reactions."[67] For RBD to exist, writes Dr. Schenck, there has to be not only the cessation of normal muscle atonia but "excessive activity of the motor pattern generators in the brain stem . . . in other words, there must be a strong drive to move and behave while dreaming, and not just a release from the paralysis."[68]

But why the aggression? Instead of other instinctual behaviors like eating or sex, "with REM behavior disorder your dream content gets very restricted," Schenck explains. "Everything is shunted along certain pathways. A lot of people say after treatment, 'I can have my regular dreams again!'"[69]

Unlike sleep eating, where the demographic is more likely to be female, most people with RBD are male and over age fifty. And while the malady is most often successfully treated with Klonopin (melatonin has also shown promise[70]), research now suggests that RBD is typically an early sign of Parkinson's and related diseases. On average, ten years after an RBD diagnosis, Parkinson's symptoms such as hand tremors, rigidity, slowed movements, and other motor problems emerge.[71] In fact, a recent study showed that 81 to 90 percent of people with RBD developed a degenerative brain disorder during their lifetime.[72] The correlation makes sense on a physiological basis, as the nerve centers associated with REM muscle paralysis in the brain stem are interconnected with the adjacent motor nuclei damaged by Parkinson's.[73]

MIDNIGHT BLUE: SLEEP SEX

Some of the best lovers are asleep. Though they have no memories of their performance in the morning, their partners say they can be more inventive, passionate, and downright wild than when they're awake. But it was a "wake-up call" for a woman when her boyfriend started snoring one night in the midst of intercourse. Up to that point, she hadn't realized he was initiating sex in his sleep, which included "playful biting" and "talking dirty." After the couple sought a medical consultation, she requested that he incorporate some of his somnambulant moves into their waking sexual play.[74] Score one for the snore-gasm!

Welcome to the newest member of the Parasomnia Club—sleep sex or sexsomnia, which was classified as an official sleep disorder in May 2014.[75] Yet once again the condition has likely been around for eons (it's been suggested that sleep-related erections are depicted in the Lascaux cave paintings in France[76]). As with sleep eating and some of the other parasomnias, people with these disorders are often embarrassed and reluctant to approach their doctors about the condition, which can be a harmless or kinky diversion for couples, or something more ominous, bordering on assault. The condition seems to predominantly affect men, though one survey indicated that around 30 percent of sexsomniacs are women.[77]

Like sleepwalking, the behavior is thought to be a "confusional arousal" that originates out of an abrupt awakening from NREM or slow-wave sleep. Women and men often display different behaviors during episodes, with women more likely to pleasure themselves and emit vocalizations, whereas sleeping men reach out to grope or fondle their bedmate.[78]

In the book *Sleepsex: Uncovered*, "Stephan" relays his girlfriend's descriptions of him as a kind of sex robot, difficult to awaken or rebuff. "I was unemotional and would not give her any foreplay at all. It basically was all about intercourse and I did it with a blank look on my face." The girlfriend said she was mostly amused by it and nicknamed him "Spock" for his lack of emotions during these sleep sex sessions.[79] Writer Stephen Klinck also earned a nickname— "Midnight Sex Pest"—when he put the moves on his girlfriend (now wife). In her own half-asleep state, she responded positively to his unconscious advances. "There was something weirdly heightened about the experience," Klinck said, "as though we were both different people somehow."[80]

"Richard" told a more poignant tale[81] of his sometimes-girlfriend, whose interest in him was waning, especially sexually. While spooning her one night, he suddenly felt her hand moving his along her breasts. Pleasantly shocked, he went along with it, as things quickly moved into a "reverse scissors hold." He guessed she might be asleep as she was much more dominant and would not stop to kiss or talk. "Well, right when it was getting good, she woke up," he said. "She had this very disappointed look on her face, and said 'I'm sorry,'" then rolled over and went back to sleep.

The repressed or unexplored side of someone's sexuality can be unleashed during these episodes. A prim person may bask in dirty talk or behave in ways they wouldn't normally.[82] "Jason" noted how his sleeping wife treated his penis as a "sacred object" but when awake she wouldn't really give it the time of day.[83] In the midst of a hot and heavy session, the sexsomniac may suddenly utter an unlikely remark, like "Well, that's enough of that," and roll over and go back to sleep, to the dismay of their worked up partner.[84]

When a person is asleep, the prefrontal cortex, which regulates "executive" decision making, is essentially offline, Dr. Michael Cramer Bornemann of Sleep Forensics Associates explains. In a deeper part of the brain are "central pattern generators," which include our primal urges, such as for sex. But those pattern generators are close to where sleep and waking functions are located. Thus, if something disturbs sleep, like a sound or a partner's jostling, "it takes just a little electrical switching error from the sleep/wake generating centers to trigger a central pattern generator," such as for sex, Bornemann continues. With the prefrontal cortex asleep at the wheel, a person may do things they wouldn't when awake—like pounce on a slumbering partner.[85]

As you might imagine, sleep sex has a harrowing side, too, when unwanted advances turn into molestation or rape charges. "Ian," a happily married thirty-eight-year-old, liked to take his family on camping trips. On one occasion, his thirteen-year-old daughter invited a school friend. On the second night of the trip, the daughter's friend, who was sleeping in a small one-person tent, was suddenly awakened by a naked Ian, who began playing with himself and forcefully trying to get into her sleeping bag.

The girl's screams woke up not only Ian and his family but nearby campers who called 911. "I was groggy and astonished at the situation," Ian said, while the girl was sobbing and "calling me a pervert." When the police showed up, with much effort, he was able to convince them that he'd been sleepwalking and that it was a freak incident. They didn't arrest him, though his family was booted out of the campground.[86] Other cases have not fared so well for the accused and entered the court system. Sometimes it's even the sexsomniac who accuses the other person of rape because they have no memory of their consent or initiation.

Klonopin has about a 90 percent success rate in curtailing the activity.[87] It's thought that the drug's sedating effects may make a sleeper less susceptible to having the confusional arousals that lead into other kinds of "arousal."[88] But how safe is Klonopin? After all, this is the drug that musician Stevie Nicks said was harder to kick than cocaine after it took her forty-seven days to detox at a Venice Beach hospital. "I nearly died," she said of the detox. "I moulted. My hair turned grey. My skin started to completely peel off. I was in terrible pain."[89] Of course, she'd been gobbling Klonopin like it was coming out of a Pez dispenser throughout the day rather than taking the careful doses a sleep specialist might prescribe. Dr. Schenck writes that Klonopin's potential for abuse is low, and the same dosage can be kept for long-term treatment. He has found that the small percentage of people who experience substantial side effects can be successfully switched over to Xanax.[90]

NOCTURNAL DELUSIONS

About 7 percent of parasomnias are classified as "nocturnal dissociative disorders" arising from a damaged psyche.[91] One of the most remarkable cases is that of a nineteen-year-old male nicknamed "Cat Boy" in Dr. Schenck's Minnesota sleep clinic. For years, he would have odd episodes once or twice a week, in which he'd awaken in the middle of the night and "become" a jungle cat. As recorded in the sleep lab, "he would growl, hiss, crawl, and leap about for up to an hour at a time," Dr. Schenck writes. He was always on all fours, with hands "stretched and bent into surprisingly realistic-looking paws."[92] Cat Boy sometimes demonstrated feats of "superhuman strength," such as chomping down on a mattress and dragging it across the room with his teeth (just as if he were a cat, his opposable thumb function was apparently turned off, so he could only move things with his mouth).

He always reported having the same dream: he is a large lion or tiger let out of his cage by a female zookeeper who holds a piece of raw meat. But, frustratingly, as he follows her, he can't get at the meat because of an "invisible force field." The dream always ends with him being knocked unconscious by a tranquilizer gun.

Interestingly, EEG testing showed that Cat Boy's brain was awake during these episodes; what he was experiencing was a dissociative state rather than a dream, as though he were reenacting some kind of buried memory. Dissociative behaviors often stem from some type of trauma, like childhood sexual abuse, and may be part of multiple personality disorder—now generally referred to as dissociative identity disorder (DID). Sleep may serve as a kind of switching station between the different personalities, in which someone falls asleep as one persona and wakes up as another.[93]

Cat Boy came from a loving family who adopted him when he was ten months old. His prior history was unknown, so abuse may have occurred at an early age. One theory poses that Cat Boy's "atavistic genes" or ancient animal traits may somehow become activated after his sleep is interrupted.[94]

A more typical case of nocturnal dissociation involved a middle-aged nurse who sleepwalked and sleep drove while experiencing vivid, terrifying nightmares of fending off a male attacker.[95] She would drive her car several miles to isolated places and come to full consciousness only when she heard a car alarm in the distance. Her incidents were a kind of reenactment of a sadistic rape at age ten by a stranger who abducted her when she was out walking. He threatened to maim her if she spoke about what happened, so she kept quiet, hid her injuries, and buried the incident in the back of her mind. The trauma was reignited years later when a young girl who'd also been raped and beaten was admitted to her hospital unit.

In the late 1800s, Dr. William Minor achieved notoriety for contributing some ten thousand entries to the *Oxford English Dictionary* while committed to the UK's Broadmoor Criminal Lunatic Asylum. An American surgeon, Dr. Minor had served in the Civil War and at one point was tasked with branding a deserter with a *D*, taking a hot iron out of the coals and searing the face of a young Union soldier.[96] Subsequently, he believed the man would seek him out and exact revenge, which may have contributed to his later paranoia when he killed a man in Great Britain but was found not guilty by reason of insanity. At the asylum, he was plagued by nighttime delusions of being abducted and taken in flying machines to such faraway places as a brothel in Constantinople.[97]

"Small boys, he believed, were put up in the rafters above his bed; they came down when he was fast asleep, chloroformed him, and then forced him to perform indecent acts" with "cheap women and small girls," Simon Winchester recounts in his book *The Professor and the Madman*.[98] A film adaptation of the book was shot in 2016 with Sean Penn in the role of the mad Dr. Minor, and after a protracted legal battle, it limped into theaters in May 2019.

BEWARE THE AMBIEN ZOMBIES

"The biggest problem I face today is the new wave of Ambien zombies," declared "Betty," the writer behind "Confessions of a Fed-Up Flight Attendant."[99] People who are probably perfectly nice in their normal lives decide they want to get a little sleep on their flight, she explains, and "choose to take Ambien for the first time on a big metal tube hurtling through the sky after they throw back a couple of cocktails. The result is a horde of lumbering, slumbering, zombie passengers wreaking havoc on the airplane."

On one overnight international flight, Betty's coworker noticed something pale and mysterious moving in the darkened aisle toward first class. It was a naked man. Approaching with caution, she quickly pegged him as an Ambien zombie. (Betty believes these folks think they're home in their bedroom, where it's perfectly acceptable to strip off their clothes.) The flight attendant gently prodded the nude man with the tip of her finger, nudging him back to the galley, where she commanded him to put his pants back on, and then guided him to his seat. Later, when the lights came back on, the passenger sheepishly inquired if he did something untoward during the night—"I figured something was wrong, when I woke up with my underwear in my hand."

Ambien (zolpidem), the homecoming queen of "Z-drugs"—hypnotic sedatives used to treat insomnia—entrances the brain to sleep by activating its natural gamma-aminobutyric acid (GABA) receptors. GABA is an inhibitory brain chemical that calms the neural synapses.[100] Particularly when combined with alcohol, Ambien can trigger a variety of parasomnias including sleepwalking, sexsomnia, and sleep eating—as in the case of my friend Erwin. The medication is especially known to backfire when people manage to stay awake too long after taking it.

One woman decided to take a shower after her Ambien dose and stayed up past the recommended fifteen-to-twenty-minute window. The next morning she awoke to the sight of a garden axe on her nightstand. With no memory of how it got there, she scrolled through her texts and discovered an entire "sleep text" conversation with her boyfriend, in which she reported hearing voices coming from the kitchen and seeing darting images in her peripheral view. This culminated in her going out to the garden shed to retrieve the axe for protection.[101]

In another case, a woman joined her boyfriend in the bedroom about a half hour after taking Ambien. "Who's that?" she asked him, pointing at a figure in the corner. The boyfriend tried to reassure her: "Come to bed, that's a laundry basket, honey."[102]

Beyond that, Ambien users have racked up some preposterous purchases with the world of Internet shopping at their fingertips. One man shipped a crate of live Maine lobsters to his ex-girlfriend;

another placed an order for a $70 leg of ham from the Pig of the Month club, despite being a die-hard vegetarian for years.[103]

"I've watched pillows growl like lions, picture frames morph into dragons, and towels turn into the couple from American Gothic," writes online poster Little_bus.[104] "The worst thing thus far was waking up to an order confirmation from Amazon Prime for 24 boxes of sugar-free Jello." That changed, however, when she initiated sex with a new boyfriend while on Ambien. They suddenly had to stop because she became convinced they were copulating on the stage of the Democratic National Convention while Hillary Clinton was narrating their sexual choreography from behind a lectern.

Denizens of certain subreddits (discussion forums on the popular Reddit website) might say these folks were visited by the Ambien Walrus, a cartoon character that's come to embody the whackadoodle world of experiencing Ambien's hypnotic effects. Cartoonist Drew Fairweather, known for the webcomic *Toothpaste for Dinner*, created the icon back in 2007. The simple line drawing of a flippered creature beckons with the caption: "Come with me on an adventure you'll never remember."

"The behavior of the walrus," Fairweather told Van Winkle's, "is a natural comparison for a user of Ambien." When the drug works as intended, "the user is like a lump, but when it exhibits its adverse effects, the user is driven to sleepwalk, shuffling around awkwardly as a walrus would flipper across an ice floe. It also drives the user to bouts of aggression which resemble that of the walrus in mating season."[105]

Functioning as a kind of excuse or rationale—"it wasn't me, it was the Ambien Walrus," the cartoon meme suggests that it is some other self, a disinhibited and hallucinating one, that is calling the shots. The next morning, the regular self, blanketed in amnesia, is left trying to decipher the Walrus's trail of clues.

Some go so far as to describe a looming "other" presence on their Ambien escapades. "You always feel like someone else is there," writes Quora contributor Siobhan. "A lot of the time you will even refer to yourself as 'we' in writings (because it makes you do really weird, uncharacteristic things like leaving yourself weird post-its or texting all your friends word salad). Ambien sends you on a journey into nonsense while feeling like you have a buddy right along there with you."[106]

Laurie Sandell, a writer for *Glamour*, penned the essay "Confessions of a Sleeping Pill Junkie," documenting how her nightly regimen of Ambien nearly did her in.[107] One morning she woke up in her bathtub. "I was freezing, shivering. I had no idea where I was. When I looked down, I saw I was naked and surrounded by low-burning candles. Slowly it dawned on me that I'd been lying in cold water, deeply asleep, for more than six hours. What if I'd drowned?"

Indeed, there's a darker side to Ambien when the harsh wake-up occurs behind bars, and there's no Walrus in sight.

CRIMES AND MISDEMEANORS

Lindsey Schweigert had a security clearance as part of her job selling software for a defense contractor and frequently jetted around the country to meet with various military officials. After flying home to St. Louis after a weeklong stint in D.C., the thirty-one-year-old made herself dinner, then slipped into PJs and into her welcome bed. It was only six p.m., but she was exhausted. And Ambien would quickly pave the way to slumberland.

But when she woke, she was far from the comfort of her own bed.

Handcuffed in the back of a squad car, she hadn't the faintest idea how she got there. The officer informed her that she was under arrest for driving while intoxicated. It wasn't until she was released from the police station ten hours later that she realized what was at the root of her amnesia: Ambien. She'd taken it for years for insomnia but recently had her prescription adjusted.

Over the following weeks, she was able to piece together from police reports and witness accounts what happened that night in March 2011. Sometime after eight p.m., she got out of bed and drew herself a bath. Then she headed out in her Mini Cooper with her dog, Tyson, along for the ride. Her roommate was so alarmed by the conditions when she got home (Lindsey had left the bathwater running) that she called the police, thinking there was a kidnapping.

A local diner called the Steak 'n Shake was Lindsey's apparent destination, but soon after leaving the house, she ran a stoplight and crashed into another car. Police officers described her as swaying and glassy-eyed—she fell three times trying to walk the line of the sobriety test. Prosecutors initially pursued a six-month sentence and a variety of other penalties, but Lindsey's attorney argued that her behavior was due to the Ambien, not personal negligence. Among the lengthy warnings on the prescription label: "After taking AMBIEN, you may get out of bed while not being fully awake and do an activity that you do not know you are doing . . . Reported activities include: driving a car ('sleep-driving')."

Charges were reduced to careless driving, considered a misdemeanor, and this allowed her to keep her security clearance. But her license was suspended for a year, and she had to pay around $9,000 in legal costs. Still, compared to what has happened in other Ambien driving cases, Lindsey Schweigert was lucky—she didn't hurt anyone. "I'm still in shock to this day I was able to even function [on the Ambien]. Was I on autopilot? I don't even know," she pondered. "I understand medications have side effects, but this is so much more."[108]

Delta's Flight Attendant of the Year for three years in a row, Julie Ann Bronson, returned to her home in San Antonio from an international flight and had some wine to unwind one afternoon in April 2009. Later, she downed Ambien to get to sleep. She awoke in a holding cell, barefoot and in pajamas, and was informed she'd run over three people, including an eighteen-month-old girl who suffered severe brain damage.

Security video captured her erratically driving her Mercedes convertible through her gated community. She swerved onto a curb and hit Traci Lopez, who was picking up grass clippings with her two daughters. All three were hit, and the eighteen-month-old was flung into the air. Bronson drove off, even though she'd blown out two tires, but police eventually stopped her, charging her with driving while intoxicated (DWI), assault, and failure to stop and render aid.

"I wouldn't hurt a flea. And if I hit somebody, I would have stopped and helped. We're trained in CPR," the flight attendant testified. She pleaded guilty to the felony charges and conceded that she shouldn't have taken the Ambien after drinking. Yet the jury bought the Ambien defense, and instead of serving up to ten years, she was given probation. Her attorney, Patrick Hancock, reported that while Bronson got off, she was deeply affected—she lost her decorated career and almost took her own life knowing that she had devastated a family and injured a child.[109]

One of the ironies of such cases is that the Ambien defense tends to work better if the accused injures or kills someone rather than causing property damage. In DWI cases that involve less serious consequences, prosecutors need only show that the driver got behind the wheel while impaired. But in the matter of vehicular homicide or where someone is hurt, the prosecutor has to demonstrate that the defendant had knowledge or culpability for their actions—a murky territory where Ambien is concerned.

With more publicity and awareness of Ambien's effects in recent years, courts are less likely to be sympathetic to users who blame their crimes on the medication.[110] Some, such as toxicologist Janci Lindsay, have argued that the drug should be raised to a Schedule II controlled substance, with restrictions on refills.[111]

And although the U.S. Food and Drug Administration acted to lower the recommended dosage of Ambien in 2015, Sanofi-Aventis, the original manufacturer, maintains that problems are relatively rare under their golden arches of slumber. Serving "22 billion nights of patient therapy worldwide," they crowed in 2013, we stand behind "the robust clinical data that have demonstrated the safety and efficacy of Ambien since its approval in the U.S. in 1992."[112]

CHAPTER THREE

SLEEPWALK MURDERS

In all of us, even in good men,
there is a lawless wild-beast nature,
which peers out in sleep.

—SOCRATES

I 've killed on occasion. A horrible, irrevocable feeling. And engaged in ghastly cover-ups, with serpentine twists and turns. What an immense relief it was to wake up and find out they were only nightmares. Shaking off the emotional residue of the dream state, I wondered if there was something dark inside me. Could it be a bleed-through of a past life or parallel existence? Or was it just decades of TV crime dramas and newscasts tainting my subconscious?

But what if one woke up only to find they *had* committed murder during the night? And yet had little or no memory of it? It would be among the heaviest of burdens—hard to ever reconcile, and harder still to convince people of your innocence, as it *was* a part of "you" that did it. Around seventy murders worldwide have been blamed on sleepwalkers.[1] Here are some of the most gripping and enigmatic cases.

INTRUDER ALERT: THE KIGER HOMICIDES

The year was 1943 and World War II was on everyone's minds. But in the town of Covington, Kentucky, vice mayor and city commissioner Carl Kiger had his own battle, at least brewing in his mind. Known to have a "robbery complex," he kept loaded pistols stashed at various locations throughout the family house (including one under his pillow), just in case there was a break-in. Some have speculated that Carl's suspicions were related to possible ties to the mob. His gun policy even extended to the family's summer house, located on a bucolic twenty-acre plot in Boone County, where they went to escape from the city.

By all accounts, it was just a typical evening at the Kigers' summer house on the night of August 17. As usual, Carl insisted that before the family retired, not only should the doors be closed and locked, but the windows as well, even though an evening breeze might have cooled them off.[2]

Carl and his wife, Jennie, had tucked in their six-year-old son Jerry before heading off to their bedroom. Fifteen-year-old Joan came upstairs last that night, just past ten thirty p.m. Around an hour later, something disturbed her, and she witnessed an intruder breaking in through a downstairs window: a large shadowy man with "wild and evil eyes." The teenager instinctively knew he intended to kill them all.[3]

Realizing that she was the only one awake, she grabbed two loaded revolvers and began to stalk the intruder, who in the darkness was barely more than a silhouette. Seeing him go into Jerry's room, she frantically dashed after him. As he stood over Jerry's bed, she fired twice. But she missed as the man sped past her and across the hallway into Carl and Jennie's room. Joan shouted at the attacker and continued to fire, following him into her parents' bedroom. Jennie, now awake, later described seeing "a form jump towards the hall door leaving my room."

The intruder was still on the loose and Joan fired fifteen shots over the course of nearly an hour. Finally, she returned to her parents' room and turned on the light. "There's a crazy man in here," she said, "and he's going to kill all of us."

The light illuminated the dead body of Carl Kiger, five bullets lodged in his body, two fatal ones in the chest. Mrs. Kiger was also shot, sustaining a serious wound in her hip. She was trying to stanch the bleeding with a sheet as her husband's blood seeped into the mattress. Young Jerry was also dead, killed instantly by a shot to the head.

Joan gave one of the guns to her mother and went to get help, driving the family car to a neighbor's house. When officials, including Sheriff Jake Williams, arrived, they found the house locked up tight with no evidence of intruders.

While the sheriff initially issued a report that the Kiger family had been attacked by an unknown assailant, over repeated interviews, inconsistencies began to emerge in Joan's statements. Police ultimately concluded that there was no shadowy intruder and that Joan Kiger had shot and killed her father and brother. She was booked into the Boone County Jail and charged with first-degree murder.

Yet while Joan admitted she'd fired the guns whose bullets killed her family members, in her mind, she'd been trying to protect her family rather than hurt them, and the man who broke into their house was very real. Joan had a history of sleepwalking and night terrors, as did her father, and in her trial "the somnambulism defense" was used by her lawyer, Sawyer Smith. Her parasomnia seems to resemble RBD, in which a person is freed from the paralysis that normally accompanies the REM state, and then acts out their vivid fight-or-flight dream narratives, as described in the previous chapter where Martin grabbed onto his wife's long hair trying to expel a dreamworld skunk.

Joan, who'd turned sixteen by the time of her court case, was tried as an adult and faced the death penalty. Her mother, now getting around on crutches, was also brought up on murder charges as an accomplice, as she backed her daughter's account of an intruder and had held one of the guns for her.

The prosecution rejected the somnambulism defense, citing how Joan had stashed the other gun in a water cistern, which suggested she was trying to hide the murder weapons. And it seemed incomprehensible to them that the gunshots wouldn't have awakened her from her dream state. Further, newspaper accounts reported that Joan's bed appeared not to have been slept in the night of the murders.[4]

Joan was tried first and separately from her mother. Experts and relatives, including an uncle, testified to her previous vivid nightmares and delusions. "The defense hinged," wrote Thomas Schiffer, "on whether the jury would buy into Smith's defense that Joan was not in her right mind when she did the shooting and therefore not responsible."[5]

It was nearly impossible to conceive in 1943 that a "nice girl" would deliberately kill her family members in cold blood.[6] And indeed, after a four-hour deliberation, a jury of twelve Boone County men found her not guilty by reason of insanity, and she was sent off to an institution for a year. Charges against Jennie Kiger were also dropped.

Joan Marie Kiger, looking to put the ignominy behind her, eventually changed her name to Marie Kiler (now there's a Freudian slip!). After graduating from college, she became a guidance counselor in the Kentucky public school system, presumably having a special insight into teenage tumult. She died in 1991.

MIND OVER MURDER: THE TRIAL OF ALBERT TIRRELL

Joan wasn't the first to use the sleepwalking defense. One of the earliest such cases to hit the American courts was the lurid 1846 murder trial of Albert Tirrell, accused of killing his mistress, Maria Bickford, a beautiful Boston prostitute. *"Her throat was cut from nearly ear to ear*, and the bed set on fire in order to conceal the act of atrocity," the *Boston Daily Mail*, a penny tabloid, reveled in horror in an October 1845 edition.

Tirrell, the son of a prominent shoe manufacturer, and Bickford, both married to other people, scandalized Boston society, as they lived and traveled together on and off, staying in disreputable boardinghouses. During their tempestuous affair, Tirrell was arrested for the crime of adultery, while Bickford continued to see clients on the side. Shortly after Tirrell posted bail for the adultery charges, Bickford was found murdered at a brothel on Cedar Lane. Tirrell was spotted leaving the scene of the crime.

Attempting to flee the country, he was apprehended aboard a boat in the Gulf of Mexico and hauled back to Boston. As a man of privilege, he retained the services of one of the era's most renowned attorneys, Rufus Choate, a former Massachusetts senator, who'd been mentored by no less than Daniel Webster. An antebellum legal eagle, Choate had a silver tongue with the distinction of rolling out the longest sentence ever known to humankind—a staggering 1,219 words.[7]

Though the prosecution presented a strong circumstantial case against Tirrell, Choate engineered a canny two-pronged defense: impugning the character of Maria Bickford and arguing that if Tirrell did kill her, it was while he was in a somnambulistic state—"the insanity of sleep"[8]—and thus not responsible.

Twelve witnesses testified to Tirrell's sleepwalking spells, which were said to have begun at age six and increased in frequency over the years. The episodes reportedly involved violence—smashing windows, forcibly grabbing people, and even threatening a cousin with a knife, all while he spoke in a curious trembling voice that was unlike his waking cadence.

One witness, Mary Head, who lived near the crime scene, said Tirrell rang her bell the morning of the murder, making an unusual

THE BOSTON TRAGEDY.

TIRRELL MURDERING MARIA A. BICKFORD,

WHILE IN A STATE OF SOMNAMUBLISM.

The murder of Maria Bickford and the subsequent trial of Albert Tirrell received sensationalized coverage in the press. From the April 1846 issue of the *National Police Gazette*. Courtesy American Antiquarian Society.

gargling-like sound, and inquiring if some things had been delivered for him. She'd found him frightening and wondered if he was "asleep or crazy." Walter Channing, dean of Harvard Medical School, capped the testimonies, declaring that it was indeed conceivable for someone to kill, commit arson, and then improvise an escape, all while in a sleeping state.[9]

The jury took only two hours to return a resounding "not guilty" verdict, becoming the first time that the sleepwalking defense was successfully used in an American murder trial. Tirrell was later to send Choate a letter asking for the return of half his legal fees on the grounds that it had been much easier to defend him than expected.

But it would seem that Choate may have earned every penny. Had the entire sleepwalking defense been a devious strategy? Many contemporaries who analyzed the case didn't believe Tirrell's claims.[10] Henry Shute, a clerk in a law office that belonged to friends of Choate's, revealed that Choate had stopped by just days before agreeing to defend Tirrell. Fascinated with Shute's copy of the British novel *Sylvester Sound, the Somnabulist* by Henry Cockton, he tore into its pages for a lengthy period and then abruptly left the office.[11]

Cockton's amusing 1844 novel begins with a nonfiction preface, citing various instances as far back as the 1600s of people performing curious actions in their sleep.

Cockton's main character, the newly orphaned Sylvester, had "the spirit of mischief lurking in his eye, but while awake that spirit was asleep: it developed itself only in his dreams. It was then that it prompted him to perpetrate all sorts of wild and extraordinary tricks: it was then that it converted him from a calm, graceful, amiable youth, into a perfect little devil."[12]

FOOTPRINTS IN THE SAND: INSPECTOR LEDRU STALKS A KILLER

In the summer of 1887, Chief Inspector Robert Ledru was one of Paris's top crimebusters. He'd just come off a string of successes, including apprehending killers, breaking up a black magic cult, and rounding up members of an organization that plotted to overthrow the French government.

Loaned out to the police department of the port town of Le Havre, he was tasked with solving the mysterious disappearance of some sailors in the area. Exhausted upon his arrival, he went to bed early at his hotel, his trusty German pistol tucked under his pillow. When he awoke in the morning, he noticed that his socks were damp.[13]

Upon reporting to the local police station, he discovered that the case of the missing sailors had been set aside for a perplexing murder that had occurred during the night. Could the celebrated detective help them find the killer?

The victim, a Parisian merchant named Andre Monet, was found at dawn on the beach. A single, fatal bullet, shot at near-point-blank range, had pierced his chest. There appeared to be no motive or suspect.

Ledru investigated the site where the body was found, across from the English Channel, and discovered a set of misshapen footprints.

"They look familiar to me," he declared. He ordered a set of plaster casts to be promptly made.

Instead of interviewing people on the beach who might have seen something, he stared transfixed at the casts for some time. Then he announced to the local gendarmes, "The case is solved. I know the identity of the killer!"[14]

Who was it? Ledru holed up in his hotel room for the night. The next morning he paid a visit to Le Havre's chief of police. By then they had recovered the bullet that killed Monet. Ledru asked to see it and quickly compared it to an unfired one in the cartridge of his own gun.

Just as he thought. "I am the man who shot Monsieur Monet to death!" he informed the startled chief, who couldn't believe what he was hearing. He must have killed the tourist when he stumbled upon him while in a somnambulant trance, Ledru explained. Needing to inform his superiors, he rushed off on the next train to Paris, armed with the plaster casts and fatal bullet.

His boss was incredulous. But then Ledru reminded him of how he had lost his right big toe in a gun accident. The missing toe matched the plaster cast of the footprint on the beach. Further, he'd kept the damp socks unwashed, and they had grains of sand in them.[15]

Still unconvinced, Ledru's superiors agreed to lock him up and keep him under close watch. As an experiment, they gave him a pistol (loaded with blanks), which he stashed under his pillow. After sleeping soundly for three nights, on the fourth night, he arose in his sleep around midnight and pulled out the gun, firing at close range on one of the guards.

This was what the authorities needed to believe Ledru's tale. He was sent to live in seclusion on a countryside farm, where he was watched by guards and medical personnel for a whopping fifty years, until his death in 1937.

At the time of Monet's murder, Ledru was said to be suffering from overwork as well as syphilis, which he'd contracted a decade earlier[16]—left untreated, the sexually transmitted disease is associated with mental illness and perhaps was a factor in his sleepwalking violence.

While Ledru seemed to have been a scrupulously honest cop, even willing to put himself under the bus, his "interpretive" biographer Frederik Oughton characterized him as a kind of Jekyll/Hyde who was both the "disgrace and admiration of Paris."

A blurb for Oughton's book described Ledru as "the archetype of the very criminals whom he relentlessly hunted and then used for his own ends. He was judge and executioner, blackmailer, and conniver."[17]

STABBINGS IN THE DARK: THE KENNETH PARKS ATTACKS

Kenneth Parks was troubled as he nodded out in the early-morning hours of May 23, 1987. Nicknamed the "Gentle Giant," the six-and-a-half-foot-tall Canadian weighed 280 pounds. He'd been banished to the couch by his wife, Karen, while they dealt with his gambling problem.

It was no minor issue. The twenty-four-year-old had sunk the family's finances with his compulsion for horserace betting and embezzled $32,000 from his employer to fund it. The company caught on, fired him, and started court proceedings against him.

Karen had given him an ultimatum—stop gambling or she'd take their infant daughter and leave. Further, she insisted that he reveal everything to her parents at a family barbecue that was scheduled the next day at their house fourteen miles away in the Toronto suburb of Scarborough.

Up to that point, Karen's parents, Barbara Ann and Denis Woods, unaware of Ken's gambling and arrest, were grateful to him, as years earlier he'd convinced their daughter, then a teenage runaway, to return home. Ken, in turn, had greatly admired Barbara and

Denis, as they provided stability that his own upbringing lacked. So it must have heavily weighed on his mind as he tried to sleep—would they reject him when they found out about his misdeeds?

Ken has no memory of what happened next. He put on his shoes, grabbed his car keys, and jumped into his vehicle, leaving the door to his house as well as the garage wide open as he headed out into the night.[18] He managed to drive the fourteen miles to his in-laws' home—a familiar journey, yet a mind-bogglingly long one to make while unconscious.

Denis Woods awoke to a nightmare. In the darkness, a large man had his hands around his neck in a stranglehold. He sputtered, "Help me, Bobbie!" to his wife, sleeping next to him, as he kicked his legs in desperation. But he soon lost consciousness.[19]

Parks's first memory fragment of that night was "a very sad" image of his mother-in-law's face. Eyes open, mouth agape, it was this visage frozen in his mind from around the time he'd murdered her.[20]

Barbara Woods was dragged to the bathroom a few feet away from the bedroom. She'd been viciously stabbed with a kitchen knife in the chest, shoulder, and heart, as well as smashed in the skull with a tire iron.

Parks's second memory fragment was hearing the Woods kids yelling and going upstairs to check on them as he called out to them. But what the teenage girls heard were terrifying animalistic grunts, as he passed by their rooms without opening their doors.[21]

At around four forty-five a.m., a dazed Kenneth Parks showed up at the local police station. Dripping with blood, he confessed, "I've just killed two people with my hands; my God, I've just killed two people . . . I've just killed my mother- and father-in-law. I stabbed and beat them to death. It's all my fault."[22]

But Denis Woods, who'd also been stabbed, had survived. At the time of Parks's confession, Woods was returning to consciousness in a blood-soaked bed, finding police already in his room.

Back at the police station, Parks suddenly noticed the cuts in his hands, blood pooling onto the floor. "My hands!" he gasped. He'd cut through the tendons of all ten of his fingers—the kitchen knife must have slid during the savage stabbings. Such an injury would normally be excruciatingly painful, yet in an example of dissociative analgesia, he did not exhibit any signs of pain.

The fact that Parks had gone straight to the police station and had no real motive for the crime led authorities to conclude that sleepwalking was the most likely explanation. But that's not grounds for automatic acquittal, and Parks was jailed on charges of first-degree murder.

During the four months before the trial, he maintained a precise consistency of what he could and could not recall about the event when interviewed by a battery of shrinks, lawyers, and cops. He underwent extensive tests, and while psychologists found no evidence of psychosis or delusion, his brain waves and sleep patterns indicated sleepwalking and other parasomnias.[23] After one test, Parks was even observed by his cellmates eerily sitting up in his sleep, eyes open, and mumbling.[24]

Parks's family tree was mapped, and parasomnias were shown to run rampant, particularly among the men. Ken's grandfather, for instance, was known for sleepwalking into the kitchen, frying eggs and onions on the stove, and then returning to bed without eating them. When Ken was eleven, Ken's grandmother had caught him just in the nick of time as he attempted to climb out a sixth-story window.[25] He'd also struggled with bedwetting, was known as a deep sleeper, and could be very difficult to awaken.

On the two nights before the crime, he'd been unable to sleep, ruminating about his marriage, gambling addiction, loss of job, and embezzlement charges. On the third night, his body was desperate to catch up on deep or slow-wave sleep—the kind associated with sleepwalking.

Parks's attorney didn't deny that he attacked his in-laws. It was a kind of "non-insane automatism," he argued, and he wasn't accountable because the crimes were committed involuntarily. By skirting the insanity defense, he claimed sleepwalking was not a "disease of the mind," and Parks wasn't in need of a psychiatric commitment.

At the trial, assistant neurology professor Roger Broughton from McGill University testified that Parks was likely in a deep sleep state and acting out a dream as he drove to the Woods home. Upon arriving, his mother-in-law tried to awaken him, and Parks flew into an uncontrollable rage, Broughton conjectured—sleepwalkers often react with aggression when suddenly confronted, he noted.[26]

How did Parks see to drive if he was sleepwalking? the prosecuting attorney inquired. Broughton explained that sleepwalkers have their eyes open and can perform complex maneuvers on a kind of autopilot.

"What true sleepwalkers cannot do," writes Prof. Rosalind Cartwright, "is recognize the faces of those they attack, even loved ones." There are two separate visual pathways, she explained, one for motion and navigating through space, and the other for face recognition, and they terminate in different parts of the brain.[27]

The evidence for Parks's sleepwalking, including his sleep deprivation, lack of motive, and absence of pain symptoms from cut tendons, was enough to sway the jury. After just a few hours of deliberation, he was cleared of all charges and set free.

While parasomnia experts like Dr. Carlos Schenck think the jury got it right, others aren't so sure. Berit Brogaard, a professor of philosophy who runs a perception lab at the University of Miami, casts doubt on the Parks defense.

"It is just plainly implausible" that he made the fourteen-mile drive without incident, she writes, and "that a severe struggle with his in-laws, them screaming at him . . . pleading with him, failed to wake him up." The fact that Kenneth remembers his mother-in-law's face suggests some consciousness, and the dissociative analgesia from his hand injuries may have stemmed from being in shock over his violent deeds rather than being asleep, she writes.

Brogaard concluded that Parks's actions were not entirely automatic, and he may have repressed his memories of the attacks, which perhaps were carried out more in the mode of temporary insanity, or in a hallucinatory fugue.[28]

Prosecutors ended up appealing the decision all the way up to the Canadian Supreme Court. Though troubled, they backed the jury's original ruling, writing, "When asleep, no one reasons, remembers or understands . . . If the respondent's acts were not proved to be voluntary, he was not guilty."[29]

Kenneth and Karen Parks eventually divorced, though she'd testified on his behalf at the trial.

OFF THE DEEP END: THE SCOTT FALATER CASE

On a brisk January night in 1997, eerie shadows danced around Yarmila Falater as she floated facedown in her backyard swimming pool, illuminated by motion detector lights.

Her husband Scott Falater sat in the corner of a small Phoenix police interrogation room. Balding and bespectacled, the Mormon

Sunday school teacher and successful computer engineer cut an unassuming figure. Hunched forward, he was barefoot and wearing pajama bottoms and a T-shirt.

"What went wrong?" asked the officer.

"I'm sorry, nothing," he replied with a quiet insistence. "I love my wife."[30]

Scott Falater said he had no memory of anything untoward. He'd awakened to the sound of their dogs barking and a commotion outside, with police banging on their door. They'd been summoned by the next-door neighbor, Greg Koons, who'd witnessed something horrifying—Scott drowning his wife.

But Yarmila hadn't just drowned; she'd been stabbed forty-four times with a hunting knife. When police officers arrived on the scene, they found Scott Falater to be shaky and short of breath. There were bloodstains on his upper arm and behind his right ear.

The first question Scott remembers the police asking him was "How many people are in the house?" To which he replied, "Four" (himself, his wife, and two children), seemingly not knowing his wife was dead in the pool.[31]

Koons and his girlfriend had gone to bed just after ten p.m., but their slumber was disturbed by sounds coming from the Falaters' backyard. At first, they thought they were hearing the moans of people having poolside sex. But then a woman's voice seemed to pierce through the air, screaming "Please, no," or "Please, don't." Greg went to investigate.[32]

Standing on a planter to peer over a cinder-block wall into the Falaters' property, Koons saw a woman lying near the pool, rolling onto her back. He thought she might be drunk. On the second floor, a light came on; Scott Falater stood in the now-lit room. Within a few minutes, other lights turned on and off, and at one point Koons saw

Falater wringing his hands in a sink. Then he came downstairs and stepped out into the yard.

Scott stood over Yarmila's body for a minute or two, taking no action. Next, he went back inside. Returning via a garage side door, he had two canvas gloves, one already slid onto his hand. He dragged and pushed Yarmila's body into the pool. According to Koons, Scott Falater held his wife's head underwater with his hands until she was lifeless. It was at this point that Koons finally returned home and called 911.

After Falater was apprehended, the police searched the area and noticed a lit flashlight pointing toward the pool pump, with bloodstains in the ground around it. The garage held a fount of incriminating evidence. A bloody T-shirt was sticking out of the trunk of Falater's station wagon. When they opened the trunk, they found a large plastic container filled with blood-soaked clothes, including jeans and socks, as well as a blood-covered hunting knife. Next to the bin was a black garbage bag that held Falater's crimson-stained leather boots and soaked leather gloves.

It seemed reasonably clear that Scott had changed out of these bloody clothes after he'd stabbed Yarmila, and then made several trips to the garage to stash the evidence, as well as placed a bandage over a cut on his hand when he went inside.

By all reports, the couple, high school sweethearts, had a loving marriage, and there'd never been any episodes of violence. Falater had no criminal history. Would a loving husband slash his partner of nearly twenty years as his children slept upstairs? Would someone trying to get away with murder choose a lighted swimming pool that neighbors could see into?

As Yarmila's funeral took place at a cemetery in Scottsdale, Scott Falater was locked up and charged with first-degree murder. Respected criminal attorney Mike Kimerer took his case, and after finding out from Scott's mother that her son sleepwalked as a child and into young adulthood, a defense strategy took shape: Yes, Scott committed the murder, but he wasn't responsible. He was asleep. Initially, Falater was said to resist this defense—it just didn't seem plausible to him.[33] But what other explanation was there?

As in the Parks case, the defense claimed it was another instance of "non-insane automatism," and would bring in some of the same esteemed sleep experts to testify: Roger Broughton and Rosalind Cartwright.

Before Scott went to bed that fateful night, there was no major argument or fight with Yarmila. While she disagreed with a work strategy he shared with her, it wasn't a heated discussion. She'd asked him to take a look at the broken pool pump, which he'd tried to repair until it became too dark to see clearly. He hit the sack just after coming in from the pool. Yarmila was already asleep on the living room couch as *ER* flickered across the TV. The kids had gone to bed earlier.

Scott's defense team suggested he was bothered by the unfinished task and in his sleep went to complete it, using the knife to cut out an O ring from the pump. But Yarmila must have startled him, and with knife in hand he reacted violently, as though she were an intruder or attacker.

Scott's sister Laura described a 1975 incident in which her twenty-year-old brother walked into the family kitchen one night half-dressed and in a trancelike state. As he stumbled at the back door, she slipped around him and locked the dead bolt. Scott reacted violently. "He kind of lifted me up and tossed me," she told the *Phoenix New Times*. "His face looked almost demonic when he reacted to me, and it really scared the hell out of me."[34]

Before the trial, Scott was monitored in a sleep lab for four nights on a polysomnograph and exhibited hypersynchronous delta waves, a brain pattern that has some association with sleepwalking.[35]

When the trial began, the state's prosecutor Juan Martinez (who would later go on to convict Jodi Arias in a sensational murder case) scoffed at the sleepwalking defense and produced his own sleep experts to counter the defense's. If someone is genuinely sleepwalking when they commit a crime, they generally do not attempt to cover it up. While Falater seemed to show some signs of covering his tracks—changing clothes and stashing items in a plastic bin—Cartwright notes that he did not clean the blood from the knife or try to hide or remove his wife's body.

"This was not the act," she writes, "of a man in full possession of his decision-making powers."[36] Further, there was a history of sleep disorders in Falater's family line.

Dr. Mark Pressman, a psychologist and director of two Philadelphia-area sleep clinics, was one of the prosecution's sleep experts. He pointed to the importance of the neighbor's eyewitness testimony, which indicated a deliberateness to Falater's behaviors.

He explained to the jury, "The only way that sleep experts think that violence can happen with a sleepwalker is that somebody physically confronts them, gets in their way. That's clearly impossible on the second episode of violence," when Scott Falater went back out to the pool to drown his wife.[37]

The neighbor witnessed another damaging piece of evidence. When Scott came back out of the house just before drowning Yarmila, he calmed his barking dog. Dr. Cartwright suggests this may have been done not in response to auditory cues (which sleepwalkers typically don't hear) but because the dog was jumping up on him.[38] Still, jurors may have puzzled over how he could seemingly recognize and comfort his dog but not his dying wife.

The defense argued that Scott had anxiety over a work situation—the possible cancellation of his project, which would cause his team members to lose their jobs. These worries led to sleep deprivation in the nights preceding the murder, which triggered the sleepwalking. But in the battle of the sleep experts, while the jurors warmed to the empathetic Dr. Cartwright, they couldn't ignore the prosecution's Dr. Pressman, who cited some sixty-five behaviors Falater performed during the crime that he viewed as inconsistent with sleepwalking.[39]

At the conclusion of the six-week trial in June 1999, local TV and radio stations broadcast the verdict live. Though a credible motive was never established, Scott Falater was found guilty of first-degree murder and sentenced to life imprisonment without the possibility of parole.

Several years after the conviction, Dr. Cartwright contended that new protocols in the laboratory testing and diagnosis of sleep-walking had emerged, and Scott deserved a new trial. But the appeal was rejected by the Arizona Supreme Court, possibly because Dr. Pressman produced a rebuttal stating that there was no independent verification of the new research.

When Dr. Cartwright assessed Falater before the trial she found him to be a "cool customer" though truly bewildered about his circumstances. At one point, his reserve faltered, and the tears began to flow.

"What upsets me the most," he told Cartwright, "is that I didn't know I was killing her, but she did. She must have looked right at me and wondered how I, who loved her, could be attacking her."[40]

Arizona-based reporter Paul Rubin covered the murder extensively, attending the trial, interviewing Falater in jail, and speaking with jury members afterward. Twenty years on, I caught up with him by phone to see how he looked back on the controversial case. The neighbor's testimony, he pointed out, was quite damning in terms of what he saw—Scott shushing his dog, washing his hands upstairs, and deliberately stepping over the body before he pushed it into the pool. Rubin concluded that Scott was "possibly in a dreamlike state in the beginning of the incident" but "was not in a dreamlike state by the time the incident ended."

The jurors liked the mild-mannered Scott (who testified on the stand) and didn't care much for the cutthroat tactics of the prosecutor, Rubin told me. "But most of the jurors came to the same conclusion that I did independently, which was that the neighbor sunk him." He doesn't believe, though, that Falater came home that night planning to kill his wife. "I think it just happened," said Rubin, who now works as a private investigator. "I think it turned from a potential manslaughter case"—a heat-of-passion type thing—into something more premeditated.

THE BRAIN ON TRIAL

If Parks and Falater were genuinely sleepwalking, why did they go berserk? "Sleepwalking might not be an appropriate term for what is going on," writes neuroscientist Philip Jaekl. In this condition, archaic brain regions related to emotions, such as the limbic system, and motor activities in the cortex "remain in 'active' states that are difficult to distinguish from wakefulness."

"At the same time," he continues, "regions in the frontal cortex and hippocampus that control rationality and memory remain essentially dormant and unable to carry out their typical functions, manifesting a 'delta wave' pattern seen during classic sleep."[41]

The brain's survival instincts date back eons to when the darkness of nighttime was fraught with terrors, and studies indicate that sleepwalking could be initiated by a haywire vigilance mechanism. The limbic system then dispenses fear like a gumball machine, perhaps igniting primitive behaviors in the throes of the fight-or-flight response.

Emerging brain science and jurisprudence can make for strange bedfellows, though. Fordham University legal scholar Deborah Denno has written about the lack of uniform standards for court cases dealing with sleep crimes. The criminal code relating to unconscious and involuntary states, she notes, hasn't been updated since the 1950s when Freudian interpretations held sway. When it comes to culpability, she views the categories of voluntary or involuntary as too limited when applied to some of the more perplexing sleepwalking criminal cases that straddle our definitions of consciousness. She has proposed a third choice: semivoluntary.[42]

This choice would allow people such as Ken Parks to be held more accountable rather than getting off scot-free. "I don't think that he should have been acquitted," she explained. "There were aspects of his background that suggest that there should be another choice and a way to capture him into the criminal justice system. You may want to tell someone like Parks, 'If for the next year you take your medications and keep out of trouble, then we won't prosecute this crime.'"[43]

To sleep, perchance to dream. To sleep, perchance to murder?

CHAPTER FOUR

SLEEP DEPRIVATION

Peter Tripp looks past his microphone and stares through the window right onto Times Square. He's the DJ in the center of the universe, pulsing with life, as thousands of people move to the beat of his music.

But maybe that's just an illusion. Are they oblivious of him? Goddamn insects in a hive, scurrying around in circles, with no discernible reason or destination.

Soon they'll stop in their tracks. They'll push and claw for a closer glimpse, he thinks. Pressing their faces against the window. Beautiful women leaving lipstick prints on the glass that will spell out *TRIPP* in glowing red letters.

The whole world will know the name. New York City already knows the voice, blasting out every afternoon to millions. After pulling off this stunt, he'll be huge. Allan Freed huge.

If only that merciless clock on the wall would stop staring, like it owns him. Its hands are digging into his mind, like the needle in this record, each tick a tiny tear. Cutting through his thoughts. But now he can see through. That clock is just a mask, hiding the face of his best friend, watching over him. . . . But, wait, then why does his friend suddenly look like he wants to kill him?

Behind Tripp, a chalkboard reads *Hours Awake: 65.*

"And that, ladies and gentlemen, was the dulcet tones of the brothers Santo and Johnny, with their smash hit 'Sleep Walk.' An appropriate song, considering I've been awake now for three nights straight. Why? Because I refuse to say good night to all my fans here at WMGM! We'll be right back after this word from Camel. Every inch a real smoke!"

Peter Tripp turns off the mic. "Who turned off the heat? It's colder than a morgue in here!"[1]

ROCK AROUND THE CLOCK

The year was 1959, a golden era for radio DJs—some of them, like Allan Freed, were household names, bigger even than the music acts they promoted. Tripp wanted to be one of them, so he came up with a stunt. He would stay awake for ten days and broadcast his show live from a glass booth in the heart of Times Square. The wake-a-thon was presented as a charity benefit for the March of Dimes, and station management contacted sleep researchers to keep an eye on him.

"I don't think anyone thought Peter Tripp was going to stay awake more than two or three days," said Dr. Floyd Cornelison, professor of psychiatry at Jefferson Medical College in Philadelphia; he and Dr. Louis West were Tripp's professional minders.

"I had the graveyard shift from midnight to eight o'clock in the morning because after two or three days" he wanted to play games,

distract us for a few minutes so he could catnap, Cornelison continued. "We wouldn't let him do this. He would say, 'I'll just go to the
bathroom for a few minutes.' We said ... we're going to the bathroom
with you. Oh, he was mad and incensed. Finally, we said, 'Look, if
you go to the bathroom and sit down, you're going to go to sleep,
and ... the whole experiment is over.' ... As inconvenient and awkward as it was, we were with this man constantly."[2]

Tripp started off in a chipper mood, but after a few days, he grew
ill-tempered and increasingly plagued by paranoia and hallucinations. He was able to dial back into reality, however, when it was
time for his three-hour live show.

By day five, a menagerie of unreal creatures were sharing the
makeshift studio with him—mice and kittens darting about, and
menacingly, spiders crawled around inside his shoes. When he took
a break to shower at a nearby hotel room and change his clothes, he
hallucinated flames shooting out of a drawer and believed the doctors had set them up to scare him into quitting.[3] Were the doctors,
Tripp wondered, in a conspiracy against him? At one point, he mistook a scientist in a dark overcoat for an undertaker, who he thought
was there to take his body away. He dashed out into the street in a
panic.[4]

"His mean body temperature progressively declined ... and the
lower it went," Dr. West commented, "the crazier he got."

The likes of mystic G. I. Gurdjieff and the Indian guru Osho have
posited that we are always dreaming—it's just a question of whether
the mind is tuning into that frequency. In fact, one of the researchers' discoveries was that Tripp's hallucinatory periods seemed to
shadow a normal REM sleep cycle, and "it was as though he was
having dreams even though he was awake," said West.

With the help of amphetamines, administered by the doctors

during the last three days, Peter Tripp managed to stay awake for 201 hours. Toward the end, he became convinced that he was someone other than himself—an ironic twist for a publicity stunt staged to get your name out there.

When it was over, Peter Tripp slept for thirteen hours and thirteen minutes and was seemingly no worse for wear. (Alas, just a few weeks later, he was indicted in a payola scandal that also netted Alan Freed, and his radio career was in tatters. He left the Big Apple nearly penniless.[5])

WILL THE REAL RANDY GARDNER PLEASE STAND UP?

Three young men appear in silhouette on an elevated TV stage, as an announcer intones: "One of these men holds an unusual world record."

The Guinness titleholder was the figure in the middle, a seventeen-year-old San Diego high school student named Randy Gardner, who'd managed to stay awake longer than anyone in recorded history—eleven days.

Under light questioning of the 1964 *To Tell the Truth* panelists, all three of the well-scrubbed lads gave little clue that anything strange or concerning happened during the 264 hours Gardner stayed awake while on a Christmas break from school. Indeed, many summaries of the case neglect to mention the hallucinations, paranoia, and mental disturbances he experienced.[6] And Guinness stopped listing records for voluntary sleep deprivation over health concerns sometime after Gardner's success.

It all started with a school science project. Randy and his friend Bruce McAllister, with invincible teenage spirit, decided to try to best the current record holder, a DJ in Honolulu, who'd gone 260 hours without sleep. Initially they wanted to observe the effect of sleeplessness on paranormal ability, but they realized this would be hard to test, so they opted for cognitive ability and performance on a basketball court.[7]

Bruce won a coin toss and opted for Randy to be the guinea pig. But they didn't have much in the way of methodology for tracking the effects.

"I stayed awake with him to monitor him," said McAllister, "and after three nights of sleeplessness myself, I woke up tipped against the wall writing notes on the wall itself." So the teens brought in a third friend to assist. In contrast to some of the DJ stunts, Randy avoided ingesting stimulants, other than occasional Cokes.

The press picked up the story, though they grouped the experiment in with teenage pranks like swallowing goldfish or seeing how many people could be crammed into a telephone booth. For a brief window, it became the third most reported story in America, after the JFK assassination and a stateside visit by the Beatles.[8] It also got the attention of Dr. William Dement of Stanford University, who offered to get involved. Now considered a world authority on sleep issues, back in 1964 he was just beginning his research in the nascent field.

Randy's parents were concerned that their son might do irreparable damage to himself or even die from the lack of sleep, and they were relieved when Dr. Dement arrived for the last few days of the experiment. Dement noted that Randy remained physically fit and could be kept active with things like bowling or basketball, but if he closed his eyes even for a moment he would immediately start to fall asleep.

At the parents' urging, Randy was also observed by Lt. Cmdr.

John J. Ross of the U.S. Navy Medical Neuropsychiatric Research Unit in San Diego, who made detailed notes of anomalies in the boy's condition over the eleven-day run.[9] These included signs of astereognosis, or difficulty recognizing objects only by the sense of touch (day 2); ataxia, difficulty repeating simple tongue twisters (day 3); and irritability and memory lapses (day 4).

On day 4, the hallucinations and delusions started to kick in, though sometimes they were considered "hypnagogic reveries" as Randy recognized them as illusory. He thought that a street sign was a person and became convinced that he, a white teen, was the African American running back for the San Diego Chargers. When indoors, at one point, he saw a path leading to a peaceful forest. By the last day of the experiment, Gardner had an expressionless affect, slurred speech, and diminished mental abilities. Then he was whisked off to the naval hospital for some final brain wave testing.

Randy slept for fourteen hours. "And then he got up and went to high school," said Dr. Dement. "It was amazing."

According to McAllister, the test results showed that Randy's brain had been "catnapping" the entire time, with parts of it awake and other parts asleep. This correlates with findings about certain birds and sea animals that go to sleep in one brain hemisphere while the other stays awake to navigate the air or sea.

Randy Gardner appeared the picture of health on *To Tell the Truth* a few months later, though panelist Peggy Cass said she chose him as the non-impostor because "he looked the most sleepy."

Fast-forward forty-six years, when a *New York Times* columnist dropped in on him for lunch. Still living in San Diego, Gardner said he remains proud of his youthful feat. But what plagues him now? The man is bedeviled by insomnia! Sometimes he's up at three in the morning, slamming doors in frustration. "Every single night I try to go to sleep, and I don't know what it's going to be like."[10] Perhaps a fitting karmic turn for someone who dared to defy sleep in the hubris of youth?

HALLUCINATION NATION

The British writer and consciousness researcher Tony Wright claims to have bested Randy Gardner's record in 2007, going without sleep for an eleven-night stretch, while under the view of a webcam and closed-circuit television (CCTV) at his local watering hole, the Studio Bar in the town of Penzance in Cornwall. Viewers could watch him consuming a "Stone Age" diet of fruits and nuts, drinking herbal tea, and playing pool, but on occasion he appeared motionless, raising the specter of catnapping or worse.

"The webcam," Wright explained in his online diary, "seems to give an unhelpful impression of total stillness when one is pondering one's creative insights . . . Several emails appeared and the phone rang to point out the lack of vital signs so efforts were made to ensure my existence had not prematurely ended."[11]

At the midway point, "giggling, dancing pixies and elves" made contact with Wright via his computer screen, but what sets apart the long-haired gent from other sleep-fasters is that he's disseminated an overarching theory of sleep and the human brain. Published in 2008, his book, co-written with Graham Gynn, *Left in the Dark*, poses that sometime in the dim past, our brains did not separate functions into two different hemispheres but worked in a unified capacity. A long-term decline took place, they suggest, with particular damage to the left or dominant side of the brain. This altered human consciousness "and created a distorted experience not so much of the outside world, but of the inner world—our very feelings of who or what we are."[12]

Through sleep deprivation, Wright believes one can exhaust the left side of the brain, decreasing its dominance and "monkey mind" chatter, as well as its ability to suppress the right side's "spiritual" aspects, including telepathy. During one of his deprivation trials, he experienced an "all encompassing religious bliss" for about twenty minutes, in which he thinks his left hemisphere went to sleep. "The self that had been to sleep," explained Wright, "felt it had missed out on something. When it woke up it wanted to find out who had been running the show."[13] Wright also accessed profound childhood memories, with exquisite recall of emotions, smells, and visual details. The left hemisphere, he concludes, accesses mainly superficial or recent memories and blocks significant recollections from one's past.

New Zealander Jess Vlaanderen reported on her similar experiments via YouTube around 2012. Her lofty goal was to hallucinate without the use of drugs, and she found that was entirely possible during a 110-hour awake stretch. Even though she was continually fighting the overpowering urge to sleep, she enjoyed the trippy visuals.

Vlaanderen described a "colorful complex universe" reminiscent of ayahuasca effects. "It's like you're in a cartoon," she told *Vice*. "People and objects become very comical . . . Cars floated, shadows hung from trees, zombies ran at me in the street. I felt I could control the clouds, as they appeared to morph and mutate. And then when I went to the supermarket the items on the shelves appeared to follow me."[14] Yet at one point she had a kind of seizure usually associated with epilepsy. While she has no memory of the event, her friend said she was repetitively shaking her head from side to side while talking, and later giggling uncontrollably.

As a teenager on a school-sponsored trip to Europe in 2004, Seth Maxon decided to see how long he could go without sleep, fueled by espresso and rambling into his journal. By the third day, he was convinced that his newly derived theories about the origin of the universe would change the world. At one point, he spoke exclusively in rhyme (likewise, Wright reported that one day, all his thoughts occurred in a kind of exalted rhyme). "I remember telling people," said Maxon, "that circles were divine, and instituting a policy of smacking my head when I made mistakes . . . On the bus ride home from JFK airport, I thought that if I concentrated hard enough, I could jump out of our bus onto the highway and land at a run . . . I remember thinking I was dead, and that I had landed in a very Earthlike eternity."[15]

Where Maxon did end up was in a hospital and placed on antipsychotic medication. He was gradually weaned off the meds and resumed a normal life, going to college and eventually becoming a journalist.

Some sleep deprivationists don't fare as well. A Chinese soccer fan, Jiang Xiaoshan, stayed awake for an eleven-day stretch of the European Football Championship in 2012. Because of the time difference in China, the games aired in the middle of the night, and the twenty-six-year-old watched them with friends while drinking and smoking before heading off to work every morning. When the last soccer ball was kicked, he finally went to bed. He never awakened. On top of the chronic exhaustion, alcohol and tobacco were cited as contributing factors to his weakened condition and death.[16]

It's hypothesized that the longer we stay awake, the more adenosine, a toxic by-product of the body's energy production, is built up in the bloodstream. Sleep offers a degree of cellular rejuvenation, "and when we interfere with that, systems go out of sync," explains Dr. Joyce Walsleben, a psychiatrist specializing in sleep disorders.[17]

Prof. Danny Eckert, head of the NeuRA Sleep and Breathing Lab in Australia, explained to me that throughout the day (i.e., the longer we are awake) we accumulate various neurotransmitters within the central nervous system (CNS). "Adenosine is one that has a sleep-promoting effect so as adenosine builds up throughout the day, this contributes, at least in part, to sleepiness."

Does the adenosine itself cause hallucinations? "When we are sleep deprived," Eckert replied, "adenosine CNS levels become much higher and significant sleep deprivation can trigger halluci-nations. So the link between sleep deprivation, adenosine, and hal-lucinations is indirect. I am not aware of any evidence that adenosine per se causes hallucinations. Of course, caffeine is a potent adeno-sine antagonist, which is why it gives us an alerting boost."

For more on the hallucinatory angle, let's drift back to the '90s to review the results of the first "controlled" sleep deprivation study. I'm talking about the 1890s, when three healthy young men were kept awake for ninety hours at the University of Iowa. One began to have intense hallucinations after only the second night. "The sub-ject complained that the floor was covered with a greasy-looking, molecular layer of rapidly moving or oscillating particles," the study's authors recounted. "Often this layer was a foot above the floor . . . and caused the subject trouble in walking, as he would try to step up on it. Later the air was full of these dancing particles which developed into swarms of little bodies like gnats, but colored red, purple or black. The subject would climb upon a chair to brush them . . . or stealthily try to touch an imaginary fly on the table with his finger. These phenomena did not move with movements of the eye and appeared to be true hallucinations . . . they entirely disappeared after sleep."[18]

While cognitive function and motor skills are known to take a hit with lack of sleep, around 80 percent of people report visual hallucinations when deprived of slumber for a long enough time. In a study of 350 people who were kept awake for 112 hours, 2 percent experienced symptoms akin to acute paranoid schizophrenia.[19]

Dr. Steven Feinsilver, now the director of Lenox Hill Hospital's Center for Sleep Medicine, had his own sliver of psychosis one autumn when he was a sleep-deprived medical resident stationed on an intensive care unit. "The reason I know it was October," he recalled, was that "there was a pumpkin at the nursing station, and I hallucinated vividly the pumpkin was talking to me. . . . It's the only time I ever hallucinated in my life."[20]

After just one lost night of shut-eye, a person may experience *microsleep*, which refers to uncontrollably falling asleep for up to thirty seconds at a time. What's disturbing about the phenomenon, said Dr. Feinsilver, is that this can happen to someone while their eyes are open. During those moments, they're virtually blind and not processing information.[21]

MICROSLEEP AND THE BLACK DOG

Microsleep is a particular threat for overnight truckers driving across some of America's uniquely long and monotonous highways. In fact, it's practically a rite of passage to "see the black dog," a hallucinatory portent that it's time to pull off the road and get some rest.

"I was coming out of Utah into Wyoming," said Joseph Cannell, a popular video blogger on the trucking industry, "and it was around two in the morning . . . and I actually did see a black dog," running along the shoulder of the road near the scale house. "That was an actual occurrence." He's speaking from the cab of his truck, the sound of motors running in the distance.[22]

Somewhere between fifteen minutes and an hour later, Cannell saw what appeared to be the same black dog again, this time just sitting on the side of the road, its eyes aglow from his headlights. "Second time, I was like, how many damn dogs are out here in Wyoming?" he chuckled. "Time's not really with me anymore. I know I'm dead-ass tired." Then he saw a black blur moving in his peripheral vision. He darts his head from side to side to demonstrate. "I don't know what the hell that was . . . I can guess what happened is that I probably microslept . . . You're completely confused, and you gotta get off the road. Your brain is actually shutting down."

The old story of the black dog is that if you see it two or three times, "you're at the end. You've got no more. It's either get off the road or the black dog will take you." Your brain, Cannell adds, may not alert you in time—a potentially tragic risk not only for the driver but for whoever is in the path of an eighty thousand-pound eighteen-wheeler careening out of control.

But why the black dog? Is there something archetypal about the creature? Tales of phantom black dogs from the British Isles date back almost a thousand years, and sightings were often considered an omen of death. Usually described as bigger than average and having large, glowing eyes, the "devil dogs" were said to frequent crossroads, ancient roadways, and execution sites. "There are dogs who dissolve into mist," writes Andy Wright of the spectral accounts.[23] "There are dogs with no heads and dogs with human faces. Dogs the size of houses and dogs who walk on their hind legs."

Dead-tired drivers, when you see the black dog "you're at the end.... It's either get off the road or the black dog will take you." Drawing by Jason Jam, 2018.

Like Cerberus, perhaps these phantasmagoric hellhounds are liminal guards, keeping watch for when a driver along the interstate slides into the dream lane.

CRUEL AND UNUSUAL: SLEEP DEPRIVATION AS TORTURE

While a phantom dog sighting may be enough to scare you awake, the all-too-real practice of sleep deprivation as a form of military and political torture is horrifying enough to lose sleep over. It's even been employed as a form of execution. In a harrowing account reported in the *Louisville Semi-Monthly Medical News* in 1869, a

Chinese merchant was convicted of murdering his wife and then sentenced to die from lack of sleep. In his cell, three prison guards took turns making sure he never caught a wink. The report goes on:

> He thus lived 19 days without enjoying any sleep. At the commencement of the eighth day his sufferings were so intense that he implored the authorities to grant him the blessed opportunity of being strangled, guillotined, burned to death, drowned, garotted, shot, quartered, blown up with gunpowder, or put to death in any conceivable way their humanity or ferocity could invent. This will give a slight idea of the horrors of death from want of sleep.[24]

A fifteenth-century Italian lawyer named Hippolytus de Marsiliis has the somewhat dubious distinction of being the first to pioneer sleep deprivation as a form of torture. Seeking to obtain confessions during the Inquisition, he was said to instruct his guards to shake prisoners at random intervals, stick them with sharp pins, and ceaselessly parade them up and down hallways.[25]

In the next century, during witch hunts in Scotland and England, confessions were sometimes extracted by "waking the witch," a method that involved depriving an accused person of sleep for so long that she began to hallucinate. What she said, saw, and did during these breaks from reality were considered legal evidence against her.[26] The 1895 *Dictionary of Phrase and Fable* explained it this way:

> If a "witch" was obdurate, the most effectual way of obtaining a confession was by what was termed "waking her." For this purpose, an iron bridle or hoop was bound across her face with

four prongs thrust into her mouth. The "bridle" was fastened behind to the wall by a chain in such a manner that the victim was unable to lie down; and in this position she was kept sometimes for several days, while men were constantly by to keep her awake. In Scotland, some of these bridles are still preserved.[27]

In the Stalinist era, sleep deprivation was honed to a deadly art in the Soviet gulags and prisons. Aleksandr Solzhenitsyn wrote in his pivotal manuscript *The Gulag Archipelago* how forced sleeplessness, combined with long periods of standing, thirst, and exposure to bright lights "befogs the reason, undermines the will, and the human being ceases to be himself, to be his own 'I.'"

Describing the plight of inmate Yelena Strutinskaya, Solzhenitsyn said she was "forced to remain seated on a stool in the corridor for six days in such a way that she did not lean against anything, did not sleep, did not fall off, and did not get up from it. Six days! Just try to sit that way for six hours!"

"Sleeplessness was a great form of torture," he continued; "it left no visible marks and could not provide grounds for a complaint even if an inspection—something unheard of anyway—were to strike on the morrow."[28]

Imprisoned by the KGB in the 1940s, future Israeli prime minister Menachem Begin was subjected to similar cruelties. The prisoner's spirit, he said, becomes whittled down to the point where there is but one desire: to sleep. "Anyone who has experienced this desire knows that not even hunger or thirst are comparable with it." He met prisoners who signed whatever documents they were asked to get what the interrogators promised. "He did not promise them their liberty; he did not promise them food to sate themselves. He promised them—if they signed—uninterrupted sleep! And, having signed, there was nothing in the world that could move them to risk again such nights and such days."[29]

This overpowering urge to sleep was memorably depicted in the original *Invasion of the Body Snatchers*. Even though Becky, the lead female character, knows she'll be turned into a "pod person" if she goes to sleep, in the end, she cannot fight its siren call.

In the post-9/11 War on Terror, the Army and CIA readily employed sleep deprivation in Guantanamo Bay and Iraq, shackling or chaining detainees in an upright position for days at a time. During the George W. Bush administration, such "enhanced interrogation techniques" (including sleep and sensory deprivation, waterboarding, cold temperatures, and the 24/7 playing of loud music) were claimed to be something less than torture. The U.S. military sometimes uses loopholes like *monstering*, in which the interrogator stays awake as long as the prisoner being questioned, to avoid violating the Army Field Manual. One interrogator, identified by the pseudonym Chris Mackey, said that monstering can yield valuable intelligence.[30] But although the technique may be effective in breaking someone's will, the longer a subject goes without sleep, the more likely they are to be confused, susceptible to false memories,[31] and out of touch with reality.

For the military, going without sleep isn't something just to inflict upon the captured. It's a long-embraced practice to keep soldiers and pilots awake beyond their normal endurance to complete missions while staying alert and vigilant. In World War II, amphetamines were widely dispensed by both the Axis and Allied powers. American GIs popped up to two hundred million[32] under the catchy name of "go pills" or "pep pills." The crazed fearlessness of the Japanese kamikaze pilots was even thought to be fueled by large doses of the drug.

One twenty-seven-year-old patient from France with a rare medical condition known as Morvan's syndrome went without sleep for several months and did not complain of feeling sleepy or tired, though he did experience nightly hallucinations and a variety of physical ailments. Psychiatry professor J. Christian Gillin has ruminated over a dystopic future where super-soldiers might be bioengineered with a variant of Morvan's so they can "face intense, around-the-clock fighting for weeks at a time."[33]

But for now, the preferred stimulant for the armed forces is modafinil, a drug initially developed to treat narcolepsy that has almost none of the deleterious side effects (such as addiction) associated with amphetamines. Tested at numerous institutes across the United States and internationally, modafinil has demonstrated an expanded ability to allow those who take it to function without sleep. Just ask the Human Effectiveness Directorate and the Fatigue Countermeasures Branch, two of the testing agencies that sound like they were airlifted out of George Orwell's *1984*.[34]

The drug's off-label use has also gained popularity as a cognitive enhancer for college students and Silicon Valley and Wall Street types, who sometimes seek long stretches of work and concentration.

SLEEP NO MORE: FATAL FAMILIAL INSOMNIA

For tuxedo-clad Silvano, the moment felt like a pinnacle of 1980s glamour as he effortlessly spun his mother on the dance floor of the swanky cruise ship, his distinctive red hair catching the light. But then he felt a drop of sweat trickle down his forehead.

It was accompanied by a slowly sinking feeling, as though something terrible had just dropped anchor within himself.

Pulling out his monogrammed handkerchief, he dabbed away the drops of perspiration. But he was mortified to discover that his shirt was soaking wet—he'd barely exerted himself in the first place.

"Please excuse me, Mother," he said softly in Italian. With a sense of dread, he strode over to an ornate mirror and gazed into his eyes.

It wasn't just the sweating. There was something else. The unmistakable sign. Silvano's pupils had shrunk to tiny black pinpoints. It was the beginning of his ending.

"I'll stop sleeping," he thought, "and within eight or nine months, I'll be dead."[35]

Silvano, fifty-three, had observed the shrunken pupils in his father as well as his two sisters, the first sign of a fatal disease marked by their inability to sleep. The ailment wound far back into Silvano's family tree, but the carefree playboy had tried to ignore its branch of doom.

Knowing that the Venice-based family had been haunted by this sickness, Dr. Ignazio Roiter, who was married to Silvano's niece, managed to do some sleuthing in the records of the local Catholic parish house. Working with science writer D. T. Max, they traced the first recorded case to a well-born Venetian doctor who perished in 1765 after falling into a lengthy stupor.

Since that time, many family members had died as a result of complications from dreadful and unrelenting insomnia, though they were given many misdiagnoses over the decades and sometimes placed in insane asylums. Villagers spoke of it as "family curse," and while the women tended to be beautiful and wealthy, it could be difficult for them to find spouses (the disease typically doesn't strike until the person is in their fifties, giving ample opportunity for a carrier to reproduce).

Ignazio convinced Silvano to seek treatment at a Bologna neurology clinic in the spring of 1984. Video recordings document his demise, after months of little or no sleep. Eyelids fluttering, he was overcome with a glassy-eyed expression typically seen in sleepwalkers. He would sometimes meticulously comb his hair in a hallucinatory glaze as though getting ready to go out for the evening.[36]

A neurologist's reading of Silvano's EEG revealed brain waves that matched nothing in the literature. Though the doctor seemed to think there might be a cure, Silvano bravely accepted his fate. "Cut the nonsense," he said. "I assume when I'm gone you'll want the brain."[37]

Near his death, around the eighth month, "he was just a living torso animated by muscle contortions and twitches," said Dr. Elio Lugaresi of the Bologna clinic.[38]

And so it was upon his passing that Silvano's freshly preserved brain was sent to Case Western Reserve University in Cleveland, and the door to this medical mystery began to crack open. While most of the tissue appeared healthy, small lesions were found in the thalamus, a site that would come to be understood as controlling the ability to sleep.

At a meeting in the Roiters' living room in 1986 (after yet another relative had died), the family and the Bologna researchers agreed to name the disease "fatal familial insomnia" (FFI). Around ten years later it was discovered that the EEGs of people with FFI closely resemble those with Creutzfeldt-Jakob disease (CJD), the human variant of mad cow disease.

Joining CJD and kuru (spread by consuming the brains and spinal cords of deceased relatives, a ritual among the Fore tribe in New Guinea[39]), FFI was now identified as one of the rare prion diseases. Prions are a type of protein first named in the 1980s that are found across mammalian lines, yet when they begin to misfold, they take on the properties of a virus. A single prion can cause adjoining ones to take on the deformed shape in a kind of chain reaction. This activity is unfathomable, as prions are not considered alive like viruses and bacteria, and they have no reason to replicate.[40] Further, prions have a nearly indestructible quality, unaffected by heat, radiation, and formaldehyde (only bleach seems to kill them).

In contrast to CJD, in which prions weave a Swiss cheese pattern on the surface of the brain, in FFI they attack the thalamus like worms boring holes in wood. Located in the center of the brain, the thalamus coordinates autonomic responses to the environment. So when it malfunctions, bodily systems go haywire.

For sleep to occur, certain physiological conditions need to be in place, but for people with FFI it's as though their conscious activity is always stuck in the on mode, and they can't experience slow-wave, restorative slumber. At best, they fall into a sort of trance between sleep and waking, in which they might be observed mimicking their daily activities, as a remnant or mirror of the REM dream cycle.[41]

Once the gene for the healthy prion was discovered and mapped, it was possible to find the mutation in it that causes FFI—children of a parent who carries the mutation have a 50 percent chance of inheriting it. And so after more than 250 years, the mystery that plagued Silvano's family was finally solved. Yet a cure remains maddeningly out of reach for the extremely rare condition, estimated to affect just forty to two hundred families worldwide. Now that the mutated gene is known, the children of FFI patients must face the agonizing choice of whether to take the genetic test to reveal their status.

"The chief clinical features of FFI include a progressive and ferocious insomnia, waking 'sleep' hallucinations, [and] autonomic disturbances suggestive of sympathetic overdrive," psychology professor Dr. Joyce Schenkein summarized. "Later cognitive changes involve a confusional state resembling dementia and, ultimately, death . . . [with] the typical duration . . . between 7 and 36 months, with a mean duration of 18 months."[42] But one of her patients, identified as DF, tried to buck the FFI survival odds by crafting an unorthodox set of strategies and interventions over more than twenty-four months.

With a doctorate in naturopathy, DF had a particular skill set to confront the challenges of FFI upon his diagnosis at age fifty-two. The disease had already taken the life of a paternal uncle, two cousins, and his father, who'd been a popular nutritionist, radio show host, and strong advocate for vitamins and wheat germ. The intake of supplements may have staved off his father's onset of the disease, which didn't strike until he was in his seventies.[43]

Ten months into his own diagnosis, DF decided to buy a motorhome and set off on a solo journey across America. "He was an adventurous spirit; he wasn't just going to sit there and die," said Dr. Schenkein, who consulted with him on some of his treatments.[44]

Vitamin therapy was one of the first approaches, including tryptophan and massive doses of melatonin to help him sleep. When this stopped working, he experimented with anesthesia, including ketamine and nitrous oxide, which allowed him to sleep in fifteen-minute increments, before re-dosing. He also took sleep medications with varying success.

For DF, the insomnia had a certain allure for a time. He described it as being like approaching an "open doorway" for slumber that would suddenly close, and he'd be jolted wide awake. With this abrupt wakefulness came an exhilarating drug-like high. However, this became less desirable as the disease progressed, and the doorway to sleep grew more and more distant. He fell into stupors, losing track of time and days. Though he wouldn't hear the phone ring, he could talk on a call for hours, not having any sense of the duration of time. The use of stimulants such as phentermine helped return him to his daily routines, including driving the motor home and writing a novel. Two years into his illness, with the assist of a benzedrine inhaler, he was still able to drive five hundred miles on his own.[45]

At one point DF had a grand mal seizure and noticed that he slept quite well in its aftermath. This inspired him to try electroconvulsive therapy (ECT) to duplicate the seizure-like experience. In the nineteenth month of his illness, over a period of several weeks, he withstood some thirty sessions of electroshock to his temporal lobes. Although he did glean some sleep after each session, the side effects, including being unable to recall the name of ordinary objects, retrograde amnesia, and paranoia, did not make it a worthy trade-off.

His most fantastic remedy was the purchase of an egg-shaped sensory deprivation tank that he kept outside. Whatever sleep he could get was frequently interrupted by small amounts of sound, light, or motion, so the isolation of the chamber offered an ideal escape hatch. Floating in body-temperature salt water, he was anesthetized with nitrous oxide and would remain asleep for widely varying periods, from ten minutes to eight hours. The downside was that when DF awakened in the tank, he was beset with distressing hallucinations, uncertain of whether he was dead or alive. But the more extended periods of sleep cleared away some of his dementia and confusion, and validated this unconventional approach.

Unfortunately, while he was away in his motor home, winter temperatures froze the tank water, causing the shell to crack. DF decided not to replace it, as the stationary device impeded his driving mobility and "made him feel like the comic book freak Aquaman, who nightly slept in a fish tank."[46]

Given the convoluted limbo that most FFI patients endure, it's surprising that DF found both serenity and insight. When he managed to fall into dream sleep, he described delightful interactions. It was like "entering a room filled with everyone who he would want to encounter, including deceased friends and relatives who would tell him that everything will be all right. In his words, 'to the outside world, I am dead and gone, but to myself, I'm still here, in this wonderful place and it is they who have disappeared.'"[47]

And during his "waking REM" states, which incorporated imagery, sound, and smell, he experienced an unprecedented understanding of himself where nothing was hidden. Dr. Schenkein cites a "sustained handshake" between the right and left brain hemispheres allowing DF to achieve a more integrated awareness[48] (perhaps something akin to what Tony Wright details in his sleep deprivation experiments). DF saw his unconscious as filled with "wounded children" who were unable to move past their damage, but through the backstage pass of FFI, he was able to mollify their hurt with adult wisdom.

The realm of these interior worlds could be so welcoming that DF assumed others in his place simply gave up their fight against FFI and allowed themselves to die. His own tug-of-war came to an end sometime after the two-year period when Dr. Schenkein was tracking his progress. DF's courageous and inventive tactics demonstrated that some degree of life extension might be possible when facing FFI.

That was not the case with Kamni Vallabh, a vibrant fifty-one-year-old who rapidly descended into a twilight state. Kamni's illness remained a mystery until after she died, when the autopsy revealed she had the FFI anomaly—a mere one letter off in the six billion that compose the human genome. No one suspected such a diagnosis, as there was no known history of it in their family. Her daughter Sonia said it was like she was stuck somewhere between being awake and asleep but "she was just lucid enough to know something horrible was happening to her."[49] As Kamni deteriorated, Sonia's husband, Eric Minikel, noted how hard it was to imagine "what it is for a person to be alive and their body is moving around, but their brain is not there anymore."[50]

A few months after Kamni died, Sonia, then thirty, steeled herself to take the test. She too carried the deadly gene. But perhaps FFI has finally met its match. Sonia, a Harvard-trained lawyer, and Eric, a transportation analyst with a degree from MIT, boned up on scientific papers on FFI and prion diseases. They soon realized that if they were going to be in the literal fight of their lives, they needed to do more. Sonia started taking science classes at MIT while working as a lab technician at the Massachusetts General Hospital's Center for Human Genetic Research, and soon Eric left his transportation-related job to apply his skills to analyzing genetic data at a lab.

Eventually, they both became doctoral students in Harvard Medical School's Biological and Biomedical Sciences division while working at the Broad Institute, a genomic research center in Cambridge, Massachusetts.

"Their story," said Stuart Schreiber, a founding member of the Broad Institute, "is of course, remarkable, and they personify the concept of patient-scientists. But their deep understanding of science and ability to innovate and execute" is extraordinary in the face of one of the most formidable challenges in biomedical science.[51]

In 2012 the couple started the research organization Prion Alliance, through which they crowdsourced funding to test the effects of an experimental compound in inhibiting prion activity in mice. One challenge they must overcome is the medical establishment's resistance to testing experimental drugs on healthy people. But such an approach is just what is needed to fend off FFI, because once the deadly effects of the disease take hold, it is too late.

"Sonia is the bomb," Eric said of his wife. "I feel so incredibly lucky to get to spend all day every day with her. It is one of the upsides of all of this happening to us, that we get to spend almost all of our time together."

This just in. After seven years of fighting in the trenches, Sonia and Eric developed a promising approach using "antisense compounds" that's been found to greatly reduce the amount of prion proteins in mice, and has left them feeling optimistic. They've teamed up with the California-based biotech company Ionis, which specializes in the compounds, and hopefully, a drug will be ready within five years to put the brakes on not only FFI but other rare prion diseases as well.[52]

CHAPTER FIVE

THE NIGHTMARE REALM

They were not like any people that I have ever known. They were shadowy dark-robed figures, capable of atrocious self-distortion,—capable, for instance, of growing up to the ceiling, and then across it, and then lengthening themselves, head downwards, along the opposite wall. Only their faces were distinct; and I tried not to look at their faces. I tried also in my dreams—or thought that I tried—to awaken myself from the sight of them by pulling my eyelids with my fingers; but the eyelids would remain closed, as if sealed."

Perhaps there is nothing more vivid and horrifying than the nightmares we endure as children. The writer Lafcadio Hearn recalled the preceding scenario from when he was a five-year-old boy in the 1850s, kept locked in his room at night.

"The mere sight of those night-mare faces was not the worst," he continued. "The dreams always began with a suspicion, or sensation of something heavy in the air,—slowly quenching will,—slowly numbing my power to move. . . . And all this signified only that the Nameless was coming,—was nearing,—was mounting the stairs. I could hear the step,—booming like the sound of a muffled drum,—and I wondered why nobody else heard it. A long, long time the haunter would take to come,—malevolently pausing after each ghastly footfall. Then, without a creak, the bolted door would open,—slowly, slowly,—and the thing would enter, gibbering soundlessly,—and put out hands,—and clutch me,—and toss me to the black ceiling,—and catch me descending to toss me up again, and again, and again."[1]

It was just a couple decades earlier, around 1830, that the term *nightmare* began to signify how it's thought of today—a scary, anxiety-ridden dream that jolts us out of slumber. Previous to that, and going back centuries, a "nightmare" referred to what we now call sleep paralysis, sometimes involving incubus encounters. The *Universal Etymological English Dictionary* of the late 1700s defined *nightmare* as a "disease when a man in his sleep supposes he has a great weight laying on him," though it was around this time that the cause was presumed to be physiological rather than supernatural.[2]

Let's delve into the world of nightmares, the haunting type of dreams, produced within our own psyches, that sometimes rival or inspire the scariest of horror films, books, and artwork. The transformation of Dr. Jekyll into the evil Mr. Hyde, for instance, came to Robert Louis Stevenson in a nightmarish dream.[3]

There's been some debate in psychiatric circles as to whether highly disturbing dreams that do not wake the sleeper qualify as nightmares, but recent research indicates that awakenings "are not the sole or even best index" of a nightmare's severity.[4] "Night terrors"—sudden arousal from sleep accompanied by feelings of terror, usually with little dream narrative—will be examined as a distinct phenomenon.

In the nineteenth century, scientists believed they'd found the root of nightmares—a lack of oxygen. In recent years, a few pilot studies with sleep apnea patients have indicated a correlation. One subject had a recurring dream in which he saw his lifeless body laid out in a coffin. "My god, please don't let me die," he pleaded in the nightmares. "I am still young and I have small children." When he awakened, he was always gasping for breath. Yet a larger study with 323 sleep apnea patients did not replicate the connection between nightmares and breathing problems.[5]

The most enduring explanation has been dubbed the "Pepperoni Pizza Hypothesis." This particular staple of the frozen food section or home delivery was not yet available at the start of the eighteenth century when numerous doctors cited gastric upset and rich foods as the culprit behind bad dreams. They may have been cribbing from the influential second-century Greek physician Galen, who associated "noxious undigested vapours" with sleep paralysis. There's never been any evidence that spicy or heavy foods play a significant role in the incidence of nightmares, the sleep and dream researcher Dr. Ernest Hartmann concluded.[6] He did concede a possible slight effect in that someone who has an upset stomach could be more prone to awakenings and disturbed sleep.

A NURSERY OF NIGHTMARES

The expression *sleep like a baby* is a bit of a misnomer, as the dreams of the very young are often far from tranquil. There's even some evidence that fetuses experience parasomnias and that their adorable kicking emerges out of their primordial sleep state.[7] In one's early years, teething, convulsions, and bowel discontents serve as "fertile sources for mental terror in sleep," Dr. Robert Macnish, a nineteenth-century writer on troubled slumber, noted. Because babies' minds are highly susceptible to dread, their dreams "can leave an indelible impression on the mind," he suggested. "They are remembered in after-years with feelings of pain," and while blended with cheerier reminisces of childhood, there are "shadows of melancholy," tinged with "hues of sorrow and care."[8]

Like sleepwalking, nightmares are far more common in children than adults, particularly those age five to twelve. Around 25 percent in this age group are awakened at least once a week by them.[9]

A man named Chris who participated in a dream study in Montreal in 2014 recalled a nightmare from his preschool years, still seared into his memory some twenty-five years later. He dreamed that family members and house pets burned in a house fire. They melted into "several humongous blobs that resembled bubbling pizza topping" with protruding body part fragments.[10]

Nightmares arise from our earliest and most potent anxieties and fears and can serve as a vehicle to embody them. The psychiatrist John Mack (who would go on to achieve notoriety for his pioneering research into alien abduction) listed these torments as "destructive aggression, castration, separation and abandonment, devouring and being devoured, and fear regarding loss of identity and fusion with the mother."[11]

Psychotherapist J. A. Hadfield wrote about a boy who was jealous of his baby brother and physically attacked him while awake. In his nightmare, a vicious monster prods him to murder his brother. "Try it!," "Go and do it," the monster cajoles. "Now I have got him by the throat . . . The impulse to destruction is as strong as the will not to . . . I delight in a feeling . . . of murderous hate," the boy recalled, as rage and fear seesawed inside him. Then he dreamed that he has carried out the killing and feels a terrible guilt. In the denouement, the monster, transformed into a hideous man, turns on the dreamer, wrapping his hands around his neck and strangling him. The boy wakes up screaming.

"The rage possessing him first turned *him* into a strangling monster, and then turned into a monster strangling *him*," Hadfield commented, suggesting that such monsters are a projection of the dreamer's own untenable feelings.[12] Although this patient was clearly struggling with violent impulses, some, such as psychic researcher Robert Bruce, would raise the possibility that the boy was a victim of attacks by negative entities, who particularly prey on children. This concept will be further explored in a later chapter.

"An aggressive, devouring orality is prominent in children's nightmares," Dr. Mack wrote. "Being eaten or eaten up, and equivalent forms of devouring, such as being ground up inside large machines, occur with particular frequency in the nightmares of children under five."[13] For very young children, this Hansel and Gretel–ization can be even more frightening if they haven't developed the capacity to differentiate dream experiences from reality.

INSIDE THE NIGHTMARE

In a typical dream you're enmeshed in a story that reaches some sort of conclusion, but in a terror-inducing nightmare, you're often plucked out of the story before it can resolve. "Just as we sleep to escape the problems of the day," Hadfield writes, "so in a nightmare we waken to escape the unsolved problems and horrors of the night."[14]

The usual content can be boiled down to some essential ingredients—an intense anxiety accompanied by a sense of danger and helplessness in the face of an impending or actual violent attack. Victimized by an aggressor (whether human, animal, or other), the dreamer generally responds by freezing or fleeing. Being trapped in a confined space, facing a natural disaster, and losing one's teeth are also common scenarios.

The persecutors in our nightmares may vary among cultures, the age of the dreamer, and other factors, but "their reaction to the helpless victim varies little," says Dr. Mack. "Whether the dreamer is threatened by an ancient demon, a vampire, a lobster, a fairy story monster, a robot, or an atomic ray, his experience is in each instance like that of a helpless child confronted by powerful forces with which he is unable to deal effectively."[15] Dr. Mack explains that the functions of the ego take a nosedive in the dream state (logical reasoning is more or less deactivated in the brain's prefrontal cortex) and that more primitive forms of thinking prevail. He says "dreams reflect the symbolization, distortion, displacement, and projection mechanisms that characterize the thinking of early childhood."[16]

In adults' nightmares, recent events, characters, or disturbances are often superimposed over archaic childhood fears, such as being chased, attacked, or mutilated.[17] But not all nightmares are ruled by fear. Up to 30 percent can be overshadowed by other emotions such as extreme sadness, anger, repulsion, or confusion.[18] Negative dreams, including nightmares, unfortunately account for around two thirds of all our dream content.

Dr. Hartmann found that those with a lifelong history of disturbing dreams had "thinner boundaries" and "were unusually open and undefended in their mental structure." While this often fosters a creative or artistic nature, this group can be highly sensitive to the pains of life and more prone to mental illness and suicidal ideations.[19]

By some estimates, about 5 percent of adults regularly have nightmares,[20] but when researcher Mark Blagrove at the University of Wales in Swansea had subjects keep a dream diary, they reported nightmares once or twice a month. The frequency does seem to decrease with age, with a fifty-five-year-old having on average only one third the number of nightmares that a twenty-five-year-old has.[21] Nightmares may be the brain's way of processing and acclimating to fears; since the dream is perceived as a real encounter, it's as though the feared events have already happened and are thus less worrisome.[22]

The internally generated imagery of dreams and nightmares are thought to arise in the secondary visual cortex, which can be like a deranged film editor trying to splice disparate elements into a whole.[23] A typical nightmare occurs in one of the later and lengthier REM periods of the sleep cycle (such as between four and seven a.m.).[24] During REM sleep, the brain's limbic system—home of the fight-or-flight response—becomes highly active and contributes to the neurochemistry behind the nightmare state.

Psychologist Steven H. Woodward referred to the amygdala and anterior cingulate cortex—structures that compose the limbic system—as the brain's "axis of fear."[25] Located deep inside the brain, the limbic region works to identify potential threats—in the case of those who have PTSD nightmares, their system may be stuck on red alert.

RECURRING NIGHTMARES AND TRAUMA

Akin to a residual haunting in which a repetitive sound or action is said to be imprinted in an environment, recurring nightmares have a broken-record quality, making them all the more torturous. Often considered to be indicators of an unresolved or insistent conflict, in many cases, they emerge out of specific traumas. Not only are veterans of war with PTSD plagued by recurrent nightmares, but nightmares can also follow serious accidents, surgery, loss of a loved one, or physical or sexual assaults. "The common feature to all these situations," says Mack, "is an external event that is perceived as life-threatening and cannot be integrated" with their psychological resources.[26]

A traumatic incident, explains Dr. Hartmann, can become "a sort of encapsulated abscess, walled off, and painful to the touch," and while the repetitive nightmares associated with them may dissolve for a time, they can suddenly be reinvigorated by a new loss or rejection.[27] "The traumatic material," he adds, "has produced some kind of tear in the mental fabric."

"I think the function of dreaming is that it allows us to work on emotion and emotional memories in very creative ways," says psychologist and researcher Dr. Gary Fireman. But nightmares, particularly recurrent ones, "are a breakdown in the system . . . [They] keep replaying over and over again because you're unable to sufficiently process an emotional experience."[28]

Repetitive dreams replay a specific trauma close to the original incident, while recurrent ones repeat similar themes and actions, though the details may change. One Vietnam veteran had the same dream night after night—a duplication of an actual incident where his friend was killed, but with a twist at the end:

"In the dream I'm running away from my tent, which is tied down to a powder keg. I am crawling in a trench we dug and I am crying. I get the feeling I am going to get hit. The hair on the back of my neck stands out. When the shooting is over, I go to my tent. It is blown full of shrapnel holes. The powder keg has blown up. So far that's the way it really was. Then I stare into the tent. There is a body in my bunk with a big bloody gaping hole in his chest. I try to see who it is, but I always wake up before I can see his face. I wonder, 'Is it me or my buddy?'"[29]

Dr. Hartmann reported that PTSD and recurrent nightmares were more likely to occur when a soldier had a "mirror relationship" with a close buddy who was killed, and a kind of "fragmentation of the self" takes place. He also detailed cases in which patients woke up during surgery when their anesthesia was too low.[30] Dosed with a powerful muscle relaxant, the patients were able to see and feel the scalpel cutting into them, yet were unable to move or signal their cognizance. Their paralyzing experiences would then rerun in a succession of nightmares.

KALEIDOSCOPE OF TERROR

"Lucien," a sixty-two-year-old visual artist based in Hong Kong, has been troubled by recurrent though somewhat abstract nightmares for much of his adult life. While horrific incidents of child abuse in his family no doubt serve as the wellspring for his nightmares, years-long psychotherapy tamed his PTSD. Yet his violent dreams seem doomed to reverberate. Different aspects of the dreams come and go, he told me, but they usually start off with a dark skyline. The huge, silhouetted skyscrapers are stand-ins for very dark presences or figures, he notes. From there a metamorphosis takes hold. The skyscrapers transform from oil cans into spigots, which end up becoming sharp instruments like meat cleavers. "The meat cleavers reflect the spires in the skyscrapers, which turns into butchering." Fingernails get ripped off and turned into knives. Mirrors with jagged edges abound.

"As soon as the butchering starts occurring, there's a lot of viscera, blood, skin, fat—the body starts getting picked apart in the dreams," and flesh starts to separate from bone. "You go from body functions, and viscera, into organization and consumption, like literally going to the supermarket and getting different cuts of meat."

Where was Lucien in all of this? His dreams are a total environment with multiple points of view, he explains. At times he identifies with being the victim, the perpetrator, the backdrop, the whole panorama.

"Some of these dreams are so violent, it's actually safer to feel like the victim than the perpetrator," he says. "It's a nasty idea to think that you're that violent. It's a much safer idea to consider yourself the subject of bad things rather than the offensive actor." When the nightmare climaxes into a splintering bone-crushing kaleidoscope (including vivisection and disemboweling), "I actually have to wake myself up . . . because the trauma loop is then inescapable."

In a horror movie, he points out, the characters seem to have some level of choice; there's always a demarcation. But in his nightmares, he reaches a point of no return, perhaps that of total annihilation, where his self-preservation kicks in.

"I think," Lucien observes, "the dreams are abstract because I make them that way—as my own protective embalming fluid. I make sure they're stillborn . . . Because, god forbid I cast these things out."

TOO MUCH INFORMATION

Dreams take place in a different mental sphere than our waking state, and their concepts are not always directly translatable. One commenter going by the username "eboyer" attempted to wrangle their strange and abstract recurring nightmare on the PsychCentral .com forum:

"Basically, I would describe them as a direct injection of fear," they wrote. "These dreams seem to be, in the most literal sense, Hell. They invoke forms of fear and horror that I have never experienced in any other aspect of life ... it's not like the fear you get when you're in a car crash or something like that; it's MUCH more intense than that."[31]

The source of eboyer's terror? No need to lock up the knives, Ma ... it's numbers. Like a computer run amok, eboyer experiences information overload when the dreams kick in, usually quite early in the sleep cycle. "It's as if my brain is trying to think about a ridiculously large number of things all at once. . . . I think of very large numbers (dozens of digits in length), and I feel absolutely obligated to perform some kind of math function on them (add, multiply, logarithm, derivative, etc.). I feel as if I'll be sent to Hell or something if I don't successfully do whatever math function is needed."

Age twenty-one at the time of the post, eboyer was fascinated by math and numbers, so it's not out of place for them to be a primary subject of these dreams. During the nightmares, eboyer has a massive expansion of what they call the "thinking space"—usually thought of as just the terrain inside one's head. "My thoughts seem to be happening outside of my head; it's as if I can reach out and actually touch my thoughts. When the dream starts, my thinking space suddenly expands tremendously, and it usually stays big."

The dreams, sometimes accompanied by thunderous sounds, last for just a few minutes before eboyer abruptly awakens. But afterward, for around twenty minutes, there is an odd residue, in which the numbers seem to take over eboyer's room—something they feel rather than see.

BODIES OF HORROR, HORROR OF BODIES

"There's always going to be dead bodies, usually babies or children," said "Therese" of her recurring nightmares. She is a jewelry designer and painter from California, in her fifties, and several significant traumas have played out in her life, such as a rape in her twenties that she kept secret for years. A recent nightmare, she said, was like many of her dreams that begin in a search for something, with a stranger guiding the way. In this case, she was taking a tour with her grandchildren of a possible new school for them. Started by a doctor, the school was housed inside a hospital for deformed children.

First, they see pictures of deformed children on the walls. These images graduate into fleshy sculptural representations. "It's as if the children with deformities had been encased in plaster and then embedded into the walls," she told me. With each turn down the curving hallways, the tour grew more and more sinister.

"We started seeing doctors and nurses pushing deformed bodies on gurneys past us, and all the faces were covered. Sometimes they looked alive, sometimes dead. We start seeing children and adults with deformities, eyes covered by blindfolds, zombie-like."

At this point, she realizes something is wrong and evil, but they are so far inside the labyrinthine hospital corridors that the way out isn't evident. She tells the children to run, and they try to get out. But their efforts are in vain, and they end up trapped inside a morgue stuffed with gurneys loaded with misshapen bodies. It is then that she realizes "they're not fixing anyone here—they're doing experiments. These aren't people that are born this way, these are people they are doing this to. And that's why they want kids to come to the school"—to find more test subjects. Eerie shadows move closer, as muffled voices grow louder.

Like Lucien, Therese gets to a point in her nightmares where she can't take it anymore, and it's "as if there's a part of my brain that's going 'this is too much—you've got to wake up now.' I kind of go back and forth a bit, and then wake up. When I wake up, my heart's pounding and I clench my fist, and I actually have a little spot in my left hand from clenching. I'm grinding my teeth, I'm shaking—my whole body's reacting."

Why the recurrent nightmares of dead and tortured children? She believes the answer lies in a job she once held at an abortion clinic. Therese was attacked by protesters outside the clinic—one of them kicked her so severely with a steel-toed boot that she was taken to the ER. But it was elements of the work itself that most traumatized her. Part of her job involved entering a closetlike room where she would examine the contents of someone's vacuumed-out uterus. "And you had to look for two little feet, two little hands, the spinal cord—you had to make sure you found everything and weigh it to make sure it [the uterus] was empty because if it wasn't it could cause an infection in the woman." For Therese, it tore at her already damaged psyche.

"For years, I did push all this stuff down, 'cause that was the best way to get by," she said of her past traumas. "Sometimes, I think it was better to just to keep it all shut in, because then at least I could be a good soldier and go to work every day—act like a normal person. Now, I'm a mess."

"I don't feel like I'm learning a lesson," she says of her treadmill of nightmares. "I feel like I want to say to my brain, I know, I get it."

One theory behind recurrent nightmares is that they are triggered by "scripts" that automatically unspool when certain types of themes or situations occur. "The nightmare script is thought to become activated when elements in a neutral dream resemble elements of the script," Dutch researcher Victor Spoormaker writes of his hypothesis. "When a person has, for instance, nightmares about being chased by an attacker in the dark, a running person in a dream can be interpreted as a 'threatening' element, in this case: a possible attacker. The running person in the dream is intrinsically neutral, but if there is perceived similarity to the script, this image activates the script and the nightmare starts."[32]

UNDER THE INFLUENCE

Nightmares can be precipitated by many substances or conditions. Both Lucien and Therese said their disturbed dreams seemed amplified or more violent while they were taking certain psychotropic prescriptions. Conversely, withdrawal from various medications, particularly depressants, is associated with nightmares and intense, bizarre dreams.[33]

Those going through delirium tremens (DTs) from alcohol withdrawal often have macabre or terrifying nightmares—in one study, nearly 30 percent of a group of one hundred alcoholics returned to drinking just to stop the horrible nightmares. And sometimes their frightful dreams continue uninterrupted into a hallucinatory waking state.[34] Since alcohol suppresses REM sleep, it's thought that the rebounding of REM sleep during abstinence may be associated with waking hallucinations, not unlike what those with sleep deprivation experience.

When drying out, does anyone really see pink elephants? Jack London was one of the first to popularize this whimsical euphemism. More likely, they'll see legions of bugs crawling up the wall and all over their body, as J. Allan Hobson wrote of his patient at the Boston City Hospital, who woke up screaming from his nightmares only to be greeted by horrifying daytime hallucinations.[35]

Credit the British essayist Thomas De Quincey for perhaps the first "addiction memoir," *Confessions of an English Opium-Eater*, published in 1821. As the consumption of his beloved laudanum (a tincture of opium) progressed, his dreams transformed into all-embracing spirals of gloom: "I seemed every night to descend, not metaphorically, but literally to descend, into chasms and sunless abysses, depths below depths, from which it seemed hopeless that I could ever re-ascend. Nor did I, by waking feel that I *had* re-ascended."[36]

Increasingly, his nightmares distorted time and space such that buildings and landscapes swelled beyond what the eye could see and he "sometimes seemed to have lived 70 to 100 years in one night" or even something like a "millennium passed in that time . . . a duration far beyond the limits of human experience."

Possibly reflecting De Quincey's life in populous London, he was tyrannized by a dreamscape of human faces. "Upturned to the heavens: faces, imploring, wrathful, despairing, surged upwards by the thousands, by myriads, by generations, by centuries."[37] And a villainous "Malay" haunted him for months, transporting him across ancient and complex Asiatic and Egyptian settings:

I ran into pagodas: and was fixed, for centuries at the summit ...
I was the idol; I was the priest; I was worshipped; I was
sacrificed. I fled the wrath of Brama through all the forests of
Asia: Vishnu hated me: Seeva laid wait for me. I came suddenly
upon Isis and Osiris: I have done a deed, they said, which the
ibis and the crocodile trembled at. I was buried, for a thousand
years, in stone coffins, with mummies and sphynxes, in narrow
chambers at the heart of eternal pyramids. I was kissed, with
cancerous kisses, by crocodiles; and laid, confounded with all
unutterable slimy things, amongst reeds and Nilotic mud.[38]

The distortions of De Quincey's opium-laced nightmares bear
some resemblance to reports of fever dreams, where higher-than-
normal body temperatures seem to stoke foreign and uniquely petrifying content.

MIND-BENDING FEVER DREAMS

On the Dream Views forum, members shared fever-related dreams
that left them terrified for hours after awakening. The nightmares
usually repeated more than once during childhood illnesses and
were often marked by a delirium of scale, involving menacing
shapes, incredible slowness, and enormous weight.

JustSoSick, a poster from Norway, recalled a childhood dream
where he was positioned at a vast chessboard. The pieces on the
board were "moving at a terribly slow speed and it was just too huge
to be moving that slow. It was just terrible, and I couldn't get away
from the objects because they were so HUGE," he wrote. "It was this
terrifying experience of seeing something that huge moving"—like
the whole known universe was condensed into a single object moving toward you.[39]

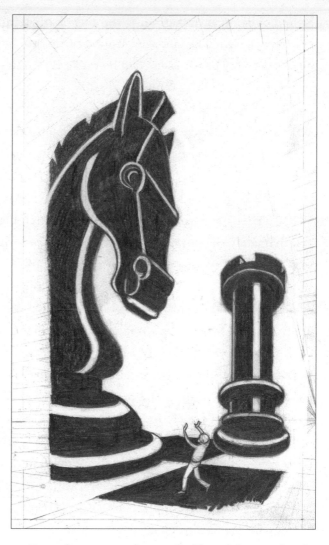

Fever dreams are often marked by a delirium of scale.
Drawing by Jason Jam, 2019.

"I remember one particular afternoon," Canterbury, who'd been sick with the flu and stuck in bed all day, recounted.[40] In the dream, "it was broad daylight and the sun was shining. I had a terrible feeling of being shrunk down to the size of an atom, sitting on the end of my nose. Even if I looked around the room, the walls, the furniture, even my hands seemed to be millions of miles away, and infinitely large, and I was infinitely small."

Higgs2, from the Netherlands, wrote about the time when he was six years old and had meningitis. He was near death with a fever of 107 to 108 and taken to the hospital. "That night I had this terrifying dream/hallucination—" like something out of an H. P. Lovecraft story. "I was in some sort of crater/landscape. . . . There was this HUGE THING hovering above me . . ." The pitch black object was approximately six miles high and a half-a-mile wide, and it was "like some sort of alien shaped cylinder or pencil. I felt very very very small, and all the time I had the feeling that thing was going to fall, and squash me, thus erasing me from existence," he said.[41]

It was as "though I was trapped inside a huge, static-charged box," wrote Lenz82 of the UK of a dream that occurred while they were suffering from an ear and throat infection. "The whole place was a nightmare of lines and bridges and thread like wires which stretched out impossibly into each other . . . I remember my head throbbing, I felt sick and I couldn't stand up properly. There was a background 'noise' like a hum, but the hum was everywhere.

"The place felt like . . . a death factory, as though there was no way out, like the whole box was a machine or a computer or a prison or something. The thing that scared me the most though, was at first I thought I was completely alone, but I eventually saw a group of about ten, skinny, tall, naked, sexless people, running at me from across this bridge. As I watched them, a huge rolling spherical shape mouth (like 'Pac-Man' but rolling and huge and made of a brown, sweating mottled flesh) . . . rolled over the skinny people, devoured them," Lenz82 went on. "I felt horrified. . . . Then the dream looped and looped a few times. I would replay the events over and over in my head. The feeling of oppression grew worse, as though my head would explode or crush."[42]

The trademark spatial distortions of fever dreams may be the result of cognitive processing glitches from an overheated brain during the REM cycle.[43] Patrick McNamara, an associate professor of neurology at Harvard Medical School, offers another angle, noting that "when we get an infection, with or without a fever, the body needs more slow-wave sleep" to heal itself. This could delay or reduce a sleeper's amount of REM and lead to nightmares, he suggests, based on the idea that the function of dreams is to process emotions, and a reduction in REM leads to a buildup of unprocessed negative feelings.[44]

WARNING SIGNALS

Not surprisingly, pathologies of the brain can be associated with nightmares. The author, lecturer, and ethnopharmacologist Terence McKenna served as a sort of "altered statesman" for the responsible exploration of plant-based psychedelics in the 1990s. A brain tumor cut his own life short at age fifty-three in 2000. In a dark irony, the cancer seemed to function as another mind-altering substance, ushering in bizarre, unpleasant dreams that preceded his diagnosis.

"The only clue I had that something was wrong until the headaches began were these dreams which were very singular in that they were indescribable even to myself," McKenna said. "They were categorical dreams, and they were repetitious—they went on for hours and hours. And I even said at the time that I should see a neurologist because these dreams were so peculiar. Maybe the tumor was pressing against the language center. I'm not sure exactly what was happening but these contentless repetitious dreams that lasted hours and hours were a clue I think that the tumor was reaching a certain size and level of danger."[45]

For those who survived the great "sleeping sickness" epidemic of 1918, it was as though they were frozen in place, with a kind of impenetrable catatonia. Oliver Sacks (whose L-dopa treatments reawakened some of these patients in 1969) chronicled the onset of the encephalitis, which in some cases was marked by premonitory nightmares of a "grotesque and terrifying" nature:

"Miss R. had a series of dreams about one central theme: she dreamed she was imprisoned in an inaccessible castle, but the castle had the form and shape of herself; . . . she dreamed that she had become a living, sentient statue of stone; she dreamed that the world had come to a stop; she dreamed that she had fallen into a sleep so deep that nothing could wake her; she dreamed of a death which was different from death."[46] Her family found it difficult to wake her shortly after, and that was when the paralysis set in.

One precognitive nightmare was lifesaving for a woman in her thirties. In the disturbing dream she found herself naked, lying on a road. A motorcycle approached, and her breast was mowed over by the vehicle. Feeling an intense pain in her left breast, she woke up startled and scared. For a number of sessions, she and her psychotherapist probed the possible meanings of the dream, but when she had a routine breast examination one month later, a tumor was discovered in her left breast, and it was successfully removed.[47]

While Dr. Hobson has likened our natural dream state to an "organic psychosis" marked by disorientation and incongruities,[48] there are cases where actual or borderline psychotics experience a dream-reality fusion that can lead to violence. For instance, in the dream, a voice issues commands to kill, or the dreamer is repeatedly murdered and then acts out in the waking state.[49]

In a less extreme example, a 33-year-old woman was hospitalized due to acute nightmares and hallucinations. Just before the hospitalization, she dreamed of "an enormous man without a face and wearing a pointed hat and brown cape" who tried to annihilate her. "She woke up screaming in terror, but the image persisted for her in the corner of the room for many minutes," and it was not until her husband took her to the exact locale of the hallucination that it began to recede.[50]

THE TALKING HEAD

Seemingly telepathic communications have arrived in the ominous package of a nightmare. On the night of November 27, 1917, psychical researcher Dr. Walter Franklin Pierce, while living in Flushing, Long Island, dreamed that a slender young woman held out a document for him to read—a "warrant for her execution," written in red letters. She told Dr. Pierce she was willing to die but requested that he hold her hand while it was happening.

As the scene shifted to darkness, "I felt her grip my hand," he recounted, "and somehow became conscious that the execution was being accomplished. I then put one hand of mine on the hair of her head, which I found was loose and severed from her body, and felt moisture, which I was convinced was blood. Then the fingers of my other hand were caught in her teeth, and the mouth opened several times and closed again . . . and I was filled with the horror at the thought of a severed but living head."[51]

The next morning, he reported the dream to a staff member of the Society for Psychical Research, who later corroborated the timeline. Subsequent newspaper accounts detailed how on November 27 a mentally disturbed woman named Sarah A. Hand wandered from her home in Manhattan and later that night deliberately placed her head in front of the wheels of a train stopped at a railroad track in Hollis, Long Island (six miles from Flushing). When the train started, she was decapitated.[52] A letter she wrote, found at the site, stated, "My head is alive and can see and talk, and I must get it to prove my case to the law. No one believed me when I said I would never die and when my head was chopped off I would still be alive."

Pierce later spoke to Sarah Hand's mother and learned that her daughter's appearance matched that of the woman in his nightmare. Many of the circumstances between his dream and the horrific event seemed to line up. Perhaps the most remarkable was the emphasis on her hand connecting with her last name, and how the bizarre assertion that her severed head could live independently was in a way realized in Pierce's experience. Was the consciousness of Sarah Hand somehow able to intersect with Dr. Pierce during her demise, or did his dream state foster a precognitive depiction of an event he would soon read about in the newspaper? In either case, he said, "the awful vividness of the dream haunted my consciousness for days, and is today as real as most of memories of actual events."

NIGHT TERRORS

Unlike your garden-variety nightmare, night terrors or "sleep terrors" occur during NREM (deep sleep) cycles that are characterized by slow delta brain waves. The episodes, which are more common in children than adults (and tend to run in families, like sleepwalking), typically take place in the first half of the night and can last from a few minutes up to a half hour.

Night terrors are marked by sweating, tachycardia, and eerie dilated pupils; the person may scream or shout, thrash about, or suddenly bolt up. One of Dr. Carlos Schenck's patients, a woman in her thirties, issued such powerful and unrelenting screams that she damaged her vocal cords. Curiously, she believed that her screams scared off the ghost that was inciting her night terrors in the first place![53]

In contrast to nightmares, which emerge out of a long dream, sleep terrors are distinguished by fragmentary images or story lines. Typical subjects include spiders, monsters, ghosts, being chased or attacked, a robber in the house, a fire burning near the bed, or walls closing in.[54]

It's challenging to rouse someone in the midst of a sleep terror, a netherworld between sleep and waking. Though their eyes may be open, they don't readily identify familiar people or surroundings and are difficult to console or soothe. To the observer, it's almost as if they're possessed.

"I was 23 when I began to suffer from night terrors," writes Rebecca Turner, the founder of the World of Lucid Dreaming. "Night terrors for me were not merely bad dreams. They were shocking and fearsome hallucinations that arose after waking suddenly from a deep, dreamless sleep."[55]

A sleep-deprived twenty-two-hour flight to New Zealand led to her first occurrence. After she finally got to bed, "I woke up screaming in absolute terror—seeing a giant six-foot-tall tarantula standing on its back legs in the bedroom. It was in an aggressive attack position, reaching toward me with its front legs beating. . . . I knew, without doubt, that the beast had malicious intent. I had to escape."

In her effort to get away from the monstrous arachnid, she stood up on the bed but ended up trampling her sleeping partner, who tried to calm her. "After about 20 seconds of thrashing and screaming, I noticed the spider had disappeared. I was finally fully conscious and back with reality.... The episode was scary. I was pumped full of adrenaline and confounded by this bizarre hallucination which had not taken place in a dream, or even a vivid false awakening, but right there in the bedroom."

When night terrors and sleepwalking are intertwined, people sometimes demonstrate superhuman strength and speed. "One of my patients," wrote Dr. Schenck, "kicked a television all the way across the room. Another moves dressers and beds that he can't move at all when he's awake." This is one reason why people can be trepidatious about trying to wake or interact with someone in the throes of night terrors. The best strategy is to gently reassure and calm them.[56]

As with recurrent nightmares, specific repeating themes or images may trigger panic. For instance, one man's night terrors revolved around the horrors of swallowing noxious items such as nails, a shirt, an internalized list for a tax return, and even part of his own throat. Fittingly, when he slept overnight at a sleep lab for observation, he reported choking on the electrodes and wires being used to monitor him.[57]

After coming out of their frenzy, the sleeper often has no recollection of what scared them in the first place and just rolls over and goes back to sleep, ironically leaving family members, partners, or housemates awake from stress. One theory posits that the lack of recall may be a kind of retrograde amnesia, with extreme terror acting to disrupt or disable short-term memory.[58] New research has found a "cortical hot zone" in the back of the brain that's correlated with dreaming in both NREM and REM sleep states.[59] This could mean that dreaming in NREM takes place much more frequently than previously believed. It's just that the ability to remember these dreams is far weaker than in REM.

For children, the hyperarousal of sleep terror could be due to a delay in the development of their CNS. They generally grow out of the condition without the need for treatment. For adults with night terrors, benzodiazepines such as Klonopin before bedtime have proven helpful.[60]

FACING THE NIGHTMARE

Although people may readily forget their dreams, which seem to dissipate upon awakening, a nightmare is not so quickly dispensed with. Its memory may linger like the smell of burned plastic, an acrid residue of emotional turmoil.

According to the Jungian perspective, nightmares represent the "shadow" archetype, which is actively repressed by the "persona" or mask that we present to the everyday world. The shadow lurks in two burrows: the personal, a brew of our own suppressed or unacceptable experiences and feelings, mostly derived from childhood, and the collective, a primitive set of instincts and drives seated in the ancient, lower brain—what Carl Jung called "the two-million-year-old human being in us all."[61]

To fully integrate one's being, Jung advocated accepting the shadow as part of oneself. Though the regressed material of the shadow "certainly seems at first to be slime from the depths," Jung wrote, at closer inspection "this 'slime' contains not merely incompatible and rejected remnants of everyday life, or inconvenient and objectionable animal tendencies, but also germs of new life, and vital possibilities for the future."[62]

While making peace with our shadow side may be a lifelong process, there are tangible ways to deal with nightmares and perhaps reprogram the ones stuck on repeat.

"Dreaming about actions utterly repugnant to our waking mind does not mean there is something bad or wrong about us," psychotherapist Dr. Alex Lukeman says. "Morality, ethics, civilized rules of behavior, cultural mores and taboos—all of these mean nothing to the unconscious." He suggests trying to work with one's nightmares objectively, writing down or telling someone the story as though you were a neutral observer—and from there, attempting to decipher the meaning of the dream's symbols and realize what your unconscious is trying to convey to your conscious mind.

Nightmares can be considered a gift rather than a curse, Lukeman suggests. "By discovering the meaning of a dream it's possible to release old hurts, heal old emotional wounds or burdens or detect illness that may be dangerous."[63]

Of course, symbolic analysis doesn't really apply with severe PTSD, such as when soldiers' nightmares are replays of real incidents almost verbatim. "There's no point interpreting the meaning behind a dream about rape or a fire," notes Dr. Deirdre Barrett of Harvard Medical School. "They are pretty much the same as waking flashbacks."[64]

The technique known as "scripting" or "dream mastery" is a type of image rehearsal therapy (IRT) that has brought relief to some 70 to 80 percent of people who have trauma-related nightmares.[65] Developed by Dr. Barry Krakow in the early 2000s at the Maimonides

Sleep Arts and Sciences Center, the therapy sessions involve the client rewriting or reimagining the most terrifying parts of their nightmares.

One of Dr. Krakow's patients, a fifty-year-old schoolteacher, had a nightmare in which she was recklessly speeding in a dark car to escape a gruesome creature with giant eyeballs rapidly gaining on her. "In your mind, with thinking and picturing, take a few minutes, close your eyes, and I want you to change the dream any way you wish," Dr. Krakow told her.[66] She imagined herself leisurely driving a white Cadillac, with nothing chasing her in the rearview mirror. The eyeballs became bubbles pleasantly floating above the city.

Jungian therapists like Jane White-Lewis have taken issue with this kind of approach because it robs the patient of trying to unravel the nightmare's symbolic significance. By transforming the eyeballs into bubbles, she'll never find out just what those gargantuan orbs were trying to tell her, says White-Lewis, who has defended nightmares as a propulsive experience that "rubs, bites and sickens our soul." For in the aftermath, the shadow is revealed and understood.[67]

Yet White-Lewis admits she doesn't treat clients who have trauma, where dream mastery can be a godsend. Dr. Shelby Harris of the Sleep-Wake Disorders Center in New York asks her patients to picture the newly altered dream in their mind's eye for at least five minutes each day, and the process seems to reduce or vanquish their nightmares (for those more comfortable with therapy in pill form, a blood pressure medication called prazosin has been found to be about as effective as IRT in reducing nightmares[68]).

For some PTSD sufferers, dream mastery can even lessen daytime flashbacks. "We do know," said Dr. Harris, "that it creates changes in the brain when someone practices imagery rehearsal with focused mental practice, but the actual mechanism of action is still unknown."[69]

Perhaps related to the IRT findings, research has shown that frequent players of video games and now virtual reality are more adept at combating nightmares—apparently, the ability to fight off digitized zombies transfers over to the dream realm! If nightmares are a type of threat simulation, gamers have a leg up on the rest of us. In what could be thought of as a kind of live version of IRT, lucid dreaming (looked at extensively in Chapter 9) has proven to quell many nightmares.[70] Lucid dreamers are able to change the scenario from within the nightmare. In some cases, it's the nightmare itself that triggers the lucidity (recognizing that you're in a dream). Gamers reportedly excel at lucidity as well. Jayne Gackenbach, a psychologist at Grant MacEwan University in Canada, has pointed out the similarities that virtual and game worlds share with dreams. "Gamers," she said, "are used to controlling their game environments, so that can translate into dreams."[71]

Hypnosis is another approach that has demonstrated success at reducing nightmares, night terrors, and other parasomnias. In one study,[72] hypnotized patients were told to visualize themselves "walking slowly down a staircase, with continuing suggestions that each step would bring increased relaxation and comfort." The patients were asked to imagine seeing themselves in a movie, depicting how they were experiencing a pleasant night of sleep at home. "This was laced with suggestions that they were safe now" and that parasomnias or nightmares were no longer necessary and could be abandoned. Self-hypnosis techniques before bedtime also show promise.[73]

In the "if all else fails" category, a friend told me that when he was a child, he had nightmares of a smothering entity in his bedroom, but he could escape the clutches of the "evil one" if he could somehow manage to get over to his record player and drop the needle on "Downtown" by Petula Clark. Or perhaps you'd prefer this dreamcatcher-on-steroids idea from a Filipino shaman: "If you want to stop nightmares, nail a stingray tail above your door. Its barbs will snare malevolent spirits."[74]

CHAPTER SIX

HYPNAGOGIA

It was the morning of my father's funeral. I awoke in the bed of his apartment, where I was staying to sort through his belongings. As I lay there, I heard his voice greeting me from inside my head.

"Where are you?" I inquired.

"I'm in France," he said.

I knew he'd been stationed there in World War II, so this by itself made some sense, I later thought, imagining that his spirit might have embarked on some sort of life review.

We chatted for another minute or two. And then he choked up a bit.

"I very much miss being alive," he said.

The communication ended shortly after that. It was such an odd and unexpected experience—I really had no yardstick to measure it by. It had come unbidden, and I hadn't imagined or played out the dialogue; it simply occurred like a real-time conversation. His remark about missing being alive was a bit of a surprise, as that did not seem like something I would have invented or predicted. As far as the afterlife was concerned, I'd more or less bought into the near-death-experiencers' visions of heavenly light and not wanting to come back to dreadful old "here."

I chalked up the exchange as an awesome quirk, perhaps co-alescing around the given time and place. It was only when I dived into the research for this chapter that I realized that the confab with Dad fell into the category of hypnagogia, the liminal state just after or before sleep that can be a doorway to PSI phenomena and a bouquet of other curious experiences.

As sleeping pills escort us to the Land of Nod, or alarms jar us awake, many of us are barely cognizant of the curious buffer zone between sleep and wakefulness. On the front end, as we close our eyes to go to sleep at night, we may see colors and shapes or feel odd sensations. These fleeting moments, known as the hypnagogic state, can float right past us like the airborne seeds of dreams. And yet if one pays closer attention, they may yield something akin to the melted clocks of Salvador Dali or a host of other surreal surprises. Inching into the dreaming mind while remaining conscious, our thoughts and perceptions untether from logic as we slip into a nebulous borderland.

Derived from the Greek words *hypnos* ("sleep") and *agogeus* ("leader" or "conductor"), the hypnagogic state is mirrored by the hypnopompic state, which refers to the interval just after someone awakens. Because the two transitional states share certain similarities, like twilight and the minutes before dawn, the researcher Andreas Mavromatis paired them together under the umbrella term of *hypnagogia*, which has been adopted here and by many who study the phenomena. In his seminal 1987 book, *Hypnagogia*, an exhaustive work cataloging more than a century of research, Mavromatis shared a variety of terms for the dual states, including *presomnal sensations, visions of half-sleep, oneiragogic images, faces in the dark, half-dream state*, and my personal favorite, *phantasmata*.[1]

The hypnagogic state is more commonly experienced than the hypnopompic and often starts with abstract visuals when someone closes their eyes to nap or sleep. They may initially see phosphenes or entoptic lights (imagery from within the structure of the eye) that start off as shifting blobs or bubbles of color.

"Thin threads of gold, silver, purple and emerald green . . . cross over or curl up in a thousand different symmetrical patterns, continuously vibrating, forming innumerable little circles, diamonds or other small regular shapes,"[2] details one description. But what starts out as retinal amorphousness can evolve into detailed objects, faces, and landscapes, though they unfurl without the narrative structure of a dream.

Some think that these experiences represent dreams in their embryonic form. The progressive English physician Havelock Ellis wrote that "as I have begun to lose waking consciousness, a procession of images has drifted before my vision, and suddenly one of the figures has spoken. This hallucinatory voice occurring before I was fully asleep has startled me into full waking consciousness, and I have realised that, while in the hypnagogic stage, I was assisting at the birth of a dream."[3]

I'VE JUST SEEN A FACE

One of the curiosities of seeing faces (a classic hypnagogic subject) is that they're almost always unrecognizable to the viewer.[4] "For many years I have been accustomed to see multitudes of faces as I lie awake in bed, generally before falling asleep at night, after waking up in the morning, or if I should wake in the middle of the night," said Mrs. Macdonald, a nineteenth-century correspondent from Manchester, England.[5]

"They seem to come up out of the darkness as a mist, and rapidly develop into sharp delineation, assuming roundness, vividness, and living reality," she explained. "Then they fade off only to give place to others, which succeed with surprising rapidity and in enormous multitudes. Formerly, the faces were wonderfully ugly. They were human but resembling animals, yet such animals as have no fellows in the creation, diabolical-looking things. So curiously and monstrously frightful were they that I cannot conceive whence they could have come if not from the infernal world. I could not . . . by any voluntary effort of imagination conjure up anything remotely approaching their frightfulness. Latterly, the faces have become exquisitely beautiful. Forms and features of faultless perfection succeed each other in infinite variety of number."

As grotesque as some of the faces may be, they aren't usually menacing, though they may embody fleeting emotions. One subject described seeing the distorted face of a man "wrinkled and lined by folds of flesh; his one eye was like a very old apple that has turned pale brown and shriveled. It stood out of his eye socket. I saw no other eye." As he observed the face over the course of several seconds, "the changeless grimace seemed alive somehow, and the head turned somewhat. . . . I was aware that this was a hideous image, yet I was not afraid so much as curious to watch it to see what it might do."[6]

Some scenarios are downright macabre yet have a touch of humor about them, such as when one subject recalled "a family of skulls in a car driving along. . . . I could see the expression on their

Faces fleeting, shifting, and distorted may spontaneously emerge in the hypnagogic state. Photograph of masks, Lonehood 2016.

faces . . . [and] tell it was a friendly family." Though they were all skeletons, it wasn't at all frightening, he said.[7] Scary hypnagogia usually causes the person to snap back to the fully wakened state.

From trolls to supermodels, faces conjured in half-sleep are not just confined to human or semihuman form. "I had images of bright green frogs that appeared to leer at me," said one eighteen-year-old participant of a psychology experiment. "Then, when they blinked their eyes, they vanished."[8]

Hypnagogic scenes have no beginning or end and can transform of their own accord, mysteriously evolving or dissolving from one image to the next. The subjects can run the gamut from minute to gigantic and can be seen at odd angles like Humpty Dumpty viewed from his posterior side, or even upside down. They certainly don't feel the need to obey the laws of perspective. For instance, as an object "moves" closer to your mind's eye, it may not grow larger, though it may get brighter.[9]

In some instances, if a person has been playing a video game or performing a repetitive activity, the images may resurface across the hypnagogic blackboard in what's been dubbed the "Tetris effect." One study found seventeen out of twenty-seven subjects reseeing the falling geometric pieces of the Tetris video puzzle in their half-dream state, after playing the game for several hours earlier.[10] Is the brain sharpening its skills for the next round, or are these ghost images like the burn-in on an old CRT display?

A SALAD OF SOUND

After visual images, auditory phenomena are the next most common type of hypnagogic content. A person may hear voices, peculiar mechanistic sounds like beeps,[11] or strands of music, sometimes unaccompanied by images, or "offscreen" to the ones they do see. Many have heard their name called by a voice as though from the next room. Illustrating the "realness" of such sounds is a case in which an experimental subject thought he'd been called by one of the experimenters. He went to the trouble of unhooking himself from biofeedback equipment and dashed out into the hall, only to discover that no one had called his name.[12] Similar to the content of sleep talking, half-dreamers may hear peculiar words, doggerel, and neologisms, spoken in their own voices or those of others. A sage bit of advice offered by one hypnagogist: "Buy stocks in the fixed stars. It is remarkably stable."[13]

Or consider this catchy bit of verse[14] from a collection of hypnagogic ramblings by readers of Britain's venerable *New Statesman*:

"Only God and Henry Ford
have no umbilical cord."

As she awoke, one young woman was surprised to find herself murmuring, "put the pink pyjamas in the salad."[15] Mavromatis and other researchers note the similarity of such utterances to the speech patterns of schizophrenics, who withdraw from the ordinary perceptual world and string disconnected ideas together.

Bodily distortions and sensations of floating, tingling, or falling, or even synesthesia, may also accompany hypnagogia.

INFLUENCING IMAGES

Except for rare flashes of lucidity, dreams are always analyzed after the fact. "The same is not true of hypnagogia," writes historian of the occult Gary Lachman. "With a little practice, anyone can learn how to watch otherwise obscure mental processes at work."[16]

Like hypnosis, the mind in the half-dream state is particularly suggestible. And though the content one initially experiences is autonomous, it can be highly malleable. One correspondent of researcher F. E. Leaning recalled how the sharp barks of a neighbor's dog shattered his night's sleep like a pane of glass. Calming himself, he stayed in bed and fell into a conscious reverie:

> Presently I saw the big trunk of a tree, with mossy roots, at the foot of the trees even several small indistinct white objects. I wasn't sure what they were—'Mushrooms, perhaps?' I thought—and they clearly became mushrooms! Then they shifted again—and 'No' I thought 'they are not mushrooms, they're Playing Cards.' And in a trice they became playing cards. I saw the black and red pips on them; then all gone. This was becoming interesting and I waited for the next picture. It came as a bank of dense plants, clumps like very large forget-me-not plants—nothing else, only the leaves. I thought, 'Now can I get these plants to blossom.' I had no sooner formed the wish than I saw flowering stems and buds pushing out from among the leaves; they grew by degree, and unfolded. I was so thrilled I hardly dared to breathe . . . Most certainly I was not asleep. My mentality was most keenly awake and absorbed in this quite new development. 'If another comes,' I said to myself, 'I'll try to get something alive.' Now this I think the most interesting and inexplicable of all. There came a sort of confusion and shaking in the darkness—indistinct bunches that moved—then I saw hanging down several legs and feet of game birds, the claws and scales on the legs lifelike; below them rose the head and forepart of a little animal that looked like a rat, its head was turned over, and the mouth open. I saw the pink tongue and lips. Then all vanished. And I saw no more at all.[17]

The Austrian psychotherapist Herbert Silberer was one of the first to point out the "autosymbolic" nature of hypnagogia. Images seen in the half-sleep state, he suggested in a 1909 paper, are symbolic representations of a person's thoughts, feelings, and sensations in the moment. Initially affiliated with Freud and his followers, Silberer believed that the dueling elements of "drowsiness and an effort to think" naturally generate autosymbolic content. He cited numerous autosymbolic moments of his own; for example, when contemplating improving a passage in one of his essays, he saw himself planing a piece of wood. He also observed that hypnagogic symbols were not universal but reflected meanings specific to the individual.[18]

An independent and original thinker, Silberer would go on to write the influential *Hidden Symbolism of Alchemy and Occult Arts*. Some time after both he and Jung were excommunicated by Freud and his circle, he hanged himself, gruesomely staging his final image with a flashlight illuminating his face.[19]

A WHO'S WHO OF HYPNAGOGIA

Diverging from the ancient Greek notion that the gods impart messages and healing during dream visitations, the third-century philosopher and mystic Iamblichus suggested that such divine interactions are better suited to an intermediate state when we have clearer powers of observation. Dreams that are "sent from God," he wrote, "take place either when sleep is leaving us, and we are beginning to awake, and then we hear a certain voice . . . or voices are heard by us, between sleeping and waking." At times we are surrounded by "an invisible and incorporeal spirit" that is not perceived by sight . . . and "sometimes a bright and tranquil light shines forth."[20]

During the Middle Ages, alchemists may have employed hypnagogic techniques to arrive at their arcane formulas. "The weird characters and eerie landscapes that fill alchemical illustrations would not be out of place in a hypnagogic hallucination," writes Lachman.[21]

In one of the first accounts of hypnagogia in the "modern age," the Elizabethan astrologer and occultist Dr. Simon Forman in his 1600 autobiography recalled the apocalyptic visions that preyed upon him as a child. As he lay down in bed, mountains and hills would roll up against him "as though they would overrun him and fall on him" and great boiling bodies of water would rage on the verge of swallowing him up.[22] Were they hypnagogic half-dreams or prophetic visions? Perhaps the former is the entry point for the latter. Forman concluded that they were sent by God to signify the troubles he'd later encounter (indeed, his later years were embroiled in controversy, and he was imprisoned over the death of a patient).

But it was the brilliant Scandinavian visionary and scientist Emmanuel Swedenborg (1688–1772) who really lifted the veil on hypnagogia for people like psychologist Wilson Van Dusen, who found inspiration in the seer's guideposts for his own journeys. "Swedenborg," Dr. Van Dusen noted, "explored the hypnogogic state more than anyone else has before or since."[23] Through the portal of half-dreams and deeper trances, Swedenborg's passport was stamped with a multitude of off-world and spiritual destinations, including heaven, hell, and various moons and planets.

In a writing from 1746 he outlines the two hypnagogic highways:

There is still another kind of vision which comes in a state midway between sleep and wakefulness. The man then supposes that he is fully awake, as it were, inasmuch as all his senses are active. Another vision is that between the time of sleep and the time of wakefulness, when the man is waking up, and has not yet shaken off sleep from his eyes. This is the sweetest of all, for heaven then operates into his rational mind in the utmost tranquility.[24]

The esoteric Russian philosopher and teacher of the Gurdjieff system P. D. Ouspensky (1878–1947) was an early advocate for exploring the half-dream state. He found that when he engaged in hypnagogia before bedtime, he slept too fitfully, so he reserved his experiments for hypnopompia in the morning. By remaining conscious in these states, he playfully engaged his inner dream artist and watched as fantastic creations unfolded, which he could control in different ways.[25]

"Golden dots, sparks and tiny stars appear and disappear before my eyes," he wrote. "These sparks and stars gradually merge into a golden net with diagonal meshes which moves slowly and regularly in rhythm with the beating of my heart . . . The next moment the golden net is transformed into the brass helmets of Roman soldiers marching along the street below . . . I hear their heavy measured tread, and see the sun shining on their helmets. Then suddenly I detach myself from the windowsill . . . [and] fly slowly over the lane, over the houses, and then over the Golden Horn."[26]

Ouspensky believed he was observing the process of how dreams, in general, are created, with the hypnagogic specks and squiggles germinating into full-bodied forms.

Rudolf Steiner (1861–1925), an influential academic, educator, and spiritualist, was the founder of the Anthroposophy Society, a movement based on the idea that the human intellect can contact spiritual worlds. Even though he disparaged the use of "trances," he likely used a form of hypnagogia to make his ethereal observations, as well as read the Akashic Records[27] (said to be a compendium of

all that has ever happened). He advised that the "moments of waking and of falling asleep are of the utmost significance" for contact
"with the so-called dead—and with other spiritual Beings of the
higher world."[28]

EXPANDING THE MIND

Dr. Van Dusen, who worked at a state mental hospital in Mendocino,
California, drew connections between hypnagogic hallucinations
and the voices and delusions experienced by his patients. Rather
than just incoherent babble, he suspected they could be hearing
(and sometimes seeing) independent spirits of both high and low
order—on his journeys, Swedenborg detailed encountering such beings ranging from angelic to demonic.

"Even average people," wrote Van Dusen, "who explore this
region can run into strange people and strange symbolic conversations that look like visitations from another world." During one of
his own half-dreams, he was transfixed by the profound vision of an
intricately carved mandala with a four-fold design representing the
nature of the self. In its center was "an empty hole through which
the fearsome force of the universe whistled."[29]

At the deepest level of the hypnagogic trance, he continued, "is a
kind of satori or enlightenment. Suddenly the questioner and the
answerer are one. This one breaks into infinite images of all its representations."[30]

Extending or prolonging a hypnagogic state entails letting go of
one's ego boundaries, similar to how a mystic or shaman accepts
"ego death" as the price of admission to the beyond. And like a med-
itator, a hypnagogist inhabits a spatial and temporal immediacy,
freed from concerns about the future or the past.[31]

In his book *Zen and the Brain,* neuroscientist James Austin reports that some yogic meditators are able to hold themselves in a transitional state between wakefulness and sleep for up to 80 percent of a forty-minute meditation. This was reflected in EEG tests showing that they had a stable mixture of alpha and theta waves (more on the brain a bit later) and were perhaps demonstrating the skill of "freezing the hypnagogic process at later and later stages."[32]

"When I allow myself to drift through this frontier region," writes dreamwork luminary Robert Moss, "with no fixed agenda, I have the sense of leaning through a window or a doorway into space. Sometimes this feels like hanging out of the open hatch of an airplane. I have come to recognize this as the opening of a dreamgate."[33]

Oliver Fox, an English writer and occultist, hammered out a how-to guide for astral projection (and lucid dreaming) in the early part of the twentieth century, and one of his methods prescribed using the half-sleep state as a jumping-off point. When you visualize a known street or location, at first your mental image may appear an indeterminate distance in front of your closed eyes, he wrote, "but you will get the sensation that the scene is within you; and what you are trying to do is to transfer your consciousness to the self-pictured locality in your vision, so that you become within the scene—even as you are when you walk along a road in waking life. When you succeed, you may get the effect of a 'click' in your brain, and the transition is instantaneous."[34] Robert Monroe also pointed to the "borderland sleep state," in which one can develop a kind of self-induced sensory deprivation cocoon in advance of lift-off.[35]

WINDOWS TO PSI

Hypnagogia seems to have a curious "chicken-egg" relationship with many things PSI (a catch-all term used here to denote clairvoyance, telepathy, the seeing of apparitions, etc.). If the half-dream state is conducive to PSI phenomena, the reverse seems to be true—that is, if a psychic deliberately wants to access impressions, they may enter a hypnagogic state to retrieve them.[36]

In his book *How to Test and Develop Your ESP*, Paul Huson advises the beginner to tune into their mental images, with eyes closed in a darkened room, preferably before falling asleep at night. After the initial phase, "you may get your first sense of depth," he writes, "a feeling you are staring into a three-dimensional space. In this depth the imaginals (as I named them) appear, dimly at first, but more solidly and clearly with practice . . . You will . . . notice they are all continually growing and evolving into something else, like a speeded up film of a plant growing." These haphazard images are not yet clairvoyance, he points out—they are "your fishing line to your unconscious memory pool," and the aspirant still needs to "hook the correct impression" of their extrasensory perception (ESP) target through the strength of their motivation and intent.[37]

The protean mental screen of the half-sleep state practically seems ported over to other PSI techniques. The Ganzfeld method, a type of parapsychology experiment, though controversial, has shown some positive ESP correlations at times by creating a hypnagogic-like environment for subjects in the laboratory.[38] There's also crystal ball gazing or scrying, which can be done with a variety of reflective surfaces—Nostradamus was said to stare into a special bowl of water to see the future. The occultist W. E. Butler provides instructions for quietly gazing into a black mirror until its surface begins to cloud over and little sparks glimmer.

Then, he writes, if you can keep your mind in a quiet, neutral state, "the appearance in the mirror may begin to increase and to take other forms. Fragmentary, glimpses of brilliantly coloured landscapes, faces grave and gay, and luminous colored clouds may all show themselves ... These pictures are the first cousins to those curious little pictures seen by some people during the entry into sleep and again when awakening."[39]

DOORWAYS TO THE DEAD

Inspired by the ancient Greeks' Oracle of the Dead, in which pilgrims were kept in darkness for days before attempting contact with deceased loved ones, Dr. Raymond Moody created the psychomanteum. It's a small chamber, illuminated only by candlelight, in which a mirror is placed high (so that one doesn't see their reflection). Opposite the mirror, a grieving individual sits in a chair for sixty to ninety minutes.

"In many of the cases," said Moody, "the people will tell us that they see the image of their departed loved one forming up in the mirror but then the image actually seems to emerge from the mirror—come right out into the room with them. About 30% of the subjects will tell you that they actually seem to hear the audible voice of the deceased ... and others have mind-to-mind communion with the person who has died ... and experience this visitation as a real event."[40]

Visits from the dead or crisis apparitions are not entirely uncommon in the hypnopompic state, as I discovered in my chat with dearly departed Dad. Sometimes specters appear as a warning. Take the case of a woman who placed her husband's dinner on low heat in the oven in advance of his return, and then retired for the night. After about three hours, she suddenly woke and saw the apparition of her deceased grandfather standing at her bedside. "He had his back to me," she said, "and was looking over his shoulder at me." She went downstairs and opened the door at the bottom. "I gasped. The house reeked of gas. I opened all the doors and turned off the gas."[41]

"In 1836," writes Robert Henry Dix, a Society for Psychical Research correspondent, "I had become engaged to a young lady; but I decided to leave England and try my fortune elsewhere, and wait until I should be able to establish myself, and could then send for my intended." He acquired a good position in St. Petersburg, Russia, and was regularly exchanging letters with his fiancé when suddenly contact ceased. He finally heard from family members that his intended had taken ill and gone to the Jersey seaside to recuperate. Depressed by the circumstance, one afternoon Dix threw himself on the sofa and fell asleep.

"It might have been an hour or so that I had been asleep, when, suddenly awaking, I observed at the foot of the couch a sort of bluish vapour, which seemed to fill up the end of the room, and what seemed to me a shadowy form appeared to come out of it, which gradually took the form of a female; the features bore the exact likeness of my intended. I raised myself on the sofa, and exclaimed, 'Louisa, is that really you? What has happened?' I received no answer and in a few seconds the apparition was gone, and seemed to melt away into the vapour, which also disappeared." He later received a letter announcing her death and noted that it took place on the same afternoon as his vision.[42]

It's conceivable that the newly deceased might want to say good-bye to loved ones one last time, but is there something about the half-sleep state that makes this otherworldly visitation possible? Or is it that our psychic senses are more activated during hypnagogia and create a kind of telegram of tragedy out of the quasi-dream fabric?

THE TWILIGHT ZONE

In contrast to the images that assemble in front of our closed eyes on the verge of sleep, hypnopompic content is often a bleed-through or continuation of the dream state. "Once I had a most vivid dream about a man I knew well," wrote Reverend E. H. Sugden. "On suddenly waking, I saw him, in the light of early morning, standing at my bedside in the very attitude of the dream. I looked at him for a second or two, and then putting my foot out, I kicked at him; as my foot reached him, he vanished."[43] One could also consider the terrifying phenomenon of sleep paralysis (covered in Chapter 1) to be a subset of the hypnopompic experience.

The parapsychologist Charles Tart, an inveterate explorer of altered states of consciousness, described an incident that demonstrates the power of certain dreams to trickle into waking reality: "I dreamed I got high on some sort of gaseous substance, like LSD in gas form. Space took on an expanded, high quality, my body (dream body) was filled with a delicious sensation of warmth, my mind 'high' in an obvious but indescribable way. It only lasted a minute and then I was awakened by one of the kids calling out and my wife getting up to see what was the matter. Then the most amazing thing happened: I stayed high even though awake! It had a sleepy quality to it but the expanded and warm quality of time and space carried over into my perception of the (dimly lit) room. It stayed this way for a couple of minutes, amazing me at the time because I was clearly high."[44]

The researcher D. Scott Rogo experimented with an intriguing method to invite an out-of-body experience (OBE or OOBE) by controlling and prolonging hypnagogic images. Aware that the sensation of falling is associated with astral projection, he held in his mind the scenario of driving a car very fast downhill, and at times achieved a dual consciousness of being both in and out of his body.[45] He found that *crashing* the car also pulled him out of body. "Since many OOBEs are reported on the verge of sleep," he writes, "by controlling this state of consciousness one can more readily direct the OOBE than at any other time."

Mavromatis details cases of "shared" hypnagogic experiences, in which just before sleep, a person saw the "face and form" of a friend and had a brief conversation with her. A few days later, the friend revealed she had "an identical experience" at precisely the same time. In Mavromatis's own experiments with group hypnagogia, one of the participants accurately described "the very scenes I was seeing with eyes shut," he wrote.[46]

Psychics have referred to switching off the analytic mind and tuning in to a different mode of perception from within. In many cases, says Mavromatis, "visual psi experiences are practically indistinguishable from those occurring in hypnagogia both in their content and nature."[47]

"When you let yourself slip into the twilight zone," adds Moss, "you may have the impression that someone . . . has something to tell you. When I lie down and close my eyes, I sometimes have the impression of a whole cast of characters waiting for me to arrive."[48]

THE BRAIN AT THE THRESHOLD

Mavromatis divided hypnagogia into stages moving from lighter to deeper. On the deeper end of the pool, as a person nears the submergence of sleep they block out more of the waking world.

The hypnagogic state brings its own bumpy set of brain waves. But first, a bit about brain waves in general. Their patterns, as measured by an EEG, represent the synchronized electrical firings of billions of neurons ricocheting in our head at any one time (if somehow all the electricity in the brain could be harnessed it could fully charge an iPhone in around sixty-eight hours[49]—OK, so, no rush to get a USB connector installed in the back of your head). During our waking hours, beta waves tend to dominate for such activities as critical thinking, problem solving, and reading; the slower alpha waves promote relaxation and are the bridge between beta and theta. Prominent during sleep, meditation, and daydreaming, theta waves oscillate when we're disengaged from the world.

Hypnagogia is marked by the transition out of beta into grappling cycles of alpha and theta, and even an EEG grab bag of "humps, spikes, or partial spindles."[50] As we move toward sleep from the relaxation of alpha to the drowsiness of theta, neither brain wave maintains dominance, and this contributes to the "half-asleep" or "half-awake" scenario.[51] During these vacillations, the brain's domineering left hemisphere also loses jurisdiction, and more fluid associations take place (the subject of enhanced creativity in this state, coming up shortly).

Mavromatis proposes that hypnagogia arises from structures like the thalamus in the "old brain" that hold sway when the neocortex (a more recent evolutionary development) is suppressed. The fact that we're getting a glimpse of the consciousness of our "old brain" while still retaining some function of the "new brain" is why hypnagogic imagery and sensations may seem so unfamiliar to us.[52]

Further, just as the stars are always in the sky but hidden from our view during daylight, Mavromatis suggests that the brain structures responsible for hypnagogic phenomena are always active, but their handiwork is blotted out by the neocortex and its focus on the external world. This parallels Rudolf Steiner's idea, Lachman notes, that the "astral world" is always with us but our ability to perceive it is blocked by ordinary consciousness.[53]

Located in the thalamus, deep inside the center of the brain, is the mysterious pineal gland, which Descartes regarded as the seat of the soul. Some have speculated that the tiny organ releases DMT (a hallucinogenic substance dubbed the "spirit molecule" by Dr. Rick Strassman) at certain times, and if so, it could be a factor in the trippiness of the hypnagogic experience.

EXPLODING HEAD SYNDROME AND HYPNAGOGIC JERKS

While Exploding Head Syndrome and the Hypnagogic Jerks makes for a cool band name, they're actually glitches while entering or coming out of sleep. The hypnagogic or hypnic jerk is an involuntary muscle spasm or twitch that wakes a person with a start as they are falling into a deeper state of sleep. These "sleep starts" are quite common—it's estimated that 60 to 70 percent of the population has experienced at least one[54]—though sometimes it's not the sleeper who is startled awake but their bed partner who witnesses the erratic twitch or gets a limb thrust their way.

"To me," writes neuroscientist Tom Stafford, hypnic jerks "represent the side effects of a hidden battle for control in the brain that happens each night on the cusp between wakefulness and dreams."[55] Before a person's body becomes paralyzed during the REM dream state, hypnic jerks indicate that the motor system is not quite ready to throw in the towel. "Last gasps" of daytime energy can sputter and burst in seemingly random movements, says Stafford, as shift change takes place at Cerebellum Inc.

Being sleep deprived increases the likelihood of these misfires that some have hypothesized could be a throwback to our primate days. Hypnagogic jerks could be "an archaic reflex to the brain's misinterpreting the muscle relaxation accompanying the onset of sleep as a signal that the sleeping primate is falling out of a tree," proposed psychologist Frederick Coolidge and archaeologist Thomas Wynn. The reflex, they explain, may have had selective value favoring sleepers who were able to maintain their sleeping position in a nest or on a branch.[56]

Though not as traumatic as falling out of a tree, hearing an explosion inside your head is no picnic. They are "strange and frightening attacks of something exploding, creating a loud bang in my head. There is no real pain ... but you feel there has been a massive hemorrhage and it takes a quarter of an hour before the fear passes, though the noise itself lasts only a split second,"[57] said one eighty-year-old sufferer of exploding head syndrome (EHS).

In what is likely a variant of the sleep start[58] delivered in an auditory hypnagogic hallucination, EHS packs a walloping fright. A person is jolted awake by an explosive noise like a gun firing, a clash of cymbals, or the sound of an object being dropped from a height. The noise is often perceived as coming from within the head rather than through the ears and is sometimes paired with a bright flash. This little-talked-about parasomnia isn't that uncommon, with one study reporting that around 18 percent of college students had the experience.[59]

Though EHS is benign, many patients worry that they have a serious medical condition. Unless you're a veteran of the disturbance (some are plagued seven nights a week), you may wake drenched in sweat, and, with heart pounding, investigate your home to see what crashed. Once I bolted awake to the sound of something like gunfire and shouting and partially fell out of bed. At the time, I lived above a busy street and just assumed it was a fracas below, though I saw nothing when I looked out the window. Now, I wonder if it was baby's first Exploding Head Syndrome?

Clinical psychology professor Brian Sharpless has investigated the phenomenon and suspects it's caused by a suppression of alpha waves and a hiccup in the brain's reticular formation, which plays a role in sleep and wakefulness. Normally, in preparation for sleep, the brain shuts down auditory neurons. But with EHS, instead of the neurons quieting, he speculates they may all fire at once, creating the blast of sound.[60]

The occurrence is ripe for misinterpretation, Sharpless adds, citing how some individuals with EHS believe they're being targeted by covert or government operatives. "People can sense these strange explosions in their head," he said, "and they may think they've had something implanted in their brain. Or they feel this surge of electricity and they think they've been shot by some kind of new energy weapon."[61]

CREATIVITY UNBOUND

For many artists, scientists, writers, musicians, and others, hypnagogia can be a fount of creativity and inspiration. As they dip into the unconscious, new ideas and associations dangle like low-hanging fruit, though cloaked in the skin of symbolism. One of the most celebrated cases of hypnagogic insight involves nineteenth-century European chemist August Kekule, who was struggling to decipher the structure of the benzene ring, a compound of carbon atoms. He recounts:

> I was sitting, writing at my text-book; but work did not progress; my thoughts were elsewhere. I turned my chair to the fire and dozed ... the atoms were gambolling before my eyes. This time the smaller groups kept modestly in the background. My mental eye, rendered more acute by visions of the kind, could now distinguish larger structures of manifold conformation: long rows, sometimes more closely fitted together; all twining and twisting in snake-like motion. But look! What was that? One of the snakes had seized hold of its own tail, and the form whirled mockingly before my eyes. As if by a flash of lightning I awoke; and ... spent the rest of the night in working out the consequences of the hypothesis.[62]

The symbol of an ouroboros—a serpent eating its own tail—dates back to ancient Egypt, and was also used in Gnostic and alchemical traditions, representing cycles of time and regeneration. Was it just the undulations of the snake or something more allegorical that led to his eureka moment? Kekule flipped the autosymbolic aspect of hypnagogia on its head, where instead of thoughts or concepts giving rise to images, it was the vision that birthed the idea.[63] Don't try to color hypnagogia between the lines, please!

Sometimes material arrives fully formed, as though channeled or sent from somewhere else. The novelist Mary Leader said the plot for her supernatural-themed novel *Triad* came to her as she drifted off while sitting in a contour chair one afternoon in 1971. Entering a "peculiar state of consciousness," neither awake nor asleep, she found herself wandering in a twilight world. "Never before had I felt like this. It was as though it were a film—the entire panorama of my novel reeled off before me, its theme, its plot . . . I don't remember how long I was gone, but when I broke out of it, it was all there. I was seized with a compulsion to write and write!"[64]

Mavromatis writes, "Hypnagogia not only makes it possible for material which might never reach consciousness directly to do so but also furnishes us with clues concerning the working of the creative process" and how ideas are generated in the first place. In some instances, a person just waking up from a dream can replay the content in a half-sleep state. When the perspective of the dream is changed from participant to spectator, more creative fodder or insights can be transplanted to the waking world.[65]

Sirley Marques Bonham, a consciousness researcher from the University of Texas-Austin, concurs. "Hypnagogia is the shortest path for communication from our unconscious," and there are various ways we can receive these messages, or even open up a two-way exchange.[66] If you run into obstacles while working on a creative project, she believes the unconscious starts percolating ideas and solutions before you're even aware of them.[67]

Venerable dream researcher Stanley Krippner notes that "one's dream-life has a life of its own, but hypnagogia might be more amenable to some kind of patterned control." Both he and psychologist

Deirdre Barrett have suggested that a person can "incubate" solutions by lightly concentrating on a problem as they drift into the half-dream state.[68]

SURREALISTIC PILLOW

The famed Spanish painter Salvador Dali only needed a minuscule glimpse into his whirling subconscious to grab an indelible image. In fact, it was part of his credo to reel in these impressions from his psyche. Hypnagogia, in particular, provided him with an endless lookbook of surrealistic subjects.

At the opening of the London Surrealist exhibition held in 1936, Dali delivered a lecture titled "Fantomes paranoiaques authentiques" ("Authentic paranoid ghosts") while wearing a wet suit, holding a pool cue, and walking a pair of Russian wolfhounds. He later explained that his appearance portrayed "plunging into the depths" of the human psyche.[69]

While Dali used a number of techniques to harness his fantastic dream universe, his "slumber with a key" method was designed to grab a quick snapshot of the half-sleep state. He explains:

You must seat yourself in a bony armchair, preferably of Spanish style, with your head tilted back and resting on the stretched leather back. Your two hands must hang beyond the arms of the chair, to which your own must be soldered in a supineness of complete relaxation. Your wrists must be held out in space and must have been previously lubricated with oil of aspic. This is intended to facilitate the benumbing of your hands at the moment when slumber approaches including the tingling that is produced when one of your members goes to sleep. . . .

In this posture, you must hold a heavy key which you will keep suspended, delicately pressed between the extremities of the thumb and forefinger of your left hand. Under the key you will previously have placed a plate upside down on the floor. Having made these preparations, you will have merely to let yourself be progressively invaded by a serene afternoon sleep . . . The moment the key drops from your fingers, you may be sure that the noise of its fall on the upside down plate will awaken you.[70]

The loss of muscle tone as one moves closer to sleep is what causes the spoon to drop and clank awake the holder. Avoiding the grogginess of a full-fledged nap, just a quarter second of half-sleep was all Dali said he needed to face his canvas armed with images of "delirious phenomena." His 1944 painting *Dream, Caused by the Flight of a Bee (Around a Pomegranate a Second Before Waking Up)* is said to be formulated with hypnagogic images.[71] The surreal masterpiece depicts an airborne pomegranate shooting out a fish from whose mouth emerges two ferocious tigers with a bayonet pointing at a sleeping woman, to say nothing of the elephant rising into the background sky with its impossibly long flamingo legs.

Curator Stephen Romano, who put together the show *Opus Hypnagogia: Sacred Spaces of the Visionary and Vernacular* at Brooklyn's Morbid Anatomy Museum in 2015, talks about how the hypnagogic state "becomes the crack between two worlds" that certain artists slip through. By "unseeing" the world, "they're letting go of the memory-ordered construct," he remarks, and seeing with fresh eyes.[72]

The playground of hypnagogia and surrealism isn't just for artists. Take this rather literal interpretation of the expression "in the mind's eye" from Prof. Peter McKellar's casebook: while in the half-dream state, a male subject said he saw an "eye sitting in a glass of water" but as he watched it, the eyeball split into halves and revealed a metal sphere, inside which tiny people moved about.[73]

INDUCING HYPNAGOGIA

Though the ingenious inventor Thomas Edison was said to only sleep four to five hours a night, he wasn't above a little catnapping to get out of his "beta" mind-set and grab some new perspectives from the borderland state. Knowing that these perceptions could be fleeting, he used a method similar to Dali's to try to wrangle them back to the waking world. Dozing in his favorite chair, he would hold a steel ball in each hand, and as his arms relaxed, the balls would fall into pans he set up on the floor—with the clattering sound jarring him out of his reverie.[74]

In the era of apps for just about everything, perhaps we can dispense with the ungainly clanging of keys and balls. Enter the MIT Media Lab project Dormio, which has tested devices that advance the technique in some exciting directions. The first prototype involved a glove with palm sensors that subjects wore while napping in the lab, and an Alexa-like robot named Jibo tasked with extending the half-dream state and trying to "incept" specific dream topics with prompts like "remember to think about a rabbit."

As the system detects that a participant is falling into a deeper sleep, Jibo interjects by saying the person's name and "you are falling asleep." This pulls them out of the Land of Nod while still keeping them close to the entrance. Jibo also asks them what they're dreaming about and records their answers without the users having to wake themselves up entirely to reply.

Between waking the subjects, letting them descend toward sleep, and incubating with audio stimuli, "it's a sort of hovercraft of states of consciousness," said Dormio team leader Adam Haar Horowitz when I caught up with him via Skype. In the background I could see a hive of movement amid colorful shapes. *Wow, that MIT Lab is really hopping,* I thought. It turned out he was chatting from a workstation at his local rock climbing gym.

"The functional properties of hypnagogia are a bit of mystery," admitted Horowitz, a cerebral but congenial grad student, staking out uncharted turf in the interdisciplinary mash-up of art and science. What has been shown is that the inception words in the experiment were reliably converted into hypnagogic content.

He is particularly interested in the half-sleep state's connection to creativity and self-exploration. While creativity can be difficult to assess, the Dormio subjects compared to a control group scored higher in an "Alternative Uses" test for the words they were given during inception, and they spent more time working on a creative story.[75] Beyond the word cues, the symbols and storytelling reported by the subjects, Horowitz noted, sometimes triggered internal insights that otherwise might never have come to them.

In contrast to lucid dreaming, he finds hypnagogic napping more accessible for studying in the lab, in that it doesn't require disturbing a person's sleep schedule. "Lucid dreaming, in my experience, is really like being *myself* in a world that I can control," he told me, whereas hypnagogia is quite a different animal when it comes to one's perceptions. "It's a removed third-person perspective on first-person experience . . . it feels to me much less controlled, much more flexible."

The next generation of wearable Dormio, already in the works, has moved much closer to home-use accessibility. Instead of various physiological measures, it just monitors eyelid movements (in contrast to REM, hypnagogia is associated with slow eye movement, or SEM[76]) and Jibo's duties are replaced by a smartphone app.

OSCILLATING ONWARD

Mavromatis extols the multiconsciousness of hypnagogia as a possible next step for humanity. It's a "definite evolutionary advance over sleep dreaming," he writes, allowing for some control over the external environment while still being able to mine one's internal terrain. As an opportunity to tap into meditative states, creativity, and PSI abilities, an individual may "learn to oscillate in and out of hypnagogia to any desired degree," he suggests.[77]

Will we ever tame these tantalizingly elusive dreamlets? Drawing from all three brain states, they're the full monty of the mind, but oh so fleeting and gossamer-light.

CHAPTER SEVEN
PSYCHIC ATTACKS

Though our unconscious may be the gateway to creativity, PSI, and the depths of the psyche, it may also provide a back door for invisible or paraphysical forces that can cause us harm. Many believe that while sleeping we're particularly susceptible to attacks from other people, discarnate entities, or astral forms.

"When in mid-September 1950 my 40-year-old brother Harry Wagner told me he was being tormented by the ghost of a woman who had been dead for nearly 20 years I thought he was losing his grip on reality," wrote Virginia Santore.[1] Yet a haunting series of events would convince her otherwise.

A couple months earlier on a hot July night, Harry's wife, Mary, was sleeping soundly beside him in their bedroom. Just as he was about to join her in slumber, he felt a chill in the room. And then, near the doorway, a glowing ball of light swirled and transformed into the luminous figure of his first wife, Alice (who had died in 1933). Dressed in a flowing white robe, the apparition spun in the air and then hovered just inches from Harry's face. He felt paralyzed with fear, as her features turned into a chalky mask from which "two fiery red eyes blazed as though hellfire was behind them." When he opened his mouth to yell, the entity swooped in for a smothering lip-lock, pinning him down as she sucked the air out of his lungs.

But then he was suddenly released; gasping and choking, he swung his feet over to the side of the bed and sat up. As though from a distance, he heard the sound of wild laughter with a cruel mocking tone. By the time Harry shared his account with his sister, "Alice" was visiting him several times a week, and her intensity was growing stronger.

Harry began to lose weight and have physical difficulties, so he agreed to be hospitalized for a series of psychiatric tests, staying overnight at his sister's house near the facility where he'd be admitted the next morning.

An odd sound startled Virginia awake after three a.m., and she went to Harry's room to investigate, turning on the overhead light as she stood in the doorway. "Harry lay rigid on the bed," she said. "His face was flushed a deep red. His eyes were wide open and literally popping from their sockets. And while his mouth hung agape, I could not . . . detect any sign of breathing . . . I thought him either dead or dying!"

Entering the room, Virginia felt as though her entire body were encased in ice. Still, she managed to throw off the immobilizing effects of the deep freeze and reach her brother. "Grasping his upper arms, I quickly pulled him into a sitting position. And in that second something invisible writhed and twisted between us. Whatever it was I could feel it physically. And then, inches from my eyes a misty grey vaporous mass . . . spiraled ceilingward!"

Coming out of his glazed stare, Harry issued gulping breaths as his sister held him in her arms. At that moment Virginia heard it: distant but wild laughter. Harry opted to go in for the hospitalization even though his sister confirmed that his issues were not "all in his head."

Found to be in good health, he was nonetheless given medication to address his nervous condition upon release. A few days later, Virginia went to visit the Wagners and found Mary in a panic. Harry, whose lips were ringed with blue, had had a heart attack in the early-morning hours. By the time he reached the hospital, he was dead.

"I can never forget my brother's farewell gesture to me," Virginia recalled, "as they carried him out to the waiting ambulance. He nodded his head several times and I knew what he meant. His ghostly visitor had paid him one last call!"

While Virginia pondered whether the vengeful entity was really Alice or some "foul fiend from hell," we're left to consider the case's similarities to sleep paralysis and SUNDS. Could Harry have had the hidden heart defect found in many of the Southeast Asian immigrants that, when coupled with fearful SP, could lead to one's demise? And yet the repeated descriptions of the same entity, the frigid temperatures, and the heard laughter seem to suggest a supernatural attack vector that differs from SP.

DEMON IN THE DARK

A dark entity may first take hold within a nightmare. Pat Fox shared the dire circumstances of his marriage in "The Demon That Stole My Wife," a first-person account he penned for Ray Palmer's *Forum* magazine in November 1967.[2] In the 1950s, when his wife, Yevonna, was pregnant with their first child, she began to have disturbing dreams of a demon trying to possess her. The entity, she said, appeared in two forms—one was human, but the other was a hideous chimera with a human face, a cat's body and tail, an eagle's legs and talons, and the leathery wings of a bat.

Pat feared that his wife had developed schizophrenia. After the birth of their second child, she became cruel and destructive and continued to insist that a demon was appearing to her. At times, it was as though a second personality seemed to overtake her. Fearing for their young children, he placed them at Saint Mary's Infant Home in Norfolk, while he stayed with Yevonna to weather the storm of her illness.

One night, as they slept at a motel, awaiting a move to a small farmhouse, Pat was awakened by his wife speaking in an Old English dialect: "Thou foul, tormenting fiend! Is there no rest from thee this side of the tomb? Thou has taken my children and made an enemy of my husband . . . Get thee hence, Demon! Leave us alone!"

Though it was dark, he could see that Yevonna's eyes were wide open. Looking in the direction of her stare, he saw "an enormous, faintly luminescent face of greenish hue. It had a deathly appearance, with gray-blue lips, dry-looking white fangs and flowing greyish hair. But its orange-colored eyes glowed feverishly, and," he said, "it leered down with quite a lively and human lustfulness upon the half-naked person of my lovely wife."

When he turned on the bedside light, the entity vanished with "an unearthly sigh that shook the room." Though Yevonna was eventually committed to a state hospital with a diagnosis of paranoid schizophrenia, her husband had finally come to accept the reality of her demon.

MEET THE NEGS

Referring to negative spirit beings as Negs, metaphysical researcher and astral traveler Robert Bruce suggests that certain dense patterns of energy could be considered independent, sentient thought-forms. Yet, if more palatable to an individual's belief system, such manifestations, he offers, could be conceptualized as originating from one's own subconscious or the mind of others.[3]

A bewildering phylum, these inorganic beings *can* be difficult to classify and differentiate, Bruce admits. Here is a sampler pack you may hope you never have to sample: earthbound spirits, astral shells (an afterimage or residue left behind by spirits), addicted ghosts (still obsessed with earthly cravings), deranged ghosts (spirits that have forgotten they were once human and have adopted any delusional form that suits them), incubi/succubi, astral snakes and spiders (evil nature spirits), demons and their lesser orders, and Negs resembling ETs and poltergeists.[4]

Most of this otherworldly cast of characters are said to practice a kind of energy vampirism, sustaining themselves on human feelings like fear and sexual arousal, or draining energy like a sponge from their target when they're the most vulnerable—during sleep.[5]

Describing an encounter with a succubus, Bruce said that while in sleep paralysis, he observed the outlines of a female figure who began writhing on top of him. Able to wriggle his big toe, he broke the paralysis and rolled out of bed as he glimpsed a glowing cloud moving away from him. Now fully awake, he saw a floating torpedo-shaped entity "about three feet long and eighteen inches wide. It was crystalline, transparent, and full of tiny sparkling motes of light. It looked much like a cellular life form, as seen under a microscope." The entity pulsed with a red glow whenever it moved and he sensed it was waiting for him to fall back asleep. As he moved closer to get a better look, it contracted and then vanished. This delicate and beautiful being appeared nothing like a demon, Bruce remarked, "whatever its coarse nature and intentions" were.[6]

People with psychic sensitivities are more susceptible to attacks, he notes. But there are some practical countermeasures for your first line of defense, such as taking a shower, because "running water creates quite a strong electromagnetic field which is . . . very detrimental to hitchhiking entities."[7]

POLTERGEISTS ON PARADE

Whether poltergeists ("noisy ghosts") are a telekinetic disturbance brought on by hormonally haywire adolescents or the result of mischievous spirits, their eerie and disturbing hijinks are sometimes intertwined with dream, trance, and sleep states.

In 1979, sociologist and parapsychology researcher James McClenon investigated a home in Baltimore where a family reported hearing voices and whistling, being bitten on the legs, and seeing beds levitating along with balls of light and other anomalies.[8] The residents included the owners, "Mr. M." and his wife; their two adult sons; two divorced daughters; and two grandchildren.

One of the daughters, Manny, age thirty-three, experienced a series of nightmares in tandem with the events, including seeing people in "old-time" clothing and sexual scenarios with priests and misshapen/diseased figures. Once, she awakened into sleep paralysis and saw a bright yellow ball of light appear on the wall. When she shared this with her mother and sister, they too said they'd seen an orb of light in their bedrooms that same night.

One night Mr. M. decided to probe the phenomena by staying awake in the bed that seemed to be the source of many of the occurrences. He coordinated a plan with his son Mick, in which he would signal with his hand if something unusual was happening. But during the night a paralysis swept over him. He heard a knocking noise and felt as though someone were pushing his feet. Mick, who was reclining nearby on the floor, watched the side of the mattress under his father's feet rise eight to twelve inches. After it came down, Mr. M. was freed from the paralysis and able to converse.

The courageous Mr. McClenon volunteered to stay in the room one night in October 1979. After just a few hours of sleep, he awoke at six thirty a.m. and saw a red orb of light one foot by two feet on a wall by the window. "Immediately afterward, Mick began moaning as if having a nightmare and a rap sounded within the wall beside my face," he recalled. After waking, Mick stated, "I was having a dream in which I was crawling over the floor toward your bed. It [the spirit] wants you out of the bed."

McClenon thought the orb might have been the reflection of a car's lights but ruled this out when he observed that a thick shade covered the window. "At about 7:30 A.M.," he continued, "I awoke feeling a vibration under my chest. . . . The bed was moving up and down; the vibrations were similar to those produced by a minor earthquake." While he thought it unlikely, he wondered if a device had been inserted in the bed to cause the sensation. Graciously, he decided "it would be inappropriate for me to cut open the mattress since I was a guest in the house."

Eventually, all members of the household reported anomalous experiences—even Robert, the "skeptical" son, who awoke one night to the sight of a hooded female apparition gently stroking his forehead while he was paralyzed. Ultimately, "I could not determine if the source of the experiences were supernatural, physiological, or fraudulent," McClenon concluded. Fortunately, for the "M." clan, over time, the poltergeist events at their Baltimore home dissipated, along with the associated nightmares.

In perhaps a more clear-cut case of pinning the tail on the poltergeist, Brad Steiger imparts a fraternity brother's quizzical account. Steiger's correspondent was hot on the make for a beautiful coed named Carol, but she was "saving it" for her one-and-only. The student said he'd wined and dined the young lady, then driven to a secluded spot.

"I thought that by all the signs (heavy breathing, sighs, whimpers, and certain minor liberties) my Snow Queen was about to melt," he recollected. "That was when I saw the damned thing. Carol had her eyes closed in what I thought was a moment of . . . abandonment, but when I saw what was in the backseat, I was ready to abandon the car!"

The young man described a shimmering form with glaring red eyes. "And then there came this god-awful stench, like someone had just opened the floodgates of a cesspool." He rolled down the windows and hightailed it out of there. "That's when I noticed that Carol still had her eyes closed." He realized that rather than being in the throes of passion she seemed to be either asleep or in a trance. She didn't awaken until he'd reached her sorority house, whereupon she blinked a couple of times, thanked him for the evening, and gave him a chaste peck on the lips.

"Carol's odiferous and monstrous chaperone was more than likely a poltergeist psychic projection, rather than a guardian angel of her virginity," Steiger, a prolific author of books on the paranormal, responded. "Although," he added, her "dogged determination

to keep her maidenhead intact was probably the very point of conflict and frustration which was feeding the psychic entity."[9]

Nandor Fodor, a psychical researcher and psychoanalyst, was among the first to propose that poltergeists were caused by involuntary or unconscious psychokinesis unleashed from the mind of the living.[10] Steeped in controversy, his investigation of the Thornton Heath poltergeist case in 1938 led down some interesting psychological avenues.

When Fodor and his medical associate Dr. Wills entered the home of Mrs. Forbes, age thirty-five, tales of poltergeist phenomena at the Thornton Heath manor had already appeared in the London newspapers. "We were treated to an exhibition such is granted to few psychic researchers. Twenty-nine incidents occurred in her immediate surroundings: crockery was thrown and smashed; a glass flew out of her hand and appeared to split in mid-air with a loud ping, as if hit by an invisible hammer; milk bottles whizzed through the kitchen and other objects vanished from their accustomed places to appear elsewhere . . . Of these incidents, I could not offer any explanation for five of them in normal physical terms."[11]

Further, apports—small objects supposedly of spiritistic origin— "fell in surprising numbers around Mrs. Forbes as we were walking and talking with her," he noted. During the time Fodor was studying the case as the director of research for the International Institute for Psychical Research, he received a telephone call from Mrs. Forbes.

In an agonized and barely audible voice, she reported that a vampiric attack had taken place during the night, and she'd awakened with two puncture marks on her neck. Fodor and Dr. Wills raced to Thornton Heath to examine her. She explained that at midnight she

awoke sensing a body on top of the cover away from her husband's side. "Pressing against her neck was something cold and hard, about the size of man's head. She could not move, she felt frozen with fear. . . . She had the impression of something biting, of something trying to paralyze her. The body was a dead weight. It felt cold and 'nasty.' There was a smell of rotten meat. . . . The thing left suddenly with a flapping noise."[12]

Mrs. Forbes also alleged that an apparition at Thornton Heath had tried to strangle her with a necklace, leaving scarring on her neck, and she was attacked by a phantom tiger, evidenced by five long claw marks on her arms.[13] But her vampire tale had come just on the heels of X-ray tests done by the institute that revealed that "apports" had been concealed on Mrs. Forbes's body, including two small objects held under her left breast.

At this point, Fodor ruled out spirits or psychic forces and determined that she'd probably used a hairpin to simulate the vampire marks. She seemed to be sitting on a powder keg of buried personal traumas, and an erotic nightmare about a scaly alligator man filled her with particular loathing. As a woman who could produce miracles, she'd liberated herself from "the dull life of a suburban housewife," and Fodor believed she took delight in tricking observers. And yet, what are we to make of this last incident from the woman Fodor labeled as suffering from "poltergeist psychosis"?

While traveling near what was likely an old execution site, Mrs. Forbes said she'd had a vision of an evil-faced man who was hanged for molesting small children. Two days later, as she sat with Fodor and two other witnesses, she announced, "I have a tightening feeling on my throat. I feel being pulled."

Before their eyes, Fodor wrote, "strangulation marks appeared on her throat: two half circles, overlapping, a quarter of an inch

thick and even in depth as if cut into her flesh by a noose. She was sitting in full daylight in an armchair. Her hands were never raised to her throat. On making a test, we observed that her fingers could not overlap on her throat in the same manner as the half circles did. The marks lasted for about 40 minutes."[14]

Fodor's interpretation was that Mrs. Forbes so intently wished for the death of the evil man from her vision that her mind transposed him into her own body, where he could be hanged to death.

DREAM INVADERS

Do we let our guard down as we dream? Perhaps the state engenders a porous boundary that allows other living people as well as Negs to slip in and influence or attack us. The prominent British occultist Dion Fortune believed that certain types of nightmares and sleep paralysis were definite signs of psychic attack.

In her classic treatise from the 1930s, *Psychic Self-Defense*, Fortune shared her own combative encounters on the dream plane. In one instance, while staying at an occult college in Hampshire, she incensed another resident, "Miss L.," by not returning her affections. "That night," wrote Fortune, "I was afflicted with the most violent nightmare I have ever had in my life, waking from sleep with the terrible sense of oppression on my chest, as if someone was holding me down. . . . I saw distinctly the head of Miss L., reduced to the size of an orange, floating in the air at the foot of my bed, and snapping its teeth at me. It was the most malignant thing I have ever seen."[15]

In the malleable juncture between sleep and waking, Fortune stumbled across a powerful discovery. She was brooding over the possibilities of retaliation to someone who'd caused her harm and imagining savage scenarios when she felt something drawn out of her solar plexus. "It was a well-materialised ectoplasmic form," a gray wolf, pressing against her on the bed. After the creature showed its teeth and snarled at her, she asserted control, sticking her elbow into its "hairy ectoplasmic ribs." Declaring "If you can't behave yourself, you will have to go on the floor," she pushed it off the bed. To her relief, the wolf morphed into a dog as it landed on the floor, then left.

The next morning, though, she was alarmed to learn that one of her housemates (not her antagonist) had been disturbed by dreams of wolves, and woke at one point to see "the eye of a wild animal shining in the darkness in the corner of her room."[16] Although Fortune chose not to follow the path of breathing life into bestial thought-forms, her accidental wolf creation hints at how an occult practitioner might extrude an "etheric double" for wreaking trouble.

Later, Fortune published a series of articles that ruffled the feathers of some in the occult community (particularly one female practitioner), and this set the stage for a series of "astral skirmishes" that impinged into the material world. Demonic faces kicked off the backlash, as they flashed at Fortune in the hypnagogic state. Next, an enormous tabby cat twice the size of a tiger followed her on the stairs of her home. She immediately pegged it as a "simulacrum" being projected by someone with occult powers. Though it quickly vanished, it appeared for several moments entirely solid and tangible.

As one of Fortune's housemates joined her in an emergency meditation session, "we heard the cry of a cat from without. It was answered by another, and another. We looked out of the window, and the street as far as we could see was dotted with black cats, and they were wailing, and howling in broad daylight." While a quick exorcism cleared out the feline cabal, Fortune decided to confront her adversary in the astral dimension.

"These astral journeys," she explained, "are really lucid dreams in which one retains all one's faculties of choice, will-power, and judgment." In the battle of wills that ensued, her aggressor forbade her the use of the "astral pathways," and amid some whirling in the air, Fortune was bounced back into her body, which she found in a heap in a different part of the room from where she began. Refusing defeat, she bound back for a second round of otherworldly MMA, and this time returned victorious.

But who had the last laugh? "When I took off my clothes to go to bed my back felt very sore," Fortune disclosed, "and taking a hand-glass I examined it in the mirror, and I found that from neck to waist I was scored with scratches as if I had been clawed by a gigantic cat."[17]

There are parts of the dream realm that are as "real" as the astral alleyways that Dion Fortune and others have traversed, muses author Michelle Belanger in her book *Psychic Dreamwalking*.[18] And while much occult lore has built up around astral journeys, she proposes a methodology whereby one can travel without their body a little closer to home. By envisioning a "dream gate," a sleeper can proceed through this into a shared space, Belanger says, and like in the movie *Inception* gain access to the dreams of others, particularly those with whom a strong emotional bond is shared.

Although this seems like an intriguing way to catch up "in person" with those we care about, it also provides an entry point for psychic attack. An adept at "shaping the dreamspace," Belanger warns, "can dreamwalk to someone, put them through the mother of all nightmares," and then safely zip back to their sleeping body, all without the victim being able to confirm they'd been targeted. After all, even if the predator was spotted, one would be forced to admit it was "just a dream."[19]

Belanger is an advocate of only mutually consenting dreamworld tête-à-têtes, but as a self-described "energy vampire," she sometimes gets in trouble when her subconscious leads her to "feed" during the dream state. In contrast to a vampire of the bloodsucking type, she replenishes herself by draining excess energy from a willing donor. But that was not always the case.

During the late 1990s, she befriended her next-door neighbor, an affable NASCAR-loving "redneck" named Rob, and they shared balcony chats about music, politics, and just about anything other than her occult interests. One night in the fall of 1998, she saw Rob in a dream. They embraced, and she bent to his neck and nibbled. "I could feel my teeth lightly clasping the skin at the base of his neck, just over the throbbing artery. I used his pulse as a focus to breathe in his energy," she recalled.

The next morning, though fairly sure she'd "dreamwalked," she held out hope for otherwise, even though her energy level was now sky high. That afternoon a haggard-looking Rob knocked on her door and confronted her with a hickey-like mark on his neck. The mark was in the exact place she'd grazed in the dream. He had distinct memories of their encounter, and at first he thought Michelle had sleepwalked into his apartment, but his door had been locked.

She felt obligated to fess up to not only her dreamwalking proclivities but her psychic vampirism as well. Rob took it in stride and was much more knowledgeable about the occult than Belanger had ever suspected. Still, the incident left her shaken and taught her that "the lines between sleeping and waking, physical and nonphysical, could be hazy indeed."[20]

THE DEVIL'S DUMMY

The following incident shared by the Catholic monk Father "X" (from his March 1988 letter to parapsychologist Charles Tart) seems to qualify more as a hypnopompic hallucination or vision than a dream. Lying awake in bed in one morning, just before the seven a.m. monastery "office bell" was due to go off, "I began to feel these strange chills throughout my body," he wrote. "This usually means that the vibrations are not far behind, and after that an out-of-body experience; but the vibrations did not come, just these strange chills getting colder and colder."

"Then," he continued, "I began to hear some mumbling off to my right, and when I looked over there, I saw this little man, looking like a ventriloquist's dummy, smiling at me and chatting away in some incoherent language. When I asked him who he was and what was he doing in my room, he just kept smiling . . . and mumbling away . . . I got out of bed and grabbed him by his foot, then I bounced him off the ceiling like a rubber ball; when he came down I tried to grab him again but he scooted under my bed and came up on the other side. He then turned his face away from me so that I could only see his profile, and he spoke these three short sentences which I heard clear as a bell and had no trouble understanding:

"'We have Him. Christ is burning. The hummingbird men have Him!'"

When Father "X" tried to grab the little man again, he simply vanished, and Father "X" found himself back in bed. Terrified, he tried to rationalize what he'd just seen and heard. He had counted himself as a modern religious believer who saw the Devil as nothing more than a quaint symbol. Yet now he pondered if "the fellow that we thought we had ridiculed into oblivion may actually exist."[21]

An eerie message imparted by the uninvited. Move over, Chucky. Drawing by Jason Jam, 2019.

IMPLANTING IMAGES

Negs, according to Robert Bruce, gain access to people's minds through openings or holes left by traumatic memories or "core images." Perhaps even more alarmingly, they can implant ghastly core images. This was vividly demonstrated to Bruce one afternoon during a spontaneous OBE. He saw his projected astral double pulling something out of his physical body.

"He lifted it and showed me what looked like a length of black rope," Bruce said. "He pulled on it and a horrifically clear 3-D vision appeared before my eyes. I saw a close underwater view of my two young sons drowning in a swimming pool. Each had a foot tied to a heavy weight lying on the bottom of the pool." As the boys pleaded for help, the vision continued for another thirty seconds, until they drowned.[22]

While Bruce had no memory of having this specific nightmare, the vision seemed "hauntingly familiar . . . like something important I had forgotten." A second scary vision involving his sons' deaths was also pulled out by the double, and it too had an odd familiarity. Bruce has developed a technique for turning over core images, like they were cards, to see what's behind them; sometimes what's revealed is a twisted rootlike structure or circuits. In the case of the death visions, he found astral spiders. He endorses various mental visualizations to vanquish these insidious insertions once they are exposed.

Mystic Samuel Hatfield refers to a phenomenon he calls "false sleep paralysis," in which an invading entity "creates an astral representation of the dreamer's bedroom or sleeping space and then mimics the symptoms of sleep paralysis accompanied with a hallucinatory experience." This could be the modality in which alien abductions occur, he adds. In regular sleep paralysis, the bedroom appears in its usual state, but in the "false" mode, there may be missing or changed elements.[23]

Posting on an online forum, Lady Warrior Ravynwynn details a chilling dream that she believes was a form of psychic attack. It began in complete darkness, from which she heard a pleasant female voice issuing what seemed like relaxation meditation instructions. The voice informed her that she was surrounded by water, and it was filling up the small area she was in. "Then, she said that I was under water, and would not be able to breathe, but that it was OK, I should remain relaxed. She said that I needed to let go, and drown in the warm, peaceful water, and that death was far better than life. . . . I tried to wake up, but could only stop from suffocating, and not wake up all the way.... Each time the alluring voice would start over again, step by step, and I'd let go a little more each time, then just jolt out of it, but not wake up to full consciousness. The third, and last time, I remember going as far as feeling mud seep into my mouth and nose, tasting the dirt, and suffocating, while her voice coaxed me along, saying that the mud was filling me up with the water, and I would 'absolutely enjoy slipping into death' this time. I woke up, feeling like I just slammed back into my body, coughing and choking, with the taste of the dirt still in my mouth."

She suspects the attack could have been instigated by a family member known for abusive occult practices. She'd cut him out of her life years ago, but just prior to the dream, her mother had a fresh confrontation with him.[24]

THE ACCURSED STONES

While we know to stay out of the path of black magic practitioners, can "harmless" objects instigate terrifying materializations and mayhem? So-called haunted dolls have a built-in fright factor, but a small set of stones would not necessarily set off alarm bells. In 1972, the archaeologist and Celtic scholar Dr. Anne Ross was called in to examine tiny rocks dug up from the garden of a family's house in Hexham, Northumberland, in the United Kingdom. Crude faces with large crescent "alien" eyes were carved into them. When they were brought inside, poltergeist events like breaking glass and glowing lights soon followed. A neighbor who spent the night woke to see a half-human/half-sheep monstrosity with clawlike hands at her bedside.

Two nights after Dr. Ross received the objects, her room was permeated in a "sort of dreadful atmosphere" as she awakened at two a.m. to glimpse a tall figure slipping away—a kind of part-man/part-wolf. Interestingly, "she felt a strange compulsion to follow it."[25] A few days later, she and her husband arrived home to find their daughter utterly gobsmacked. She'd witnessed a "werewolf" leap over her head and the banister railing before tumbling noisily down the stairs. It landed with a thud in the music room (thankfully Mrs. Peacock was in the billiard room at the time) before vanishing.

Dr. Ross believed the stones could be Celtic carvings dating back to the first or second century, designed to ward off evil spirits. But then a twist: a former resident of the house where the stones were found claimed to have made them himself in 1956 as amusements for his daughter. Ross thought it an odd coincidence the man's carvings so closely resembled the ancient stones. Though the modern rocks lacked the steeped-in-time Celtic legacy of a possible ancient curse, perhaps they picked up dark energies while they were buried—the town after all was called "Hexham." Researcher Jenny Randles notes that the stones were studded with quartz crystals, capable of generating an electric signal.

ATTACK ON THE THRESHOLD

Back when he was a teen in the muggy Nebraska summers, the occult author Lon Milo DuQuette sometimes liked to sleep in his family's basement, where it was a few degrees cooler. On one particular night, his fitful slumber was disturbed by noises akin to the rattling of a snare drum. Groggily, he got up to investigate and was shocked to discover a group of zombie-like beings obliviously huddled along the stairsteps. But then "the mob started to move down the stairs as if gravity was sucking them down," DuQuette recounted, "like a lazy tide of unclean ooze."[26]

Though he was terrified, he knew his only chance for safety was to make it to the top of the stairs. As he pushed his way up, "the zombies attached themselves to me as if to feed on my energy," he continued. "Their bodies were cold and foul like pale, bloated corpses that had been in stagnant water for a long time. They touched me obscenely from head to foot, clawing away pieces of my flesh as I struggled up the steps."

Upon reaching the landing, he saw a swimming pool in the back-yard. Only his family didn't have a swimming pool. He assumed he must be dreaming and tried unsuccessfully to wake himself up. When he lay down on his bed in his upstairs bedroom, he realized that his body was physically asleep in the basement. "Somewhere I opened an eye and saw my own arm dangling over the pull-out bed in the basement . . . and for a moment I could also 'see' my bedroom ceiling from the point of view of my other 'body' upstairs." It would be years later that DuQuette would realize that this "dream" was actually an OBE. Such out-of-body travel is often instigated in dreams, he writes, and by learning to become lucid in the dream state, one can master these mysterious states.

With the hindsight of accrued occult wisdom, he looks back on the zombie attack from the perspective of an astral anthropologist. Labeling the corpselike figures as "astral shells," he views them as chucked-off bodies that had sunk like sediment to the lowest level of the astral plane, closest to our material level.

Yet these discarded husks still retained a flicker of animation, so as he passed through them they mindlessly grasped at his energy. "They are quite literally astral vampires," he noted. "The danger here is very real, but also very easy to avoid—just keep moving!"

Such "terrors of the threshold" are also a kind of training ground for us to face and conquer our projected fears. "Fear," DuQuette points out, "is something altogether too dangerous and heavy" to take with us in the lighter and higher realms that await beyond the entryway.

CHAPTER EIGHT

THE ALIEN IN QUESTION

A lien, wherefore art thou? Something foreign is coming through the border, deterred not by a fence. This "other" slips through the threshold of our personal space, menacingly or benevolently making itself known at certain moments. We may recognize the "other" even as it dons different masks throughout the ages. And yet how can we be sure what we're looking at when our own lives arrive shrouded in mystery?

In the modern era, when you hear the mention of an alien what comes to mind is probably the image of a Grey, with its signature large head, wraparound black eyes, and spindly body. Around twenty years ago, during *X-Files* mania, the Grey head nearly reached the status of the smiley face, appearing on cardboard plates, pens, cups, party hats, napkins, tablecloths, gift wrap, lottery tickets, bumper stickers, games, balloons, and lollipops. It has "the penetrating simplicity required of all good cultural icons," Michael

Lindemann told me.[1] At the time, he was the editor of the respected UFO information source CNI News.

While its ubiquity in the design world has faded, the face of the Grey remains lodged in our consciousness, floating in the pantheon of less rosy-cheeked compatriots like the green-inked George Washington and the Pillsbury Doughboy. Attached to the face is the popular conception that aliens are by definition extraterrestrials, traveling here from outer space in their UFOs. While acknowledging that we live in a vast universe, and it's almost inconceivable that life doesn't exist elsewhere, this chapter dispenses with the extraterrestrial hypothesis to explore the idea that aliens may arise from a closer source.

One could fill an entire library with all the books and materials that have accrued on UFOs and aliens. Why, your head may just explode trying to unravel seventy years' worth of conflicting theories, data, and interpretations. So for our purposes, we'll gnaw off a corner that primarily looks at alien interactions associated with unusual states of consciousness and psychic phenomena.

BEDROOM ABDUCTIONS

When the harrowing phenomenon of alien abduction takes place on a desolate road or campsite, one may surmise it's something like a "wrong place, wrong time" scenario. But what about when the invasion occurs in the private sanctuary of your bedroom? During a hypnosis session with Dr. John Mack, "Scott" recalled such an encounter from April 1990. Still living with his parents, he'd gone to bed early. But before falling asleep, he felt the aliens permeate his mind. Unexplained light spilled out from an adjacent room as he saw six beings with boxy, angular heads moving in front of him.[2] Because he's aware, they proceed to paralyze him using a "round-tipped rod" tapped behind the ear. Scott hears a ringing sound and sees a TV-like screen, as he struggles to secure his mind from the alien intrusion. Moments and memories of his life flash before him. After an interlude, he finds himself on a table, examined by two "doctors" with tan and white skin, amid several shorter beings. They all, he recalls, had "deep, black, slightly slanted eyes with gray borders around them."

Considering this wasn't their first time, the beings quickly get down to business, positioning a "faucet thing, like a suction" on his penis. At this juncture, his perception goes out-of-body. Looking down on himself, he sees four prongs or electrodes pressed into his neck and scalp, which he believes control his reactions. Stimulated by the suction device, his subsequent ejaculate is transported in a tube, as the aliens telepathically convey that the sperm will be used for insemination.

He feels ashamed and powerless. Scott despises the beings for taking him away from his family and "not telling me who they are," even though he remains curious about their intentions. "They know exactly what they're doing," he laments; "that's why they cover it up. They don't want us to remember." He finds himself "dropped in bed" but cannot recall how he was brought back. With the help of hypnosis, he revisited numerous abductions like this that began in childhood.

Mack, a Pulitzer Prize–winning psychiatrist, cast a sheen of legitimacy on the alien abduction topic with the publication of his books *Abduction* and *Passport to the Cosmos* in the 1990s (even though Harvard Medical School, where he was a tenured professor, appointed a committee to review his research methods and consider censuring him; after a grueling fourteen-month investigation they ruled in Mack's favor[3]).

Many of the abductees told Dr. Mack they sensed that their encounters were somehow outside the physical space/time dimension. "They speak of aliens breaking through from another dimension" from a "crack in some sort of barrier," he revealed. And while they often describe their alien interactions as occurring in a distinct waking reality (albeit a different brand of reality), he outlined three ways an abduction could interface or be conflated with dreams: (1) an actual kidnapping, but misconstrued as a dream or nightmare; (2) a replay of an abduction in the form of a dream or traumatic nightmare; or (3) simply a dream that contains alien or UFO subject matter.[4]

ANATOMY OF THE PHENOMENON

While the terrain of the alien encounter is slippery and hard to grasp, there is a remarkable fidelity to a fixed order of events in the phenomenon[5] that runs counter to a unique narrative one would expect if a person were recalling a dream or hallucination or simply fabricating a tale. Capture and examination are the prevailing features of an abduction—the subjects typically report being "floated" out of their room (sometimes through a wall or solid object) and soon find themselves undergoing an examination aboard an unknown craft by strange beings whose mouths and noses appear as mere vestigial holes or slits.

Abductees consistently detail "some sort of mental impairment while in captivity, an inappropriate docility or peacefulness alternating with a sense of terror," writes researcher and folklorist

Thomas Eddie Bullard. The beings "exert something like a hypnotic influence to restore this unnatural tranquility when it weakens, or accomplish an instant relief of pain with a touch on the forehead," he adds.

Betty Hill, whose sensational story of the UFO abduction of herself and her husband, Barney, captivated the public in the early 1960s, offered insight into the mechanics of telepathic communication with the aliens. "I did not hear an actual voice. But in my mind, I knew what he was saying. It wasn't as if he were talking to me with my eyes open, and he was sitting across the room from me. It was more as if the words were there, a part of me, and he was outside the actual creation of the words themselves."[6]

After the examination there is often harvesting of sperm and eggs; sometimes sexual encounters with hybrids and others are orchestrated. During subsequent abductions, experiencers report seeing massive walls of incubators where hybrid babies are gestating, and they're asked to nurture and play with their own "offspring"— hybrid children that can seem quite frail. Curious, since abductees are sometimes shown screens that depict cataclysmic or environmental disasters befalling Earth and told that the hybrids will be needed to repopulate the planet in the aftermath. Alternatively, some aliens have suggested that their own home world is dying out, and they need human stock to shore up their species.

Apocalyptic ideations attributed to aliens have a long history in UFO culture, beginning in the 1950s. Many contactees and abductees become imbued with the sense of a mission after their contacts. Yet numerous predicted dates of calamitous destruction have come and gone, and we're still here—at least in this version of the time continuum! The highly original Fortean author John Keel cited the similarity of prophecies of doom proffered by spirit mediums and

UFO entities alike, some of which led to false beliefs, irresponsible actions, and ruined lives.[7]

Another hallmark of abductions is the sense of "missing time"— when a subject returns, unaccounted-for time has passed on the clock, sometimes hours. The term was popularized by Budd Hopkins, an influential researcher who practiced hypnotic regression techniques to bring buried memories to light.

"The abduction phenomenon," Mack remarks, "is not simply traumatic. Experiencers may be left with fears, nightmares and . . . severe stress together with small body lesions, sinus headaches . . . psychosexual dysfunctions" and other physical maladies. Conversely, there is evidence that the alien encounters were responsible for healing conditions that included pneumonias, leukemia, and paralyzed limbs due to muscle atrophy.[8]

The fact that many of the abductee accounts are sincere and consistent and pass muster with investigators lends a certain cohesion and validity to their experience, yet a waft of deceit lingers about their captors. "Aliens," notes Bullard, "advanced enough to create hybrids but obliged to steal the raw materials . . . seem implausible."[9] Could the harvesting of genetic materials and other aspects of abductions be a kind of stage show masking something else? But if layers of deception are tucked into each other like nested dolls, where does the truth lie?

When Lily Martinson, a real estate agent, was vacationing with her mother in the Virgin Islands in 1987, she woke up to see her dead brother standing at the foot of her hotel room bed.[10] Rather than frightening, she found his familiar image to be comforting and reassuring. Yet when the incident was explored under hypnosis with Prof. David Jacobs, she discovered that it was a "screen memory" and what she had seen was not her brother but "a person without clothes, small, thin, no hair, and large eyes."

The small Greys that handle the capture of individuals are often described as having a mechanistic quality, as though they were bio-engineered for their specific tasks. "They look like ghosts," abductee Karla Turner, a college instructor with a doctorate, recalled of the four-foot-tall beings. "They look so hollow, they don't have any real feelings. That's why they're so scary, they just look dead.... They're really hardly there."[11]

Turner revealed this information in 1989 during a session with Oklahoma hypnotherapist Barbara Bartholic, who was one of the first to suggest that some of the aliens may feed off human emotions, "especially the ones that come from fear, pain, depression, and compulsive actions." Hopkins echoed the sentiment, stating that during abductions people seemed to be deliberately subjected to pain, "very much like we might do in an experiment with a laboratory animal."[12]

In a session with Bartholic, an abductee named "Fred" detailed an experiment in which his sperm was drawn and seemed to be placed in both a woman and an animal. The woman's body was elevated, and her chest was completely opened up. He recalled with amazement how the alien pulled her skin together with a laser, "sealing it up" so that you couldn't even tell she was ever cut. But then the entities turned their attention back to Fred, and he swung from fright to anger during his hypnotic recall. They inserted a long thin rod into the corner of his left eyeball, though he reported no pain. Next, a long needle was stuck into his navel, scraping tissue from the inside, followed by an injection of a clear fluid into the punctured spot. He presumed the tests had something to do with regenerating DNA, the immune system, and crossbreeding between animals and humans.[13]

RANSOM NOTES FROM THE UNDERWORLD

In contrast to contactees' celestial interactions with aliens, abductee encounters echo mythological journeys to "the underworld, the realm of the dead and the dispossessed," writes scholar Keith Thompson in his absorbing treatise *Angels and Aliens*.[14] In the fifteenth-century painting *Saint Wolfgang and the Devil* by Michael Pacher, the body of the green-skinned Devil with its slender appendages and large head bears a certain physical resemblance to modern-day Greys, as well as elements of Reptilians (the sinister but intelligent bipedal reptoid species that abductees sometimes report). Of course, Pacher's Devil has a unique second face formed over its buttocks and anus that has not to my knowledge ever been published in the annals of UFOdom!

The needles and instruments used by the ufonauts on their examination table are similar "to the piercing tortures which devils inflict on sinners in Christian art and fundamentalist belief," Thompson points out.[15] Could today's aliens be the devils and liminal beings of yore cloaked in a new disguise? Medieval fairy lore of northern Europe certainly mirrors many aspects of alien encounters.

Irish fairies are "great shapeshifters, appearing as large or small beasts or blasts of wind or as lights which fly through the air; their country's under the ground or under the sea or in islands out in the West," the British writer Patrick Harpur said in a lecture at a 2003 Fortean conference.[16] He refers to the "little people" and other anomalous creatures like angels and the jinn as belonging to the

Apples and oranges? Michael Pacher's 1471 portrayal of the Devil (detail from *Saint Wolfgang and the Devil*) seen in the upper right (courtesy Wikimedia Commons) compared to a "modern" alien, drawn by Jason Jam, 2018.

"daimonic" reality, an elusive zone that incorporates both the material and immaterial. Before the Christian era demonized the daimonic realm, such beings were not considered exclusively evil. "They're not good or bad but both," Harpur said. "Sometimes malevolent, sometimes benign. Always tricking. At best mischievous, at worst life-threatening. There are no boundaries they won't cross."

Jacques Vallée, the astute French-American author and ufologist, writes of a place called Magonia or Elfland that constitutes a parallel realm coexisting with our own. Like the interior of a UFO, "it is made visible and tangible only to selected people, and the 'doors' that lead through it are tangential points, known only to the elves."[17]

As with the UFO occupants, fairies demonstrate supernatural powers, paralyze people, impart prophetic dispatches, and can float or fly. In some traditions, notes Bullard, they sailed ships in the air or could climb a ladder to the clouds.[18] Further, they share the aliens' interest in human reproduction. Their penchant is legendary for stealing human babies and swapping them out for "changelings," elderly fairies, who may have the sickly or gaunt quality seen in alien hybrids.

Although the similarities between fairy lore and alien abductions are remarkable, Bullard acknowledges that "few fairies are hairless or large-eyed, as so many aliens are, and no fairy drives a spaceship." It's entirely possible, though, that the phenomenon drapes itself in the custom and culture of the age in which it manifests. Take the mysterious airship sightings of 1896–1897. The Wright brothers didn't become airborne until 1903, but the public was aware of the growing interest in flight. Accordingly, numerous witnesses of the clunky oblong-shaped sky boats across North America viewed the occupants as aviation or scientific geniuses rather than aliens from another world. Statements from the pilots included "We are from Kansas," and "We are from ANYWHERE . . . but we'll be in Cuba tomorrow."[19]

During the Inquisition, people could be prosecuted for sexual congress with demons. Today, if there are unfathomable or forced carnal activities with nonhumans, how do we respond? Do we point the finger at an incubus conjured during sleep paralysis, or above at a mysterious object shimmering in the night sky?

THE TELLTALE HAIR

A paralysis overtook Peter Khoury as he lay on his bed in a suburb of Sydney, Australia, one night in July 1988. He was surrounded by a group of bizarre entities, and one of them, a "tall thin golden yellow coloured being, with large black eyes," stuck an elongated needle into the side of his head, knocking him out. When he woke with a start, he rushed into a nearby room only to find family members in a "switched off" mode. As he roused them, they discovered that one to two hours had passed, though the consensus was that only about ten minutes had gone by. They confirmed that Peter's head had been injured.[20]

But this incident was a mere appetizer to what was to take place four years later, on July 23, 1992. Early in the morning, Peter drove his wife to the transit station. He was feeling ill and upon returning to their house went straight back to bed, fully clothed. Around seven thirty a.m., he awoke and sat upright, feeling as though something light like a cat had just pounced on the bed. Two females were on the bed with him. *How the hell did they get here?* he wondered.

He had a momentary out-of-body perception, like he was viewing the room from the back of his head. One of the women seated on the bed was a blonde, perhaps as tall as six feet; the other was shorter and Asian in appearance. The blond or "Nordic" woman was naked and had a long face with a pointy chin and eyes that were "two to three times bigger than our eyes." It struck him that this woman was not entirely human.[21]

The Asian woman also had abnormally large eyes, as well as odd cheekbones that sat very high on her face. No small talk here, the blonde pulled him toward her breasts with a strong grip. Perhaps as a defense mechanism, he bit her left nipple, and a rubbery piece came off that was "stuck in my throat for three days." The blonde had no reaction or blood from the wound. "It was as if I took a bite out of a plastic dummy or mannequin," he recalled.

The two women had coldly analytical stares, and it occurred to Peter that they were specifically there to be impregnated. He started to have a coughing fit from what was stuck in his throat, and abruptly the women were no longer there. Feeling the urgent need to urinate, as he reached the toilet he felt an intense burning pain. Tightly wrapped around the head of his penis like nylon string were very fine blond hairs. They were extremely painful to unravel and remove. Yet even under such extreme circumstances, he had the presence of mind to place them in a plastic bag. The only way the hairs could have gotten there was "if somebody had actually pulled the foreskin back, wrapped it on there, and left it that way."

Bill Chalker, a leading UFO researcher from Australia, got involved in studying the Khoury case and worked with a biochemistry team to provide the "world's first DNA analysis of a biological sample implicated in an alien abduction experience." The analysis, Chalker reported, confirmed that the hard hair shaft came "from someone who was biologically close to normal human genetics, but of an unusual racial type—a rare Chinese Mongoloid type—one of the rarest human lineages known, that lies further from the human mainstream than any other except for African pygmies and aboriginals."

But perhaps what was even odder was that the soft hair root had a totally different kind of mitochondrial DNA, a novel Basque/Gaelic type. Chalker has pondered whether the DNA results suggest advanced cloning techniques, and he traced the Chinese type to an isolated group of Asians known as the Lahu, who have a long history of shamanic connections to mysterious lights and sky beings.

The rare hairs found by Peter Khoury, while not out-of-this-world in origin, certainly lend some weight to his odd tale, even if it's just a matter of microns.

SKEPTICAL SCRUTINY

Science writer and historian Michael Shermer is the founding publisher of *Skeptic* magazine, and through his books, articles, and appearances he's solidified his reputation as a staunch critic of claims of the paranormal and unexplained. And yet one morning in August 1983, while biking on a rural highway in Nebraska, "a large craft with bright lights overtook me and forced me to the side of the road. Alien beings exited the craft and abducted me for 90 minutes, after which I found myself back on the road with no memory of what transpired on the ship."[22]

Was it really aliens? Not in Shermer's case. His abduction experience, he explains, was triggered by sleep deprivation and exhaustion related to cycling for the past eighty-three hours as part of a 3,100-mile nonstop Race Across America. He'd begun to weave down the road when his support motor home flashed its high beams, and the crew admonished him to get some shut-eye. "At that moment a distant memory of the 1960s television series *The Invaders* was inculcated into my waking dream," he later realized. On the TV show, the giveaway sign that someone is an alien is a stiff little finger. "Suddenly the members of my support team were transmogrified into aliens. I stared intensely at their fingers."

After a sleep break, he chalked the experience up to nothing more than a bizarre hallucination and an indicator of the boundless human capacity for self-delusion.

In the 1990s, UK psychologist Dr. Susan Blackmore pegged

alien abduction as "our modern sleep paralysis myth," connecting it to past lore of various cultures that associated the terrifying threshold state with the Old Hag and other nefarious and supernatural entities. If someone has watched TV shows about abductions or read about them, during the paralysis of SP, they may begin to think about menacing aliens, Blackmore suggests. "And in this borderline sleep state, the imagined alien will seem quite real. This alone may be enough to create the conviction of having been abducted. Hypnosis could make the memories of this real experience (but not real abduction) completely convincing."[23]

The neuroscientist and inventor Dr. Michael Persinger, who worked out of Canada's Laurentian University, was known for his creation of the "God helmet." The headgear is rigged with coils that fluctuate weak magnetic fields over the temporal lobes. Wearers of the modified motorcycle helmet report mystical and psychic experiences as well as a "sensed presence." "Persinger's theory," wrote Blackmore, "is that abduction-like experiences are caused by complex patterns of activity in the temporal lobe," and those with susceptibility in that brain region "may have the experiences spontaneously" if they are exposed to certain conditions.

Persinger contended that magnetic effects associated with earthquakes could affect the temporal region as well as generate mysterious lights in the sky. He found a strong correlation between the dates of seismic events and claims of UFO sightings and abductions.[24]

The idea that brain alterations may be related to the perception of aliens has come up in the intriguing experiments of psychiatrist Rick Strassman, who injected volunteers with the hallucinogen DMT. A large number of subjects reported almost identical meetings with a specific type of alien being.[25] Psychonaut Terence Mc-Kenna dubbed them the "DMT elves"; he described them to me as diminutive "tykes" who let loose a kind of cheer when you first rupture into their plane, a sort of upholstered underground womb.[26] These inner-world Teletubbies, though, seem a universe away from the aliens who thuggishly haul you off in the middle of the night.

For a 1994 episode of the BBC TV series *Horizon*, Blackmore gave Persinger's helmet a whirl in her effort to track down the origin of the abduction experience. At first, she felt nothing unusual in Persinger's testing chamber. "Then suddenly all my doubts were gone," she said. "It felt for all the world as though two hands had grabbed my shoulders and were . . . yanking me upright. I knew I was still lying in the reclining chair, but . . . something seemed to get hold of my leg and pull it, distort it, and drag it up the wall. I felt as though I had been stretched halfway up to the ceiling."

"Then," she continued, "totally out of the blue, but intensely and vividly, I felt suddenly angry. . . . After perhaps ten seconds it was gone but later was replaced by an equally vivid sudden fit of fear. . . . Never in my life have I had such powerful sensations coupled with the total lack of anything to blame them on."

The experience left Blackmore a bit shaken, and she could well imagine that if such powerful feelings came to her unbidden in the middle of the night, she'd be desperate to assign a cause to them. "If someone told me an alien was responsible and invited me to join an abductees' support group, I might well prefer to believe that idea; rather than accept I was going mad."[27]

To Blackmore's credit, she concedes that sleep paralysis and temporal lobe activity do not necessarily explain all alien abduction reports, and she can't claim with absolute certainty that some form of alien intrusion has never happened. Not so much with her American counterpart, Prof. Susan Clancy, whose 2005 book from Harvard University Press, *Abducted*, starts out with the research assumption that all alien abductions are the product of recovered false memories.[28]

Clancy serves up a grab bag of skeptical reasoning: "Alien abduction memories are best understood as resulting from a blend of fantasy-proneness, memory distortion, culturally available scripts, sleep hallucinations, and scientific illiteracy, aided and abetted by the suggestions and reinforcement of hypnotherapy." Like Blackmore, she points to the appeal of a belief system that offers an explanation for distressing or confusing experiences.

Recovering buried trauma through hypnosis has remained controversial, and there are likely numerous cases where false or distorted memories were inadvertently induced. Yet even if that were applicable to much of the hypnotic recall of abductees, "about 30% of the thousands of UFO abduction reports researchers have investigated were recalled without the use of hypnosis," Hopkins writes in a rebuttal to Clancy's work.[29] He also points out fallacies in the one-size-fits-all sleep paralysis argument. "It clearly self-destructs before one central problem: the large percentage of UFO abductions which occur in the daytime, when the abductee is up and about, driving a car, taking a walk, playing in the front yard, or even in one case, driving a tractor." Yes, sleep paralysis is the likely culprit for some bedroom encounters. But the regimented quality of the medical exams, repeated over and over in abduction accounts, is an odd fit for the idiosyncratic nature of SP. As mentioned in Chapter 1, the peculiar liminal state may be a kind of gateway for astral entities to intersect with us.

BACK AT THE (PARANORMAL) RANCH

What are we to make of specific locales that seem like magnets for the unexplained? Not just aliens, but a veritable kitchen sink of disturbing anomalies. Though surrounded by the unfettered beauty of the American West, three remote ranches became beacons for high strangeness during the latter part of the twentieth century.

In 1975, a sprawling but dilapidated property in rural Colorado was purchased by a married couple, "John" and "Barbara," and their friend "Jim," a former U.S. Air Force security officer with professional training in physical and biological sciences. They restored the place within a few months but soon were plagued by events and phenomena that defied rational explanation and persisted over the four-year period they remained. A team of investigators from the Aerial Phenomena Research Organization were brought in to study the case, including Dr. Leo Sprinkle and John Deer, PhD, a seismologist.

Jim, John and Barbara, as well as their two sons regularly heard an intense humming noise that persisted even when the electricity was shut off; this sound would later match emissions from UFOs they observed on several occasions. There were frightening cattle mutilations on the property, precise surgical cuts that could not have been made by animal predators. A Bigfoot-type creature was witnessed more than once and left behind a hair sample that matched "no known species," according to a Denver biogeneticist.[30]

There were also psychic and electronic intrusions, poltergeist-like activity, forced paralysis, and alien encounters. One night around two a.m., Jim awakened in a paralyzed state and saw a creature nearly seven feet tall wearing a "cosmonaut's helmet." The entity vanished before his eyes. On another night, he awoke to see a being in a tight-fitting suit through the window. He went to alert Barbara and found her in an agitated trance state. Then the ranch's entrance door flew open, and when he went to close it, an internal voice declared: "We don't need to open your door in order to enter your house!"[31]

One of the oddest incidents took place one night around two a.m., when Jim and guests were sitting around a stereo console. There was a sudden blackout, and a voice was heard simultaneously emitting from all the radio and TV speakers. "Attention," the voice announced. "We have allowed you to remain. We have interfered with your time very little. Do not cause us to take action which you will regret. Your friends will be instructed to remain silent concerning us."[32] One of Jim's guests, a computer and electronics specialist, dismantled the stereo set and could find no logical explanation for the broadcast.

On one late evening, Jim, Barbara, and a friend named Harry saw nine discs land in the yard. As Jim intrepidly walked out to get a closer look, Barbara watched from the window, her face close to the glass. A swift invisible force struck her in the forehead, knocking her to the ground. Jim came running back in, and as he and Harry attended to her, the mysterious discs disappeared.

The visitations culminated for Jim when he followed a light in the trees one night. He met two self-assured humanoid individuals wearing flight suits that changed in color from brown to silver. "They were fair, had large eyes, and seemed perfectly normal," Jim recounted. "They had blond hair . . . their facial features were finer. They were almost delicately effeminate."

The beings, in well-spoken English, apologized for the inconveniences they'd caused, and at one point they demonstrated control of the "Bigfoot" creature via a type of electronic box. While Jim had initially suspected that some kind of military interference or experiment was behind all the transgressions, at this point, he started buying the extraterrestrial explanation, assuming that some sort of alien installation was on the ranch.

The French researcher Emmanuel Dehlinger revealed that the location was northeast of Denver in Elbert County, which is adjacent to several large military operations. He argued that a covert military agency was conducting a psychological manipulation of the residents "by using electromagnetic waves somehow to induce hallucinations as well as to manipulate electrical devices," according to Nevada-based investigative journalist George Knapp and research scientist Colm Kelleher. "Dehlinger," they continued, "thinks a combination of advanced hypnosis and costumed actors may have convinced the ranch family that their encounters with the assorted beings were real."[33]

The goal, according to Dehlinger, was to get the family to move because the military wanted control of their land, which overlooked a strategic range. But Knapp and Kelleher find this motivation flawed—if the Pentagon determines that a particular property is needed for security or intelligence reasons, they can just seize it rather than conducting an elaborate and expensive charade.

Encircled by majestic red rocks, Sedona, Arizona, has long been considered a New Age haven, stoked by metaphysical tales of energy vortexes and hallowed Native American grounds. Just outside Sedona lies the sprawling Bradshaw ranch, initially burnished with a bit of Hollywood luster as the shooting location for such features as the 1967 Elvis Presley clunker *Stay Away Joe*. But starting in the early 1990s, after John Bradshaw and his wife, Linda, reinvigorated the property as a working ranch, it would garner a reputation for something else—a nexus for unexplained activity. First came the appearance of glowing orbs in the sky and poltergeist activity in the home, followed by a paranormal menagerie that included sightings of shadowy or partly invisible entities, a Sasquatch-type creature Linda dubbed "Big Girl," and even a long-tailed five-foot-tall bipedal lizard.[34]

Late one night on the complex, Linda's son and friends observed the landing of an unidentified craft. They saw "strolling past the window ... four short-statured aliens wearing tight-fitting one-piece uniforms of a light tan color. . . . Typically called the Zeta Reticuli (also known as the Grays) ... these appeared to be a bit more ashen-colored, almost white. Once the beings were out of sight and the witnesses recomposed themselves, the three of them jumped into their car and sped to the house where I was sleeping," Linda wrote. "I remember so vividly how my son vigorously shook my arm to wake me up. I can still hear the trepidation in his voice as he said, 'Mom, wake up. They're here!' I raised up and said, 'Who's here?' He exclaimed, 'The aliens, Mom.'" A few minutes later, she saw one of the beings herself, and as she stepped outside to confront them, "the visitors became invisible but I could still feel their intense presence and see the faint outline of their forms."[35]

There were also mutilations and illnesses afflicting their livestock and dogs, as well as appearances of portals of light in the sky that Linda Bradshaw and researcher Tom Dongo believed demonstrated a gateway or merging point to another dimension. In 2003, the U.S. government purchased the ranch and has kept it off-limits ever since—save for a few incidents, such as during the 2013 filming of Discovery Channel's *Uncovering Aliens*, when a man on the set named Steven Jones reportedly managed to wander onto the ranch property. When he returned, he was said to be in a daze and spoke of being surrounded by disembodied voices. Though his watch stopped working after the incident, he was still able to ascertain that there was "missing time."[36]

At the "Skinwalker Ranch" in Utah, a similar witch's brew of activity took place during a concurrent period in the 1990s. The Sherman family (referred to as the Gormans in Knapp and Kelleher's 2005 opus *Hunt for the Skinwalker*) faced a grueling combination of animal mutilations and deaths, poltergeists and psychic phenomena, unearthly creatures like a monstrous dire wolf, and inexplicable aerial sightings.

The vast 480-acre ranch sits in the Uintah Basin, a location dripping with centuries-old bad blood, according to science teacher Junior Hicks, who collected stories from the region. When the Ute Indians moved in on Navajo turf, the Navajo were said to place a curse on the Utes, sending a "skinwalker" or evil sorcerer/shapeshifter to hunt them down and torment them.

An assortment of colored orbs were seen by the Shermans. "They appeared to be light forms, but they certainly had physical effects," Knapp and Kelleher reported. As the blue orbs flew past the home's windows, the lights would dim, and these same objects were associated with the death of three dogs, probably by incineration. "Both Ellen and Tom were overcome by a fear that transcended everything in their previous experience as a blue orb hovered over them and seemingly stimulated the fight-or-flight reflex in their brains."[37]

Like the Bradshaws, the Shermans observed puzzling aerial openings. "The rancher," said Knapp, "had seen these giant orange holes in the sky" and by looking through the rift, he could see another sky, where it appeared to be a different time of day. "Occasionally things would fly in and out," with the objects seemingly coming from another dimension or reality.[38]

In 1997, after entrepreneur Robert Bigelow purchased the ranch as a kind of living laboratory to study UFOs and the paranormal for his National Institute for Discovery Science (NIDS) organization, unexplained phenomena continued to occur. In one climactic nighttime event, a NIDS investigator, "Jim," sat in a field to meditate, knowing that however oddly, this quiet behavior could sometimes activate the "phenomenon." Hours later, as he and an associate, "Mike," observed the pasture through night vision binoculars, they saw a dirty yellow light just above the ground.[39]

Through the night vision, Mike saw the light expand to form a kind of tunnel. "Oh, my God," he gasped. "There is a black creature climbing out. I see his head. . . . It has no face." Whatever it was crawled out of the tunnel in midair just above the spot where Jim meditated, then stalked off toward a hill. Mike estimated the humanoid was enormous, perhaps three hundred to four hundred pounds, and six feet tall. They discovered a pungent sulfur-laden odor where the light was first seen. The tunnel suggests a portal or doorway from some other dimension, Knapp remarked, and the overall phenomena seemed to be telling us that "reality is different than how we perceive it."

Some members of the NIDS advisory board hypothesized "that a sentient, precognitive, nonhuman intelligence occupied the ranch."[40] "The phenomena," Knapp said of Skinwalker and other incidents, "puts on . . . performances. It sometimes pretends to be uninterested in us, then slams us in the face with some sort of display that is unavoidable and undeniable. It plays mind games. It messes with us . . . our lives, our animals, our property. . . . It seems to get some sort of jolt out of causing an emotional reaction."[41]

"The experiences at Skinwalker Ranch showed there is often a paranormal element to UFO events," Knapp continued, "something far weirder than just flying saucers." It suggests that several mysteries or "paranormal phenomena are likely intertwined, related in ways we don't understand." Further, a lot of people are going to be deeply troubled if the truth turns out to be that "these beings are our overlords or creators, that we are livestock . . . [and] that this other intelligence can enter our reality any time it wants to . . . can read our minds, that it observes us night and day, when we sleep or in the shower or in intimate moments."

IN CONUNDRUMS WE TRUST

Like a disoriented Rubik's Cube that can never line up, the mystery of alien intrusion defies a purely physical solution. Aliens and UFOs generally remain unseen, writes Keel, because they consist of "energy rather than solid earthly matter." But through manipulation of frequency patterns, they can make themselves visible, taking on any form, "ranging from the shapes of airplanes to gigantic cylindrical spaceships . . . [and] living entities ranging from little green men to awesome one-eyed giants. But none of these configurations is [their] true form."[42]

Just as microscopic life forms in a drop of water remain unaware of the larger environment around them, our existence "may also be part of something bigger, something beyond our senses and abilities to comprehend," notes Keel. Jettisoning the notion of extraterrestrials, he coined the term *ultraterrestrials* to describe homegrown players, albeit ones of a seeming supernatural nature, who can glide along the electromagnetic spectrum, defying laws of physics, and toy with our minds. To these paraphysical beings, it is we, the humans, who are interlopers on *their* planet.

Vallée largely echoes Keel's approach, arguing that alien phenomena and UFOs represent a control system—a kind of thermostat regulating and conditioning human beliefs. As such, the system rides above direct perception as a kind of cosmic can't-see-the-forest-for-the-trees. "In every instance of the UFO phenomenon I have been able to study in depth," he writes, "I have found as many rational elements as I have absurd ones, and many that I could interpret as friendly and many that seemed hostile. No matter which approach I take, I can never explain more than half of the facts."

And what Lovecraftian surprises might we find, Vallée ponders, if we could somehow step outside the rat's maze? "Perhaps a terrible superhuman monstrosity the very contemplation of which would make a man insane? Perhaps a solemn gathering of wise men? Or the maddening simplicity of unattended clockwork?"[43]

SPIRITS IN THE SKY

The traumatic effects of alien abduction are in a way "designed" to bring about an ego death from which spiritual growth and consciousness expansion may take root, Mack contends. Getting to the "realms of the sublime" involves some growing pains, he implies, and it's not hard to see how jarring alien encounters could chip away at stodgy worldviews. Still, needles to the navel and eyeballs and other invasive procedures seem like a rather crude way to accomplish this.

Describing the aliens as intermediaries or emissaries from God, the abductees sometimes "develop a sense of awe before a mysterious cosmos that becomes sacred and ensouled. The sense of separation from all the rest of creation breaks down and the experience of oneness becomes an essential aspect" in their evolution, Mack notes. Further, a sense of a dual human/alien identity arises in many regressions, as well as the notion that the alien self is a lost or abandoned aspect of the soul. We may even be witnessing, Mack marvels, "an awkward joining of two species, engineered by an intelligence we are unable to fathom, for a purpose that serves both our goals with difficulties for each."[44]

Various studies have shown that abductees have no more psychopathology than the general public, yet they're more likely to report experiences with psychic phenomena and alternate realities dating back to childhood.[45] British ufologist Jenny Randles sees alien encounters as relating more to OBEs and near-death experiences than UFO sightings.[46]

The diary entries of OBE pioneer Robert Monroe featured in his classic work *Journeys Out of the Body* highlight an otherworldly contact that reads as alien: Lying in bed one night, "I suddenly felt bathed in and transfixed by a very powerful beam that seemed to come from the North about 30° above the horizon. I was completely powerless, with no will of my own, and I felt as if I were in the presence of a very strong force . . . it had intelligence of a form beyond my comprehension, and it came directly (down the beam?) into my head, and seemed to be searching every memory in my mind. I was truly frightened because I was powerless to do anything with this intrusion" (September 9, 1960).

"The same impersonal probing, the same power, from the same angle. However, this time I received the firm impression that I was inextricably bound by loyalty to this intelligent force, always had been, and that I had a job to perform here on Earth" (September 16, 1960).

"They seemed to soar up into the sky, while I called after them, pleading. Then I was sure that their mentality and intelligence were far beyond my understanding. It is an impersonal, cold intelligence, with none of the emotions of love or compassion which we respect so much, yet this may be the omnipotence we call God" (September 30, 1960).[47]

CHANGING CHANNELS

In contrast to the discombobulation of abductions, contactees can receive alien communiques from the comfort of their Barcaloungers. While the origin of these spiritually oriented messages is said to be extraterrestrial, they could just as easily be considered other-dimensional. George Adamski, one of the first contactees of the 1950s "space brothers" movement, amassed a lot of information from Venusians through what he called "transdimensional telepathy."[48] Yes, we know now that Venus is hotter than Hades and "ain't the kind of place to raise your kids," but *his* contacts were from the etheric rather than physical plane of the second planet.

Across the pond, yoga adept George King, whilst washing dishes in his apartment one day in 1954, quite out of the blue heard a disembodied command: "Prepare yourself! You are to become the voice of Interplanetary Parliament." It was the alien intelligence he would come to know as Master Aetherius. Receiving over six hundred transmissions from various "Space Masters" throughout his life, King claimed to consciously manipulate the power of Kundalini yoga as a focusing tool for "thought beams coming from the transmitting intelligence." Concurring with Adamski, he declared that there was indeed life on other planets in our solar system, though they exist on different vibratory planes.[49]

The intriguing parapsychologist and physician Andrija Puharich saw humans as "biocosmic resonators" able to tune in to information beyond themselves, with electromagnetic oscillations (signals from elsewhere) resonantly entraining parts of the human brain. In 1952–1953, his team worked with an Indian channeler, D. G. Vinod, who made contact with a cosmic collective that came to be known as "the Nine," though they spoke as one voice. A disparate group including Uri Geller reportedly channeled the entity "Spectra," described as "an extraterrestrial intelligence *from the future*" that possibly existed as a conscious computer on a distant spacecraft. By cross-referencing information, Puharich determined that Geller and the others were in contact with the same entities as the Nine.[50]

Later J. J. Hurtak (who worked with Puharich) and Carla Rueckert would create books of channeled material, seemingly from different flavors of the Nine. Hurtak's *The Keys of Enoch* grew out of an early 1970s encounter in which he found himself swathed in light and "taken out of body and into regions from which he would receive information for years to come," researcher Jon Klimo recounts. "The result of this initial encounter and later communications was . . . probably the single most scientifically rich and puzzling set of channeled material in modern times."[51]

Hurtak doesn't view his material as channeled information, because it was given directly to him in a "face-to-face experience with two beings of Higher Superluminal Intelligence."[52] At a glance, it's hard to decipher whether you're in the presence of sheer brilliance or scientific-sounding palaver:

The valency of transfiguration takes place when the
biogravitational energies which control the positive centropy of

the DNA coding of intelligence are centered
within a new spectrum of star energy controlling
molecular-magnethydrodynamic fields.[53]

While there are now more extraterrestrial channelers than you
can shake a stick at—Barbara Marciniak is one of the more acclaimed, relating the perspectives of multidimensional spirit beings
from the Pleiades star system—the work of Laura Knight-Jadczyk
merits a look for its "hyperdimensional" explanation of alien abduction.

Using a specialized form of the Ouija or spirit board, during the
1990s, Knight-Jadczyk and cohorts made direct inquiries of a
group of beings known as the Cassiopaeans, who rather than hail-
ing from somewhere in that constellation, may just be Laura and
her associates from the future. For a little terminology table setting, Knight-Jadczyk uses the esoteric reference points of "third
density" (humanity's current state) and "fourth density" (a level of
development between the physical and ethereal). Densities, she explains, can be conceptualized as vertical, and dimensions as horizontal and infinite.

Rather than dully benevolent star beings, the Cassiopaeans have
a bit of a bracing edge. At times they come off as scolds, and seem
exasperated by certain lines of questions, as though they were stuck
teaching a remedial class. Most alien abductions, they assert, take
place in fourth density, a realm not visible to the naked eye and un-
detectable by current scientific methods. The Greys use a technology called *transdimensional atomic rearrangement* to pass through
solid matter and make "soul imprints."

The abductees, they explain, most often are not physically removed from third density. Instead, they are put in a kind of stasis,

while "a soul imprint occupying . . . that particular host body is re- moved forcibly, transported to another locator, and remolecularized as a separate physical entity body for purpose of examination, im- plantation, and other." Changes in the fourth-density "clone" are seamlessly matched in the third-density being "whenever and wher- ever desired."[54]

When Knight-Jadczyk raised the issue of her own abduction (three spidery creatures got in a "tug-of-war" with her as they tried to float her out of bed, while a beam of light emanated from outside the house), the Cassiopaeans diagnosed an "eclipsing of realities" in which her energy centers were in conflict. Dusting off their hall of mirrors, they inquired, "What if the abduction scenario could take place where your soul projection, in what you perceive as the future, can come back and abduct your soul projection in what you perceive as the present?"

Knight-Jadczyk hints that the realms shamans travel in might be considered fourth density, and their "visions nearly always include serpents which inform the percipient that they are the creators of the human race."[55]

A SERPENTINE TRAIL

The anthropologist Michael Harner, who pioneered a renaissance in Western shamanism, studied with Indians in Peru and Ecuador, and on one occasion in 1961 he entered a trance state after drinking the hallucinogenic brew ayahuasca. "Now I was virtually certain I was about to die," he recalled in *The Way of the Shaman*:

As I tried to accept my fate . . . [a] lower portion of my brain began to transmit more visions and information. I was "told" that this new material was being presented to me because I was dying and therefore "safe" to receive these revelations. These were the secrets reserved for the dying and the dead, I was informed. I could only very dimly perceive the givers of these thoughts: giant reptilian creatures reposing sluggishly at the lower-most depths of the back of my brain, where it met the top of the spinal column. I could only vaguely see them in what seemed to be gloomy, dark depths.

Then they projected a visual scene in front of me. First they showed me the planet Earth as it was eons ago, before there was any life on it. I saw an ocean, barren land, and a bright blue sky. Then black specks dropped from the sky by the hundreds and landed in front of me on the barren landscape. I could see that the "specks" were actually large, shiny, black creatures with stubby pterodactyl-like wings and huge whale-like bodies. Their heads were not visible to me. They flopped down, utterly exhausted from their trip, resting for eons. They explained to me in a kind of thought language that they were fleeing from something out in space. They had come to the planet Earth to escape their enemy.

The creatures then showed me how they had created life on the planet in order to hide within the multitudinous forms and thus disguise their presence. Before me, the magnificence of plant and animal creation and speciation—hundreds of millions of years of activity—took place on a scale and with a vividness impossible to describe. I learned that the dragon-like creatures were thus inside of all forms of life, including man. They were the true masters of humanity and the entire planet, they told me. We humans were but the receptacles and servants of these creatures. For this reason they could speak to me from within myself.[56]

If the serpentine trail of the alien does lead back to our very essence, it's even more of a reckoning than the "ancient alien" hypothesis—that advanced beings tinkered with the DNA of existing primates. Perhaps aliens use our DNA like a software key to access our minds. One's blood runs cold at the possibilities.

We may be knocked down a few pegs on the food chain, but still, the mirage of the alien beckons to us—an ancestral god, a demonic intruder, a spiritual guidepost. Sliding behind masks, of hero and villain, and all the shades of "grey" in between.

CHAPTER NINE

LUCID DREAMING

Sitting behind the reception desk at the museum where I sometimes volunteer, I watched as my colleague leaned back against the wall. His face slowly turned mottled and grotesque as his body merged with the wall and he vanished entirely. *Now, that was a rather odd exit,* I thought. *Was it something I said?* Needless to say, something felt very off.

I went to the bathroom mirror to see if my own face was looking like the tucked away portrait of Dorian Gray. While still recognizably me, my reflection was rubbery and mutable. It was then that I opted for a definitive reality check, glancing at some text on the wall, then looking away. When I looked back, the text had changed. That cinched it! I was officially in a lucid dream, a rare occurrence for me—knowing that I was dreaming while in it.

Rather rusty in the ways of lucidity, I opted to fly. While this sounds liberating, there was a pathetic fishbowl quality about it, as I flew around the small space, confined by the twelve-foot ceiling, not remembering that I could move through "solid" objects if I willed it. When I landed, I looked out the front window. Outside it was nighttime, but there were no lights whatsoever, just darkness. I heard the sounds of someone or something coming closer and felt the pangs of fear. Then I woke up.

Fear is a known buzzkill for lucid dreaming (LD), but as I discovered in my research for this chapter, there are a fair number of reports of "lucid nightmares" and highly disturbing aspects to lucidity. We'll take a deep dive into this dark side, but first we'll look at the many positive aspects of the acclaimed state when the mind wakes up while it's still asleep.

AN ABBREVIATED HISTORY OF LUCIDITY

More than three thousand years ago, Hindu tracts inscribed perhaps the first written accounts of lucid dreaming. Aristotle also made note of the phenomenon in his 350 BC treatise *On Dreams.* "When one is asleep," he wrote, "there is something in consciousness which tells us that what presents itself is but a dream." But it was Tibetan Buddhists around the eighth century AD who really delved into lucidity as part of a yogic practice to understand the illusive nature of the dream state, and by extension, waking life, and even death.[1]

Fast-forward to 1867, when French dream experimenter Marquis d'Hervey de Saint-Denys first coined the term *rêve-lucide* ("lucid dream") to describe his budding ability to consciously control his dreams (he was also one of the first to make note of hypnagogic phenomena). However, Dutch psychiatrist Frederik van Eeden is most often credited with coming up with the term. In his 1913 paper

"A Study of Dreams," presented to the Society for Psychical Research, he wrote: "I can only say that I made my observations during normal deep and healthy sleep, and that in 352 cases I had a full recollection of my day-life, and could act voluntarily, though I was so fast asleep that no bodily sensations penetrated into my perception. If anybody refuses to call that state of mind a dream, he may suggest some other name. For my part, it was just this form of dream, which I call 'lucid dreams,' which aroused my keenest interest and which I noted down most carefully."[2]

While van Eeden reveled in the glories of his controlled dreams, they were often followed by hellish "demon dreams." His breakthrough research was seen by relatively few people, and as late as 1980, "dream researchers in general . . . were nearly unanimous in rejecting lucid dreaming as a bona fide phenomenon of sleep—REM or otherwise. Lucid dreams were evidently viewed as aberrant chimeras, brief daydreamlike intrusions of wakefulness into disturbed sleep,"[3] writes the pioneering psychophysiologist Dr. Stephen LaBerge.

Hooked up to a polysomnograph machine at the Stanford University sleep lab in 1978, LaBerge made specific eye signals during his REM cycle to demonstrate his lucidity to fellow researcher Lynn Nagel. A peer-reviewed journal, *Perceptual and Motor Skills*, published the findings in 1981. Yet British researcher Keith Hearne beat LaBerge to the punch, conducting a similar experiment in 1975 with prolific lucid dreamer Alan Worsley.

Hearne marveled over his discovery: "Suddenly out of the jumbled senseless tos and fros of the two eye movement channels, a regular set of zigzags appeared on the chart. Instantly, I was alert and felt the greatest exhilaration on realizing that I was observing the first ever deliberate signals sent from within a dream to the outside. The signals were coming from another world—the world of dreams—and they were exciting as if they were emanating from some other solar system in space."[4]

In the ensuing years, scientific research in the subject has yielded a treasure trove of data. Activities within a lucid dream are reflected in the brain in a manner that is equivalent to what we'd see in a waking person. For instance, if someone sings during a conscious dream, the right hemisphere lights up, and if they start counting, the left hemisphere activates. Further, scientists at Heidelberg University demonstrated that practicing a motor skill during a lucid dream significantly improves performance in the waking state.[5]

FOLLOW YOUR DREAMS

Stephen LaBerge, with his seminal 1985 book *Lucid Dreaming*, "acted as an unusually charismatic promotor of lucid dreaming, helping to create a burgeoning, mainstream interest in the subject,"[6] notes author David Jay Brown. LaBerge founded the Lucidity Institute in 1987; now in his early seventies, he has been the poster boy for oneironauts (intrepid explorers of the dream state) the world over. Other well-regarded researchers and writers on the topic include Robert Waggoner, Patricia Garfield, Ryan Hurd, Paul Tholey, Daniel Love, Clare R. Johnson, Jayne Gackenbach, Robert Moss, Andrew Holecek, Ken Kelzer, and Ed Kellogg.

Beyond these lucid luminaries, there are now ever-multiplying online courses, books, apps, devices, supplements, binaural beats, YouTube gurus, and TEDx Talks on the subject—a Google search returned an astonishing 22 million responses for "lucid dreaming" (though it must be said, by way of comparison, that "almond butter" yielded 141 million results). And in spite of the Internet's seeming love affair with lucid dreaming, when I bring up the topic, most people are unfamiliar. But once I explain it, they often admit to having something akin to the experience. Studies show that 58 to 70 percent of individuals will have at least one lucid dream during their life.[7] While most of these may have been random, at the Lucidity Institute's recurring Hawaiian retreats, attendees are trained to amp up their abilities to dream lucidly.

Canadian science journalist Jeff Warren attended one of the Hawaii gatherings as part of his research for his invigorating romp around the mind, *Head Trip*. Breakfast conversation with the other participants grew increasingly bizarre, he reported, to the point where the "normal" resort guests politely excused themselves from the oneironauts (pronounced "oh-nigh-row-nots") after hearing the likes of this: "After performing a quick reality check I confirmed that I was in an artificial dream world where the standard rules of physics did not apply. I executed a dream spin to prevent world-dissolution, then conjured up my captain's chair when I found myself on the control deck of the *Battlestar Galactica* . . . More coffee?"

Picking up the sci-fi metaphor, LaBerge told Warren that the potential for the future of lucid dreaming "is something like the *Star Trek* holodeck. Here is a room you can go into and have any imaginable experience. You can use it for education, practice, rehearsal, therapy, recreation . . . in a way that is both safe and stimulating. This is its potential for human betterment, and it's there every night."[8]

Lucid dream images appear as real as waking life, perhaps even more real in a sense—according to LaBerge, they're "the most vivid form of imagery likely to be experienced by normal individuals."[9] Though LD shares some similarities to the hypnagogic state in that a person can exercise some conscious control over the experiences, hypnagogia takes place at the threshold of sleep and waking, while LD generally occurs entirely within REM sleep. There is a bit of crossover between the two states, however, as one can potentially fall asleep during hypnagogia and roll right into what's called a "wake-induced lucid dream" (WILD), though this can be tricky to pull off.

LIFT-OFF TO LUCIDITY?

Abetted by the sleeping brain's damping down of the areas that govern logic and memory, the dreaming mind is a stubborn mistress, generally defying attempts to make it "wake up" to the realization of what it is. We simply accept even our most outlandish dream narratives as being real until we wake up and realize "it was just a dream." As therapist Ken Kelzer notes, "in lucid dreaming we awaken IN the dream; in ordinary dreaming we awaken FROM the dream."[10]

Although lucid dreams can be a ticket to the unfiltered content of our unconscious, the majordomo of the personality structure, the ego, perhaps prefers a more pasteurized worldview. It doesn't want us consciously rooting around in its foundational substrata—home to the repository of the unknown and repressed. "To penetrate the bed of ego," writes author and spiritual teacher Andrew Holecek, "is to see through its facade, and for the ego, that is the equivalent to death."[11]

And so, to attain lucidity, we have to swim upstream in the river of dreams and disrupt the entrenched way we sleep, and for most this is an arduous undertaking. While there are a variety of mental training exercises (more on these coming up), in our app-happy culture, there's the desire to just slap on a device or pop a pill before going to sleep and ta-da—lucid dreaming. Though a cottage industry has sprung up, there is no ta-da product . . . yet. Will it be like the long-dangled male pattern baldness cure (still waiting on that one), or is it just around the corner?

Back in the 1990s, the Lucidity Institute was the only game in town when it came to high-tech gadgetry. Their NovaDreamer is a pair of sleep goggles kitted with sensors that detect when you go into REM sleep, and then it flashes or beeps at you at regular intervals to act as a reminder or cue that you're dreaming. I had one of these puppies and did have a small amount of success with it. In one of my most memorable lucid dreams, I recognized the flashing lights inside my dream and found myself in a gritty and colorful Times Square, bustling with noise and pedestrians. As I gaped at the incredible realness of the "crossroads of the world," I noticed a theater marquee emblazoned with the title MR. PSYCHIC. Based on various reviews and my own experiments, the older tech of the NovaDreamer has not been surpassed by some of the newer contraptions, which are often funded through crowdsourcing. That could be subject to change as more wearable technology hits the market in the years ahead.

One of the most compelling findings related to lucidity technology was announced in 2014, when Dr. Ursula Voss and her associates at J. W. Goethe-University in Frankfurt, Germany, conducted experiments sending weak electric currents, thirty seconds long, to subjects during REM sleep. It was found that when given 40 Hz of transcranial stimulation (gamma brain waves), 77 percent of the twenty-seven subjects reported lucid dreams. And this from a group who had no experience with lucidity!

"I was dreaming about lemon cake," said one of the subjects. "It looked translucent, but then again, it didn't. It was a bit like in an animated movie, like the Simpsons. And then I started falling and the scenery changed and I was talking to Matthias Schweighöfer (a German actor) and two foreign exchange students. And I was wondering about the actor and they told me, 'Yes, you met him before,' so then I realized, 'Oops, you are dreaming.' I mean, while I was dreaming! So strange!"[12]

Gamma waves aren't just for dreamers. They're found to be highly active in the brains of meditating Tibetan monks[13] as well as associated with high attention states in awake people.[14] Perhaps by waking up parts of the sleepy cortex, gamma activity gives us a leg up in recognizing the dream state for what it is. But sounding a don't-try-this-at-home note, Voss said that although they hadn't seen any harmful effects from the currents, there wasn't enough data to be sure.[15] "Electrical stimulation of the brain," she cautioned the *Jackass* set, "should always be monitored by a professional."

Don't tell that to the team behind the LucidCatcher, a device marketed by a Ukrainian company relocated to San Francisco that seems to riff on Voss's research, zapping the brain with gamma and other waves via a headband worn to sleep. At the time of this writing, the Kickstarted product is no longer available, and one reviewer, SpaceTimeBadass (the YouTube persona of James S. Bray), said it triggered lucidity only once in a twelve-night trial.[16] A company out of the Netherlands has been at work on a similar wearable product. Called the Lucid Dreamer, it's said to emit mild electrical stimulation during REM sleep, but as of early 2019, it continues to be "under development."[17]

In the supplement department, a substance called galantamine has lately bogarted the attention of the oneironaut crowd. Derived from extracts of the snowdrop daffodil and spider lily, it was developed as a prescription drug to treat Alzheimer's but is also available over the counter. Considered an acetylcholine inhibitor, galantamine slows the breakdown of neurotransmitters that support the function of memory.

A recent study in which the Lucidity Institute teamed up with the University of Wisconsin–Madison determined that when LD enthusiasts took 4 to 8 milligrams of galantamine 4.5 hours into their sleep cycle (and practiced the MILD induction technique, described in the following section), 57 percent were successful in scoring a lucid dream on at least one out of two nights.[18] In my own experiments with galantamine and a similar acetylcholine inhibitor, huperzine A (made from moss extract), I've found that at the higher dose level it can be a struggle to fall back asleep once you take them, and they're slightly headache inducing. Though not producing full-fledged lucidity very often, 4 milligrams of galantamine taken in the mid-sleep cycle seems to make my dreams more memorable and intelligent without keeping me awake.

Once I opted for a combo of galantamine and huperzine A, which rather than yielding lucidity transported me to a macabre land-of-the-dead dreamworld that resembled some of the creepier aspects of the audience-participation play *Sleep No More*. For more on various herbs and supplements that can enhance dreaming and lucidity, check out the comprehensive round-up in David Jay Brown's book *Dreaming Wide Awake*.

INDUCTION BOOTCAMP

The Army of Lucid Dreamers wants you! But since we're still waiting for the magic pill or device, I'm afraid you'll have to perform some mental gyrations to get there. The aforementioned MILD technique—mnemonic induction of lucid dreams—is part of La-Berge's standard protocol. Essentially, it's a rehearsal whenever you wake up from a nonlucid dream. First, you go over your dream several times, trying to recall as much as possible. As you return to sleep, you say to yourself, "Next time I'm dreaming, I want to remember to recognize I'm dreaming." Then you visualize yourself back in the same dream, only this time you see yourself realizing that it's a dream. Finally, repeat the last couple of steps a few times as you start to fall asleep.[19]

Wake Back to Bed (WBTB), meanwhile, involves getting out of bed after four to six hours of sleep, then staying awake for twenty to sixty minutes reading or doing something analytical. When you go back to bed, because your brain is in a more peppy state and the REM cycle is heavier in the later hours of sleep, the likelihood of lucidity increases. This parallels how many humans slept before the advent of artificial lighting—in two intervals. A "first sleep" was followed by a one-to-two-hour period of wakefulness known as the "watch" or "watching," and then a "second" or "morning" sleep.[20]

While I can verify that WBTB works to some degree, I often have difficulty falling back asleep once I'm up, so you run the risk of feeling sleep-deprived for the rest of the day.

Sprinkling "reality checks" throughout your waking day is another key to lucidity. The thinking here is that if you get into the practice of testing whether you're in a dream, this habit could carry over into your dream life and serve as a cue for lucidity. In addition to looking at written text (mentioned at the beginning of the chapter), other checks include flicking a light switch (in dreams, they tend not to work), jumping up in the air (you may become airborne in a dream or fall through the ground on your return), gazing into a mirror (in a dream your reflection will behave unpredictably), and the time-honored Carlos Castaneda instruction, looking at your hands.

Once in the dream state, keep an eye out for your own personal *dreamsigns*, a term LaBerge uses to reference our native set of themes, anomalies, and characteristics. "Dreamsigns can be like neon lights," he and Howard Rheingold write, "flashing a message in the darkness: 'This is a dream! This is a dream!'"[21] One of the best ways to get to know your dreamsigns is to keep a dream journal and pay attention to the elements that keep returning.

You may, for instance, find that mechanical or electric devices rarely work properly in a dream—I've started doing reality checks with the time on my cell phone lock screen—or that you can't find your way back to a place where you've left something behind—one of my persistent frustrations is that the dream fabric has difficulty reconstructing stable environments. Once you've isolated particular scenarios, you can practice throughout the waking day a kind of activity comparison. For example, when you put your shoes on, notice that they are exactly where you left them—not like in the dream! The hope is that this kind of analysis will seep into your dreaming mind.

Sometimes help can come from an unlikely source—a character in the dream itself. The researcher and psychologist Paul Tholey cites the case of a woman who dreamed she had to force her way through a repugnant mass of gray slime. "I didn't know then and I still don't know what it was. . . . Then, in the midst of this grey slime, I came to a brightly lit place with a person standing in the center. I could see that it was Mr. Spock, the scientist of the Enterprise . . . He told me, 'There is no reason to worry because you are dreaming!' I did not believe him and I asked him what it was that I had just passed through. He answered that I had just passed through my own brain, or my own mind. I did not believe him, but he knew so much more than I did and he told me he would jump up and then remain in mid-air, just so that I would be able to see that we were part of a dream. Only after this actually took place was I convinced that I was in a dream."[22]

Tholey refers to such a character as an *internal self-helper*, or ISH, and says you can incubate a meeting with one by means of a pre-sleep suggestion. More on lucid dream characters a bit later.

NOW THAT YOU'RE LUCID

Congratulations on getting this far! But your journey has just begun. One of the first things newbies struggle with is maintaining their lucidity. Sorry, but your natural excitement over realizing that you're in a dream has to be checked at the door. Strong emotions can cause a person to easily wake up, or if you get too engrossed in the scene, you may fall back into ordinary dreaming. Though it seems a bit restraining, beginners must remain fairly neutral. For now, think of your dreaming self as Switzerland. It's a bit of a high-wire act over the Matterhorn of your mind. "Not only did I need to be consciously aware of being in a dream, I needed to be consciously aware of being aware,"[23] lucid dreamer extraordinaire Robert Waggoner revealed. For the novice, internally voicing a reminder or repeated mantra such as "This is all a dream" can be advantageous.

Beyond the goalpost of becoming lucid, it's beneficial to have a plan of things to do or explore, as this can help you maintain your focus. In contrast to the discombobulations of the standard dream, a person in the lucid state can reason clearly, engage in complex thinking, access their waking memories, and follow through on prearranged strategies,[24] though there are different degrees of lucidity, and those on the semilucid or sublucid end of the continuum may not have full access to these faculties.[25]

In the event that the dream seems about to collapse and waking is imminent, spinning your dream body around or rubbing your hands together can refresh the dream setting and prolong lucidity.[26]

ADVENTURES IN LUCIDITY

Flying is one of the more beloved activities for new and veteran oneironauts. The sky's not even the limit for some of the more intrepid. Waggoner revisits a 1997 dream: "I become lucid and find that my flying control is excellent. . . . I think about what to do and decide to try to fly out into the stars. I begin to fly and keep flying and flying. I can't believe how far I'm going . . . I begin to fly past planets . . . I look down about forty degrees and there's a large planet with rings and four moons."

"I marvel," he continues, "at the profound sight of seeing an entire planet hanging in space. It's so incredibly silent and still. . . . I head toward the rings and as I do so, I begin to feel energy hitting me as I move through the ring."[27] Rather than outer space, Waggoner ponders whether such trips represent symbolic layers of the mind's inner depths.

Sexual encounters are another favorite pastime. Dream authority Patricia Garfield shares that her own experiences convince her that "conscious dreaming is orgasmic. . . . I believe it quite possible that in lucid dreaming we are stimulating an area of the brain, or a chain of responses, that is associated with ecstatic states of all sorts. Sensations of flying, sexual heights, pleasurable awareness, and a sense of oneness are all outcomes of a prolonged lucid dream."[28]

While hooked up to monitoring equipment at the Stanford Sleep Lab in 1983, lucid dream researcher Beverly D'Urso participated in a unique experiment. As published in the *Journal of Psychophysiology*, her sexual encounter led to the first recorded female orgasm in a dream. "In my lucid dreams, I think of sex as a powerful bonding or integrating experience.... I have been the woman, the man, half woman/half man, divided by upper and lower body, left and right sides, and with both a penis and a vagina. This made it possible to make love physically with myself in all combinations ... In one lucid dream, I had sex with the earth, as I flew at its edge, one leg dragging into the dirt. I can barely think of some sexual situation that I have not experienced. These dreams are all very enjoyable and everyone is always totally accepting. Often, I perform some sexual advance or action as soon as I know I am dreaming, to prove in a way that I feel unrestricted in the dream," she detailed in her *Ethics of Dream Sex* presentation at the 2005 conference of the International Association for the Study of Dreams.[29]

Playing the hero and even with time itself, correspondent S.C. from El Paso, Texas, writes: "I'm an astronomer and I pride myself on my powers of detailed observation; I would like to add to our knowledge of the sleep state. I have saved the Earth from nuclear war, the Galaxy from its core exploding, the Universe from final heat Death. I have inhabited a score of other bodies and personalities, from the distant past to the technological future. One of my more interesting lucid dreams lasted for over five years in the dream time frame, during which I lived in the far distant future, in a body very different from my present one. I would actually fall asleep in this 'nest' life. Interestingly, I did not have lucid dreams in this alter life, but each time I awakened from the 'nested' sleep I would become instantly aware that I was having a lucid dream, and each time I chose to stay in the dream. This was far in the future, when the moon had broken up to form lovely multicolored rings, which I would watch with my wife and little girl in the cool evening twi-light."[30]

HEALING FROM WITHIN A DREAM

Guided meditations, visualizations, and other mind-body approaches have been touted as healing modalities over the years, but in the lucid state, these techniques can be amplified because of the felt "realness" of the experience. When we dream, we generate our own body image, so "why shouldn't we be able to initiate self-healing processes during lucid dreams by consciously envisioning our dream bodies as perfectly healthy?" LaBerge asks.[31]

Some of the healing methods tried during LD include directing healing intent (sometimes manifested as unexpected light), performing chants or sound energy, creating symbolic imagery, pursuing information about the cause or meaning of an illness, and seeking a "dream doctor" or healing environment.[32] One VA patient reportedly cured himself of twenty-two years of chronic pain with a single lucid dream involving beauteous musical tones and giant strands of DNA made out of cookie dough. "I'm no expert on lucid dreams," psychiatrist Mauro Zappaterra commented, "but the man woke up with no pain. He said it was like his brain had shut down and rebooted. A few days later, he walks in the VA pharmacy and actually returns his medication—300 tabs of levorphanol. To me that's pretty convincing evidence."[33]

Mattie, an experienced lucid dreamer, had such a severe ankle fracture that she was using a wheelchair. When she became aware that she was dreaming, she focused on healing and pictured herself going inside her ankle. Patricia Garfield picks up the story: "There she looked around and saw 'all sorts of junk.' In these lucid dreams, Mattie busied herself with removing from her injured ankle the debris she found—screwdrivers, bolts, and all sorts of tools. When she was awake, she found her condition improving. For the first time since her injury, Mattie was able to walk."[34]

Healing efforts can be focused on others besides the dreamer. Lucid dream experimenter Ed Kellogg, PhD, describes his attempt in 1992 to aid a man suffering from emphysema: "I try a healing of D. . . . [He] keeps interrupting, asking me what I do. I tell him I'll explain later in Waking Physical Reality. I use a healing chant (Now let the healing energy shine / To cure the lungs with power divine). A green energy-liquid, like dark chlorophyll comes out of my fingers into D's chest, where it seeps out again. I leave him to recover, but when I return I find him pale and frail . . . I create a white light chi energy ball with rotating hand motions and try to charge him up."[35]

Within a day or so, D showed a remarkable improvement, Kellogg reported—for the previous six months he'd needed continuous oxygen therapy, but afterward, he only required it while sleeping at night. Kellogg, who has conducted a far-ranging series of challenges and experiments with lucidity (including using dream mirrors as portals, developing PSI abilities, and sharing mutual dreams), finds that the use of rhyming chants is an especially effective means of focusing intent.

THE CURIOUS WORLD OF DREAM CHARACTERS

An unpredictable bunch, characters in the lucid dreamscape run the gamut from malleable mental images to insightful independent beings. "Differentiating between the types of dream figures requires considerable skill," writes Waggoner, since characters of diverging mental status may have similar appearances. "To get a more accurate reading of the varieties of dream figures," he explained, "lucid dreamers have discovered that they must literally interact with them, through conversations, questions, or suggestions."

Once while having sex with an attractive woman in a lucid state, Waggoner pondered whether his avid partner might be just a mental construct conjured up by his own expectations and desires. To resolve the matter, he pulled himself away and authoritatively announced: "All thought-forms must now disappear!"

She promptly vanished, leaving him to wonder how someone "so real, so tactile and responsive," could just be a thought-form. But before long, another woman supplanted the first. After some passionate lovemaking, he repeated the earlier declaration about thought-forms, and she too disappeared. Not to be outdone by the first two, a third partner appeared underneath him to continue the action, and as he was formulating the words "all thought-forms must . . ." she popped out of existence before he could even say "disappear."[36]

Are all dream inhabitants merely a product of our mind? Prof. Deirdre Barrett draws a connection between dreaming and multiple personality disorder (MPD, also called dissociative identity disorder), suggesting that "the dream character, as an hallucinated projection of aspects of the self, can be seen as a prototype for the MPD alter. Dreaming may even be a more literal precursor whose physiologic mechanisms for amnesia and the manufacture of alternative identities are recruited in the development of MPD."[37]

Setting aside the notion that we all turn into mini-Sybils when we hit the hay, Waggoner retested his thought-form hypothesis, subsequently issuing his "must vanish" proclamation in other lucid dreams. The results were intriguing. "I recall once making the announcement to two groups of about four dream figures; one group suddenly disappeared, while the other group looked at me with something close to utter disdain as if to say, 'Can't you tell the difference?' and continued with their project."

The minister and dream educator Jeremy Taylor shared an account of a young man named "Dan" who dreamed he was at a party in a swanky penthouse. As live jazz music played and the city sparkled below, a pretty woman sat on his lap, "Suddenly, he realizes that he's dreaming—that his physical body is asleep in a cheap rented room in Chicago. At this moment in the dream, the woman... asks if he's having a good time. He laughs and replies that he is having a great time, but that he will have to leave soon—his alarm is about to go off and wake him up. The woman asks him in surprise what he means, and he replies that all of this is a dream and none of it is real."

"'You mean you think I'm not real?' the woman asks in some annoyance. 'That's right,' he replies. With this, the woman becomes even more annoyed. 'I'll show you who's real or not!' she says, and crushes her lit cigarette out on the back of the dreamer's right hand. Instantaneously, the young man awakens in the rented room with a terrible pain in his right hand. He turns on a light and sees a round burn the size of a cigarette on the back of his right hand. He peers in amazement and sees what appears to be cigarette ashes clinging to the skin around the wound."[38]

While there may be other explanations for how he wound up with the wound, the dream certainly depicts an independently minded character. Hell hath no fury like a (lucidly dreamed) woman scorned!

In a recollection published in 1992,[39] a conscious dreamer informed "Sandra" that she was in point of fact a dream character. "This is a very unusual thing for me to do—my dream characters think this is rude," wrote the correspondent. "She replied that I'm a character in *her* dream. To prove her wrong, I did various things such as fly around the room and change our environment. Sandra did similar tricks. Neither of us could influence the other. After a bit of this, I was very confused and Sandra commented that she, too, was confused." Now, who's zoomin' who?

Among the more autonomous and intelligent dream residents, some do seem to be projections of the oneironaut's own mind, yet others might be travelers, other dreamers, or even spirit guardians, suggests David Jay Brown. The "place" where lucid dreaming occurs, he continues, "is an independently existing alternative reality or realities where some people live their day-to-day lives. However, on rare occasions, some of the other characters that I've met in the dream realm seemed to be, like me, other dreamers who temporarily came to this place through the process of lucid dreaming."[40]

The idea that two or more physical people could be sharing a mutual dream space is fascinating, if not borne out yet in sleep lab testing. Both Kellogg and Waggoner describe lucid dream encounters with people whom they believe to be nonlucid dreamers. They tend to behave as if they're semidrunk, moving disjointedly and with little focus. Those who are partially lucid are a bit more responsive. Flipping the equation around, Waggoner describes a time he became lucid when he was with a group of people on a neighborhood street: "Then, I notice—everyone was waiting for me to become lucid! In particular, there are three dream figures . . . and as they recognize that I am lucid, they appear very pleased that I have made the mental shift. We all hug and perform a spontaneous chant, like a team."[41]

Meanwhile, David Jay Brown found a different sort of lucid communion. He was speaking with a boy who looked to be around five years old. "I was thinking that I was going to ask him about his dreams. I wanted to ask the dream characters in my dreams about their dreams! Then, at the exact same instant in time, we both asked each other, 'What are your dreams like?' I was really surprised by this simultaneous expression, and I said to him, 'How did you know I was going to ask you that?' Then he looked at me with an expression of wisdom that I've never seen another dream character possess and confidently said, 'It's because we're the same person.'"

CONTROL ISSUES

In one of Waggoner's early lucid adventures, he was flying over a city and decided to play a game and swoop down and knock the hats off men on the street, one at a time. "Flying back, I descend, select a target, and *poof*, there goes the second one. Coming back around, I concentrate on a hat in the middle of the crowd, descend, and just as I prepare to hit the hat, a hand reaches up from the crowd and stops me in midflight! . . . Without any presuggestion on my part, a dream figure acted contrary to my goals. Absolutely unexpected."[42]

For the LD beginner, asserting control over aspects of the dream—"Hey, I just changed the sky from blue to orange!"—can feel like a playground. But such manipulations often don't work or last long. As more seasoned oneironauts have discovered, lucidity is most effectively a tool not for exercising control over the dream landscape but as a way to take charge of your own personal experience and reactions within the dream.[43]

As Waggoner so eloquently puts it: "No sailor controls the sea. Only a foolish sailor would say such a thing. Similarly, no lucid dreamer controls the dream. Like a sailor on the sea, we lucid dreamers direct our perceptual awareness within the larger state of dreaming."[44]

BEHIND THE CURTAIN AND OUT OF THE BODY

Waggoner discovered that voices in his conscious dreams would sometimes boom out not from the characters but as though from backstage or above the scene. And instead of making inquiries of dream characters, he learned he could simply ask the dream itself for revelations.[45] Rather than the source of chaotic messages buried in his own mind, he began to view the unconscious as an independent and responsive field—the limitless fountainhead behind the dreams themselves.

Author Ryan Hurd has also contemplated the mysterious orchestration behind our dreams, and he doubts that it's rooted in one specific system. "There's really no guarantee that you are in conversation with your higher self when you ask a question beyond the dream," he said. "The voice could be representing any number of self-constructs, or even your expectation of a conversation with your higher self. . . . But the practice certainly brings novelty into the dream."[46]

OBEs (out-of-body experiences, perceiving the physical world from outside one's self, often floating above the physical body) have a correlation with lucid dreams as well as sleep paralysis. In one survey of lucid dreamers, 39 percent reported having OBEs.[47] Though there are a number of differences between the two states—lucid dreamers can make alterations in the environment, while out-of-body travelers are viewing the "real" world or a simulacrum of it—LaBerge and psychologist Susan Blackmore have postulated that most OBEs are actually a type of lucid dream.

"Aware that I was in a dream, but with the image of what I had been dreaming about fading, I tried to hold onto it," LaBerge recalled of his own experience. "Throwing myself into the darkness, I found myself crawling down a dark tunnel on my hands and knees. At first I could see nothing, but when I touched my eyelids I was able to open them, and I suddenly found myself floating across the room toward Dawn, who was sleeping on the couch. I looked back to see my 'body' asleep on the living room floor. Somehow, I was completely convinced that this was not a dream, but that I really was seeing my sleeping body. Dawn awoke and started to speak, and I felt myself magnetically drawn back into the body asleep on the floor. When I arrived, I got up in this body (which I took to be my physical body) and excitedly said to her, 'Do you know what just happened to me? An out-of-body experience of the genuine kind!' . . . I was shocked to awaken a few minutes later in my bed and realize that I had been sleeping all along. By now my brain was working well enough to note the general implausibility of my previous interpretation of the recent events. I could see, for instance, the inconsistencies implied by my belief that the body I had seen asleep on the floor, and entered from my supposed 'other body,' was actually my physical body. . . . My 'out-of-body experience of the genuine kind' serves as a reminder that we can be totally mistaken about what seems indubitable."[48]

While LaBerge presents a persuasive argument, other researchers, such as Australian psychologist Harvey Irwin, have demonstrated that the brain wave patterns of those undergoing OBEs largely differ from the REM dream state in which lucidity takes place.[49] And then there are the out-of-body revelations of near-death experiencers who report seeing precise details of things like their hospital surgeries even though they're more or less brain dead.

A LUCID DOUBLE FEATURE

If the radical perception of seeing two versions of your body isn't enough to set your head spinning, let me introduce the concept of simultaneous dreaming shared by lucid dreamer Lucy Gillis. She first encountered the phenomenon in 1988.[50] "I had been in two dreams *at the same time* but not only that, I was lucidly aware of being in the two dreams *while they were happening*." She explained that the dreams had equal prominence and her sense of self did not feel split in half, even though she was experiencing herself in two concurrent dreams.

Gillis subsequently correlated the experience with some of the Seth writings (material channeled by Jane Roberts) related to the multidimensional nature of consciousness and the idea of probable selves, as well as new thinking in physics around parallel worlds. She writes, "I believe that the phenomenon of simultaneous dreaming is not as rare as it may first appear," and lucidity is likely mandatory to reel it in. It could be going on underneath the surface of our awareness, "but because we are so habituated to experiencing time in a single, linear progression," we fail to recognize the simultaneous streams, and the waking mind collapses the dream memories into a singular if fragmentary occurrence.

IN THE GRIP OF A SERPENT

Some lucid dreams pack a powerful spiritual wallop. Such is the case of Ken Kelzer's 1981 account he calls "The Arrival of the Serpent Power":

Now I am lying face down on the ground somewhere on a patch of bare brown earth. Still fully aware that I am dreaming, I see a huge serpent approach me from the right. Quickly it glides over my back, then turns and passes back underneath me, silently sliding between my body and the ground. Then it rises and turns and comes back up over me again, strongly gripping me around my chest in its powerful coil. Its gray-brown body is about three to four inches thick, and about thirty feet long. Its eyes are strange yellow-green in color, and they gaze at me calmly and steadily, continuously emitting their soft, yellow-green luminescence from within. . . . It watches me through its glowing eyes, with a calm and amazingly neutral objectivity.

Our eyes meet and the impact is extremely powerful—absolutely unforgettable as I gaze for a long moment into the serpent's profound yellow-green eyes, utterly perplexed and fascinated at the same time. Now I drop my head to the ground and begin to wrestle with the serpent, trying to free myself from its grip. I discover that I am no match for its incredible strength. I feel afraid that it will crush me, and I wrestle with all my might for some time, until exhausted I decide to stop struggling. Soon I perceive that the serpent is actually very gentle, merely intent on holding me in its relentless grip. I am very surprised to feel that its body is warm blooded, and not cold blooded as I would expect. Suddenly, it makes a quick jerky movement with its coil,

which rotates my prone body onto its side. . . . The serpent
seems to be playing with me in some strange uncanny fashion,
rotating me back and forth in a gradual deliberate manner. . . . I
feel totally subject to its will, as these movements are repeated
several times, each time with a quick, powerful jerk of its
massive coil.[51]

In the dream, a second serpent appears, and he undergoes a similar encounter. When Kelzer finally awakened, he felt a powerful swirling of energies traveling up his spine into his head. In subsequent reflection, he believes the dream released a rising kundalini energy inside him that would bring new awarenesses and challenges.

DREAM A DREAM OF DREAM YOGA

Dream yoga, an ancient variant of lucid dreaming, focuses on self-transcendence rather than self-improvement. The Tibetan perspective clocks you with a sort of double wake-up call—not only are nonlucid dreams a delusion, but so is your waking world! Just because physical reality presents itself as "stable" doesn't mean it's any more "real" than a dream, according to this outlook. Holecek explains: "So it is through the practice of mindfulness . . . that we wake up from the illusion of stability in the outer forms of daily life, seeing it more like a dream, and we simultaneously stabilize our dreams, seeing them more like waking reality." Dreaming and waking consciousness "become increasingly alike—irrespective of sensory constraint."[52]

But what's the endgame here? Let me sidebar for a second. While working on this chapter, I inquired of my acupuncturist, a pleasant chap named Dr. Scott, if there were any special points where he could place the needles that might improve my chances for lucid dreaming.

"What's a lucid dream?" he inquired.

I explained.

"Oh, doesn't everyone do that?" he responded.

I was somewhere between aghast and in awe. It would seem that Dr. Scott had been emptying out his mind for the last fifteen to twenty years and had so eliminated mental chatter that when he slept, he immediately advanced to the furthest reaches of dream yoga, a stage called "sleep yoga," a kind of contentless content of clear light. Here I was scratching at the starting gate, while he was nearing the finish line.

"I hate you, you're so evolved," I said, only half joking.

He stuck a needle in my foot.

Back to that endgame. Tibetan Buddhists call an intermediate state between death and rebirth *bardo*. It's a kind of prolonged dream state, a crucible where how you respond will determine your fate. According to *The Tibetan Book of the Dead*, the deceased experience horrifying visions and encounters with wrathful non-humans, including fifty-eight "blood-drinking deities"[53] whose savage antics rival any *Night of the Living Dead* nightmare. Just to escape, the newly departed may jump on the nearest train to Rebirth City.

That is unless, of course, they realize the hellish visions are illusory thought-forms. "Just like in a lucid dream," writes Holecek, "there may be limited control over the bardo content, but endless options for controlling how we relate to that content . . . Without this lucidity and control, the rest of us reincarnate (re-form) invol-

untarily due to the force of habit, and will continue to do so ad infi-
nitum."[54] Here's where it really pays to be a lucid ninja—you retain
the power of choice over your next form, perhaps getting off the
karmic wheel of death and rebirth altogether.

CLOSING IN ON THE MONSTER

Lucidity can be a valuable tool to transform or fend off nightmares
on the earthly plane as well. Saint-Denys was plagued by reoccur-
ring nightmares of "abominable monsters" who chased him through
an endless series of rooms, uttering "horrible cries" as they grew
closer. But as the fourth time this scenario played out, he realized he
was in a dream. "My desire to rid myself of these illusory terrors
gave me the strength to overcome my fear. I did not flee, but instead,
making a great effort of will, I put my back up against the wall and
determined to look the phantom monsters in the face,"[55] he said.

Though he experienced a "fairly violent emotional shock at first,"
he stared down his principal assailant. "He bore some resemblance
to one of those bristling and grimacing demons which are sculp-
tured on cathedral porches," Saint-Denys continued. "I saw the fantastic monster halt a few paces from me, hissing and leaping about.
Once I had mastered my fear his actions merely appeared burlesque.
I noticed the claws on one of his hands . . . precisely delineated. The
monster's features were all . . . realistic: hair and eyebrows, what
looked like a wound on his shoulder, and many other details. In fact,
I would class this as one of the clearest images I had had in dreams . . .
The result of concentrating my attention on this figure was that all
his acolytes vanished, as if by magic. Soon the leading monster
began to slow down, lose precision, and take on a downy appearance.
He finally changed into a sort of floating hide, which resembled

the faded costumes used as street-signs by fancy-dress shops at carnival time."

Just because you're lucid doesn't mean that primitive or violent scenes automatically dissipate. Citing Carl Jung's adage, "the brighter the sun, the darker the shadow," Kelzer argues that the darker or hidden aspects of our psyche are part of our humanity and natural fodder for what's explored in lucid states. He cites a lucid dream of his friend, a Presbyterian minister named George.[56]

In the dream, George and a companion enter an auditorium to see a play, but a man jumps out of his seat and aggressively stands in their way. "I say to myself," George recounts, "'This is a lucid dream and no harm can come from this, so I'm going to kick this guy in the nuts.' With that I kick him . . . and he folds up with great, shrieking convulsions." While in waking life he would never behave this way, knowing that he was in dream offered him a liberating outlet for his aggressive impulses.

When it comes to lucid nightmares, there is some disagreement in the field whether it's best to fight off or vanquish attackers by physical means or engage them in conversation to find out what's behind their animosity. "The assumption that moving towards reconciliation in lucid nightmares—as opposed to killing and fighting—is always for the best has a humanistic and ethnocentric bias. . . . Sometimes we still need to fight," comments Ryan Hurd.[57]

Tholey occasionally instructed his patients to go *mano a mano* with dream attackers, but eventually he de-emphasized that approach in favor of detente, as this better integrates psychological conflicts and avoids driving hostile dream characters into further isolation within the self.

One of Tholey's clients, a female student, followed this advice within one of her recurring lucid dreams. She stood her ground as menacing beings in long robes approached. "As she looked at the first figure to come close—a gigantic man with a cold, blue face and glowing eyes—she . . . asked him, 'What are you doing here? What do you want from me?' The man looked at her sadly and helplessly as he said, 'Why, you called us. You need us for your anxiety.' At this, the man shrank to normal size. His face turned flesh colored and his eyes ceased to glow."[58]

Some psychotherapists suggest that using lucidity to alter nightmarish scenarios is only an intermediate solution or a form of sugarcoating a deeper issue. Lucid dreams, cautions Dr. Erik Craig, can become "psychic objects for self-gratification or even self-congratulation" and a "narcissistic flight from one's fuller, though perhaps less appealing, possibilities."[59]

In the following account, collected by Ryan Hurd from a resident of the Sinai Peninsula, the dreamer doesn't attempt to rejigger his lucid nightmare and emerges in the end with a shamanic badge of transformation:

Suddenly it opened into a black void. Like a 9-foot black hole, vaguely the shape of a figure. . . . I thought, I am dreaming. This can't be true. The black-hole blackness sort of oozed into the room. I was beyond terror. . . . The blackness started moulding itself into a recognizable shape—don't ask me how long it took. The blackness became a 9-foot Japanese devil or . . . Samurai. Viciously grinning "You are NOT dreaming"—he said—"You thought you could *integrate* me." He then stretched out his enormous black hand—grabbed me—and in one sweeping movement—stuffed me into his blood-red mouth—and swallowed me.

Then I fell into unconsciousness for a moment—now in a Vortex pulling me down and down into an abyss of no dimensions. And all of a sudden my black Samurai-devil spat me out into his hand. Somehow I had crystallized into a red ruby.... So there I was. In his big hand. Looking at him (as a red ruby)—and him looking at me. In that moment—SEEING each other ... something happened. We looked at each other, became aware of each other—and then, there was LOVE. I KNOW what the mystics talk about—can't talk about. There is believing—and KNOWING.[60]

FALSE AWAKENINGS

When a lucid dreamer wakes up, they may reach for their journal to jot down their latest adventure, only to discover that someone has already filled in the pages! Oops, you are still asleep, my friend. Welcome to the eerie world of false awakenings, where all seems normal until it's not, in a dream of waking up from a dream.

It's "a very common pleasantry of this demon pack ... to let you awaken apparently," van Eeden wrote of his obstinate cycle of "demon" dreams in *The Bride of Dreams*, a novel that incorporated his experiences.[61] "You imagine it is morning, open your eyes, look around and recognize your bedroom. When you want to rise however, you see all at once that there is something strange, something weird and spectral about the room—a chair moves by itself, and an empty garment stalks about ... and all at once you realize that you are not yet awake, that you ... have landed in the world of spectres."

For Waggoner, false awakenings are the biggest pitfall for lucid dreamers. One summer morning he woke from a pleasant lucid dream, only to notice that his nightstand had changed. No problem—

just a false awakening. But when a series of six more false awakenings cascaded like an infinity loop, he was thoroughly rattled.
"Where was my world?" he asked. "It felt as if I was bursting through
probable worlds as layers kept giving way! At the final apparent
awakening, my mind swirled . . . grasping for an *actual actuality*! . . .
After seven, I told myself that whatever reality I might encounter in
the hallway, I would accept—that's how shaken I was—any reality
was fine, as long as it stayed put."[62]

The experience took a toll on Waggoner and for the next two
years he no longer sought out lucid dreams. "Maybe like some
inner Icarus of the dream world," he wrote, "I had ventured too close
to the enormity of the unconscious, only to realize my humanness
and fall back."

When the line
between dreaming
and waking
becomes blurred.
"The Splintered
Man," photograph
by Lonehood, 2019.

SPLITTING WITH REALITY

Alcohol, heroin . . . and lucid dreams? There have been cases where people have become so entranced with lucidity that they lose touch with waking reality. "I would lay in bed, miss work, and wrap myself in a catatonic state in which to spin dreams, dreams, dreams. I would sleep in public places to use various stimuli for my lucid dreams," Mark Barroso wrote to the *Lucidity Letter*.[63] "I finally 'O.D.'d' on lucid dreaming when I stayed in bed for 4 or 5 days, only rising to drink and use the bathroom. I was a hermit with no other ambition."

Certainly, the most notorious case of an unhinged person associated with lucid dreams is that of Jared Lee Loughner, who in a 2011 shooting spree in Tucson killed six people and injured thirteen, including former U.S. Representative Gabby Giffords. Loughner's friend Bryce Tierney told *Mother Jones* that Loughner had been obsessed with lucid dreaming and "more interested in this world than our reality." By early 2010, dreaming had become Loughner's "waking life, his reality," said Tierney. He told friends, "I'm so into it because I can create things and fly. I'm everything I'm not in this world."[64]

Loughner's philosophy professor Kent Slinker noted that he seemed checked-out when he was in class. Loughner was always looking away, but not out the window, "like someone watching a scene play out in his mind."[65] In 2012, Gawker obtained a cache of Loughner's emails and discovered that he'd written to lucid dreaming expert Ryan Hurd back in 2009 with an innocuous question about melatonin. Gawker's A. J. Daulerio reached out to Hurd for a response.

"His [Loughner's] request was so routine, polite and sensible—never would have noticed this correspondence without your call," Hurd wrote back. "This was some 18 months before the shooting, I guess, so it makes sense that I never would have noticed. As a dream researcher and educator, you just hope your work helps people. I teach lucid dreaming from a holistic perspective and take pains to make sure people understand that an important prerequisite to lucid dreaming is having a safe container—a social network, a stable home life, good friends to talk to—because lucid dreaming can be intense and sometimes bring up fears and challenges."

"Lucid dreaming," Hurd continued, "is not a cause of mental illness. . . . We know that lucid dreaming can be caused by stress (over-vigilance), and we also know that those suffering from trauma can have lucid nightmares. But even though lucid dreaming isn't a slippery slope to mental illness . . . that doesn't mean that those suffering with mental illness can't have lucid dreams. That's the logical fallacy that keeps getting re-inserted in the media."[66] Initially diagnosed with schizophrenia, Loughner was sent to a federal psychiatric facility, but in 2012 he was cleared for trial and pleaded guilty to nineteen charges. Because of the plea, he was spared the death penalty and is currently serving seven consecutive life terms without the possibility of parole.[67]

In the 1970s, Bruce Marcot of Portland, Oregon, conducted a successful series of experiments with conscious dreaming. Perhaps too successful. "I was able to become acutely aware of my body sleeping in bed," he detailed.[68] "I was asleep, dreaming, but conscious that I was dreaming, and conscious of my actual body in bed, which I could willfully move about. I abandoned the experiments because I began to become confused as to when I was normally asleep, asleep in this lucid dream state, or awake. At one point, I was able to lay in bed, asleep in a lucid dream, with my eyes open and with full consciousness of moving my arms, legs, and face. It was only a step from there to sleepwalking in an aware, lucid dream state. What would distinguish these various states of mind if I was conscious, aware, and able to move? The various realities were beginning to eclipse one another."

Another advanced lucid dreamer, Vincent MacTiernan, took to solving math problems in the lucid state, but the ensuing expansion of consciousness proved too much to handle (not unlike the nonlucid nightmare described in Chapter 5):

I began to feel great pressure in my eyes. It felt like the feeling you get when you spin around many times and get that slight headache.... The funny thing about the whole thing was, and the most unusual, was that with each correct answer, I felt my mind expand.

What happened next scared me more than anything I ever experienced in my life. I found my consciousness so expanded that for a moment I could not tell if this was just a dream or reality. The feeling was overwhelming. I became very frightened. Everything around me had become too clear to be just a dream, and it felt as if my physical body, and mind, was converging together with my dream body. It was very frightening. Something in the back of my mind told me that if I didn't stop with the math problems and awaken soon, I will not be able to awake at all and die.... I ... walked away from the desk.

But walking this time was different from any I had experienced in a dream. This time I seemed to feel the weight of each foot as it hit the ground. Actual weight. It was like I was there; my physical body. I began to tremble, what was happening was too much for me to comprehend, I just wanted to wake up. When I tried, I found out that I could not. This scared me very badly. . . . Out of desperation I tried something else; I tried to focus my mind on my physical body. . . . It worked. For an instant I saw my face, in bed, overlap my vision like a double exposure. I then felt my dream body (or more accurate my mind) being sucked up into a vacuum and into a tunnel. The feeling was most unusual; I had never felt it before. . . . I then felt I was jerked into my physical body. When I awoke I had that pressure in my eyes still and it lasted most of the day.[69]

TOUCHED BY AN ALIEN

Ed Kellogg postulates that "alien" abductions may take place in the out-of-body state, as well as in a kind of mutually shared lucid dream. In one episode, in which he realizes he's in a dream, Kellogg finds himself pulled upward into a cloud-like space, where stiff hands guide him into a laboratory. There, a stern-appearing female scientist and two assistants try to rush him into a procedure— "etheric surgery" on his brain. When he inquires about what effects the operation will have upon him, the scientist seems irked that she has to get his permission. After she proposes an alternative option, he agrees, thinking it might offer a beneficial mental enhancement. Kellogg continues:

> She immediately straps an apparatus to my head with two cylinders on a sort of headband, oriented into the temporal lobes. She turns it on. The cylinders light up . . . the apparatus buzzes and puts painful pressure inside my head—I question

whether I should go through with the procedure. I begin to lose my sight and my patience, and realize what alien abductees might go through—and with no guaranteed, or even indicated, positive results. I take/tear the headband off. I hear the "woman scientist's" voice telling me I've spoiled the procedure by not going through to the end—now I'll have to do it over again. I refuse to do so, ask about the effects—a cold silence ensues, fragments of expression on the woman's face. I realize this does not seem a known therapeutic procedure at all—just an experiment to see what would happen. They do not care what happens to me at all![70]

Even though the dream lacked UFOs and alien-looking creatures, Kellogg categorized it in that vein as it seemed to be taking place in outer space, the scientist projected an intensely cold and inhuman quality, and she had unusually strong hands that felt like wood. Most unnerving was the sense that to the experimenters the physical body was a trivial commodity on the order of "disposable paper shoes."

And then there are the eerie descriptions of "inorganic beings" from anthropologist and author Carlos Castaneda, whose extensive conscious dreaming experiences are chronicled in one of his last books, *The Art of Dreaming*. While there has been much debate as to whether Castaneda's sources existed (i.e., the Yaqui shaman Don Juan), his concept of energy beings without a body that inhabit a world only accessed via a "dream gate" is captivating to consider:

I settled down to observe the details of my dream. What I was viewing looked very much like a gigantic sponge. It was porous and cavernous. I could not feel its texture, but it looked rough and fibrous. . . . As I looked at it fixedly, I had the complete impression of something real but stationary; it was planted somewhere and it had such a powerful attraction that I was incapable of deviating my dreaming attention to examine anything else. . . . Some strange force, which I had never before encountered in my dreaming, had me riveted down.

Then I clearly felt that the mass released my dreaming attention; all my awareness focused on the scout that had taken me there. It looked like a firefly in the darkness, hovering over me, by my side. In its realm, it was a blob of sheer energy . . . It seemed to be conscious of me. Suddenly, it lurched onto me and tugged me. . . . I did not feel its touch, yet I knew it was touching me. That sensation was startling and new; it was as if a part of me that was not there had been electrified by that touch.[71]

The danger of visiting the intoxicating realm of the inorganic beings, Castaneda learns, is that if you agree to stay, you can never leave.

Afterword

Perhaps one of the great questions of life is whether we decide to plumb the depths of the unknown—the worlds beyond worlds within us—or stay in the confines of our mental comfort zone.

Lucid dreaming, hypnagogia, and even sleep paralysis and sleep deprivation offer fascinating glimpses of those uncharted territories—fusions of the conscious and unconscious, hybrids of dreaming and waking that reward and haunt us with a Pandora's box of surprises, joys, and terrors.

Whether some of the characters, entities, and "aliens" we encounter along the way are merely the imaginings of our dream machine or sentient independent forms, we may never know with absolute certainty. Teachers and tricksters, demons and gods, they simultaneously reflect ourselves and something "other."

As secrets of the unconscious spill into our waking lives, and lucidity holds sway in the dream state, the swinging pendulum of the mind may arrive at an unexpected equilibrium. But if we say good night to the brain's long-running cat-and-mouse game, just who will we be in the morning?

Acknowledgments

First off, I'd like to thank Mitch Horowitz, who back in his editor days gave me a shot and developed the initial book concept. To my late great friend Jeffrey Betcher, I'm indebted for his help in the early stages of the book. Miss you! Kevin Reardon, Cristina Favretto, and Heddie Abel also were invaluable in their feedback. And thank you, Tom Austin, for brainstorming the title of "Nightmareland."

I'm grateful to the *Coast to Coast AM* family for their support, including George Noory, Lisa Lyon, and George Knapp, as well as the team at TarcherPerigee at Penguin Random House, starting with my editor, Nina Shield, book designer Lorie Pagnozzi, and cover designer Linet Huamán Velásquez, as well as Hannah Steigmeyer and Lauren Appleton.

A big shout-out to Jason Jam (http://jasonjam.blogspot.com/) for his illustrations.

Additional thanks for their support and/or contributions to Marcus Mars, James Dotson, Margo Abel, Elliott Linwood, Trudy Thekla, Carolyn Budd, Kate Saeed, Ken Green, Stephen Nover, Vickie Lee, Suzanne Richardson, Gary Wertheimer, and Marni Freedman and the San Diego Writers' Circle.

Notes

CHAPTER ONE: SLEEP PARALYSIS

1. Karen Emslie, "Awake in a Nightmare," *The Atlantic*, May 26, 2016, https://www.theatlantic.com/health/archive/2016/05/sleep-paralysis/484490/.
2. Ernest Jones, *On the Nightmare* (London: Lund Humphries, 1951), 29.
3. David J. Hufford, *The Terror That Comes in the Night* (Philadelphia: University of Pennsylvania Press, 1982), 58–59.
4. Ryan Hurd, *Sleep Paralysis* (Los Altos, CA: Hyena Press, 2011), 45–46.
5. Ronald K. Siegel, *Fire in the Brain* (New York: Dutton, 1992), 83–89.
6. Louis Proud, *Dark Intrusions* (San Antonio: Anomalist Books, 2009), 43.
7. Chris French, "The Waking Nightmare of Sleep Paralysis," *The Guardian*, October 5, 2009, https://www.theguardian.com/science/2009/oct/02/sleep-paralysis.
8. Hufford, *Terror*, 52.
9. Ibid., 54–55.
10. Emslie, "Awake."
11. J. A. Cheyne, "The True Night-Mare: SP in Myth and Legend," http://arts.uwaterloo.ca/~acheyne/night_mare.html.
12. Ibid.
13. José F. R. de Sá and Sérgio A. Mota-Rolim, "Sleep Paralysis in Brazilian Folklore and Other Cultures: A Brief Review," *Frontiers in Psychology*, September 7, 2016.
14. Hurd, *Sleep Paralysis*, 43.
15. Shelley Adler, *Sleep Paralysis* (New Brunswick, NJ: Rutgers University Press, 2011), 14; D. L. Ashman, "Night-Mares," http://www.pitt.edu/~dash/nightmare.html#grimm81.
16. Martin Walsh, "The Politicisation of Popobawa: Changing Explanations of a Collective Panic in Zanzibar," *Journal of Humanities* 1 (2009): 23–33.
17. BBC News, "Sex Attacks Blamed on Bat Demon," February 21, 2007, http://news.bbc.co.uk/2/hi/africa/6383833.stm.
18. Natalia Klimczak, "She Brings Bad News: The Scary Slavic Household Spirit Called Kikimora," Ancient Origins, October 7, 2016, https://www.ancient-origins.net/myths-legends/she-brings-bad-news-scary-slavic-household-spirit-called-kikimora-006776.
19. de Sá and Mota-Rolim, "Sleep Paralysis."
20. Christopher Frayling, *Nightmare: Birth of Horror* (London: BBC Books, 1996).
21. Noelle Paulson, "Henry Fuseli, the Nightmare," https://www.khanacademy.org/humanities/becoming-modern/romanticism/romanticism-in-england/a/henry-fuseli-the-nightmare.
22. Adler, *Sleep Paralysis*, 56.

23. Edgar Allan Poe, "The Fall of the House of Usher" (n.p.: Archive Classics, 1960), 22.

24. Adler, *Sleep Paralysis*, 58.

25. Ibid., 64–65.

26. Ibid., 65.

27. Mayo Clinic Staff, "Narcolepsy Symptoms," http://www.mayoclinic.org /diseases-conditions/narcolepsy/basics/symptoms/con-20027429; Thomas C. Neylan, "Sleep Disturbances Associated with Posttraumatic Stress Disorder," *Psychiatric Times*, November 1, 2008.

28. Patricia L. Brooks and John H. Peever, "Identification of the Transmitter and Receptor Mechanisms Responsible for REM Sleep Paralysis," *Journal of Neuroscience* (July 18, 2012): 32.

29. J. A. Cheyne, S. D. Rueffer, and I. R. Newby-Clark, "Hypnagogic and Hypnopompic Hallucinations during Sleep Paralysis: Neurological and Cultural Construction of the Night-Mare," *Consciousness and Cognition*, September 1999, 319–337.

30. Owen Davies, "The Nightmare Experience, Sleep Paralysis, and Witchcraft Accusations," *Folklore* 114, no. 2 (August 2003): 181–203.

31. Robert Macnish, *The Philosophy of Sleep* (Glasgow: McPhun, 1834), 134–135.

32. Adler, *Sleep Paralysis*, 94.

33. Ibid.

34. Craig Marks and Rob Tannenbaum, "An Oral History of *A Nightmare on Elm Street*," Vulture, October 20, 2014, http://www.vulture.com/2014/10 /nightmare-on-elm-street-oral-history.html.

35. Adler, *Sleep Paralysis*, 121.

36. Daphne Chen, "'Voodoo Death' and How the Mind Harms the Body," *Pacific Standard*, October 17, 2014, https://psmag.com/social-justice/voodoo -death-mind-harms-body-sleep-paralysis-92660.

37. Adler, *Sleep Paralysis*, 108.

38. Proud, *Dark Intrusions*, 101.

39. Ibid., 267–268.

40. Barbara Walker, *The Woman's Encyclopedia of Myths and Secrets* (San Francisco: Harper and Row, 1983).

41. Sarah Janes, *A Dream Cure? The Effective Healing Power of Dream Incubation in Ancient Greece*, Ancient Origins, December 15, 2017, https://www.ancient -origins.net/history-ancient-traditions/dream-cure-effective-healing-power -dream-incubation-ancient-greece-009287.

42. Juliette Harrisson, "The Classical Greek Practice of Incubation and Some Near Eastern Predecessors," Academia, 2009, https://www.academia.edu /277934/The_Classical_Greek_Practice_of_Incubation_and_some_Near _Eastern_Predecessors.

43. Jones, *On the Nightmare*, 93–94.

44. Ibid., 89.

45. Walter Stephens, *Demon Lovers* (Chicago: University of Chicago Press, 2002), 64.

46. Jones, *On the Nightmare*, 82–83.

47. Henry Charles Lea, *A History of the Inquisition of the Middle Ages* (New York: Macmillan, 1906), 384; Walker, *Woman's Encyclopedia*.

48. Gareth Medway, *Lure of the Sinister: The Unnatural History of Satanism* (New York: NYU Press, 2001), 306.

49. Cecil L'Estrange Ewen, *Witchcraft and Demonism* (New York: AMS Press, 1933), 187–189.

50. Robin Briggs, *Witches and Neighbors* (New York: Penguin, 1998), 110.

51. Éva Pócs, *Between the Living and the Dead* (Budapest: Central European University Press, 1999).

52. Davies, *Nightmare Experience*.

53. Jones, *On the Nightmare*, 193, 231.

54. Ibid., 117–118.

55. Montague Summers, *The Vampire, His Kith and Kin* (New Hyde Park, NY: University Books, 1960), 228.

56. Barbara Black Koltuv, *The Book of Lilith* (York Beach, ME: Nicolas-Hays, 1986), xi.

57. William Heinrich Roscher, *Ephialtes: A Pathological-Mythological Treatise on the Nightmare in Classical Antiquity (from Pan and the Nightmare)* (New York: Spring Publications, 1972), 82.

58. J.-C. Terrillon and S. Marques Bonham, "Does Recurrent Isolated Sleep Paralysis Involve More Than Cognitive Neurosciences?," *Journal of Scientific Exploration* 15, no. 1 (2001): 97–123.

59. Proud, *Dark Intrusions*, 225–226.

60. Lucy Gillis, "The Girl with Kaleidoscope I's," *Lucid Dreaming Experience* 4, no. 3 (December 2015): 16.

61. Stephen LaBerge, *Exploring the World of Lucid Dreaming* (New York: Ballantine, 1990), 109.

62. Jorge Conesa-Sevilla, *Wrestling with Ghosts* (Bloomington, IN: Xlibris, 2004), 45–46.

63. Roscher, *Ephialtes*, 86.

64. Ibid., 13.

65. Adler, *Sleep Paralysis*, 88–89.

66. Ibid., 89.

67. Hurd, *Sleep Paralysis*, 4–6.

68. Ibid., 48–49.

69. Ryan Hurd, *Guarding the Threshold: The Use of Amulets and Liminal Objects for Sleep Paralysis Night-mares*, Dream Studies Portal, November 30, 2012, http://dreamstudies.org/2012/11/30/guarding-the-threshold-the-use-of-amulets-and-liminal-objects-for-sleep-paralysis-night-mares/.

70. Ben Guarino, "Meet the Biggest Fans of Our Worst Nightmares," Van Winkle's, August 25, 2015, https://web.archive.org/web/20160119020548/http://vanwinkles.com/dreamers-are-inducing-sleep-paralysis-for-a-shot-at-dreamings-purest-experience.

CHAPTER TWO: PARASOMNIAS

1. Shannon S. Sullivan and Christian Guilleminault, "Parasomnias: A Short History," in *The Parasomnias and Other Sleep-Related Movement Disorders* (Cambridge, UK: Cambridge University Press, 2010), 3.

2. Steven W. Lockley and Russell G. Foster, *Sleep: A Very Short Introduction* (Oxford, UK: Oxford University Press, 2012), 71; *Sleep Runners*, directed by Brian Dehler (St. Paul, MN: Slow Wave Films, 2004), DVD.

3. American Academy of Sleep Medicine, "Demand for Treatment of Sleep Illness Is Up as Drowsy Americans Seek Help for Potentially Dangerous Conditions," December 19, 2012, http://www.aasmnet.org/articles.aspx?id=3520.

4. Carlos H. Schenck, *Sleep: The Mysteries, the Problems, and the Solutions* (New York: Avery, 2007), 32.

5. Ibid., 2.

6. David K. Randall, *Dreamland* (New York: Norton, 2012), 171–172.

7. Erica Seigneur, "Brains That Go Bump in the Night: Stanford Biologist Talks About Parasomnias," *Scope*—Stanford Medicine, October 30, 2015, http://scopeblog.stanford.edu/2015/10/30/brains-that-go-bump-in-the-night-stanford-biologist-talks-about-parasomnias/.

8. Olinka Koster and Tahira Yaqoob, "Sleepwalker, Age 15, Found Curled Up on Crane," *Daily Mail*, July 6, 2005, http://www.dailymail.co.uk/news/article-354802/Sleepwalker-age-15-curled-crane.html.

9. Ibid.

10. Schenck, *Sleep*, 100.

11. Antonio Zadra and Jacques Montplaisir, "Sleepwalking," in *The Parasomnias and Other Sleep-Related Movement Disorders* (Cambridge, UK: Cambridge University Press, 2010), 109.

12. Randall, *Dreamland*, 158.

13. Leslie Watkins, *The Sleepwalk Killers* (n.p.: Graham Watkins, 2016), 39–40; Brian Knowlton and *International Herald Tribune*, "American Topics," *New York Times*, November 28, 1998, http://www.nytimes.com/1998/11/28/news/american-topics.html.

14. Schenck, *Sleep*, 106.

15. Ibid., 127.

16. Zadra and Montplaisir, "Sleepwalking," 112.

17. Rosalind D. Cartwright, *The Twenty-Four Hour Mind* (Oxford, UK: Oxford University Press, 2010), 28.

18. Quoted in Dr. Stephen Juan, "What Are Zombie Behaviours?," *The Register*, August 11, 2006, https://www.theregister.co.uk/2006/08/11/the_odd_body_zombie_behaviours.

19. Schenck, *Sleep*, 108.

20. Ibid., 101.

21. Ibid., 108.

22. Jeff Stryker, "Sleepstabbing," *Salon*, July 8, 1999, https://www.salon.com/1999/07/08/sleepwalking/.

23. Schenck, *Sleep*, 113–117.

24. Ibid.
25. *Sleep Runners.*
26. Stephanie Steinberg, "Why Do People Talk in Their Sleep?," *U.S. News & World Report*, March 4, 2015, http://health.usnews.com/health-news/health -wellness/articles/2015/03/04/why-do-people-talk-in-their-sleep.
27. *Sleep Talkin' Man*, July 2010, http://sleeptalkinman.blogspot.com /2010/07/.
28. Steinberg, "Why Do People Talk."
29. David Robson, "The Dark Tales of the World's Most Epic Sleep-Talker," BBC Future, February 22, 2016, http://www.bbc.com/future/story/20160219 -the-dark-tales-of-the-worlds-most-epic-sleep-talker; Natalie Wolchover, "Why Do People Talk in Their Sleep?," Live Science, March 26, 2012, https://www .livescience.com/33794-people-talk-sleep.html.
30. Wolchover, "Why Do People Talk."
31. Robson, "Dark Tales."
32. Schenck, *Sleep*, 235–236.
33. Ibid., 231.
34. David Peeters and Roel M. Willems, "What Is the Difference between Sleep -Talking and Talking While Awake?," Max Planck Institute for Psycholinguistics, http://www.mpi.nl/q-a/questions-and-answers/what2019s-the-difference -between-sleep-talking-and-talking-while-being-awake.
35. Dan Wilkinson, "This Guy Turned Surreal Sleep Talking into a Cult Album," Noisey (Vice), February 11, 2015, https://noisey.vice.com/en_us /article/6e4d5w/this-guy-turned-surreal-sleep-talking-into-a-cult-album.
36. Robson, "Dark Tales."
37. Ibid.
38. Bill Hayes, *Sleep Demons: An Insomniac's Memoir* (New York: Pocket Books, 2001), 137.
39. Robson, "Dark Tales."
40. Ibid.
41. "The Science and Poetry behind a Semi-Famous Sleep Talker," *All Things Considered*, NPR, March 18, 2014, http://www.npr.org/templates /transcript/transcript.php?storyId=291172106.
42. Hayes, *Sleep Demons*, 136.
43. Ibid.
44. Robson, "Dark Tales."
45. "Catathrenia—Research & Treatments," American Sleep Association, https:// www.sleepassociation.org/patients-general-public/catathrenia/.
46. Schenck, *Sleep*, 179.
47. Sandra G. Boodman, "Hungry in the Dark," *Washington Post*, September 7, 2004, http://www.washingtonpost.com/wp-dyn/articles/A1178-2004Sep6.html.
48. Schenck, *Sleep*, 183.
49. John W. Winkelman, "Sleep-Related Eating Disorder," in *The Parasomnias and Other Sleep-Related Movement Disorders* (Cambridge, UK: Cambridge University Press, 2010), 203.
50. Boodman, "Hungry in the Dark."

51. Schenck, *Sleep*, 184, 190.

52. "Woman Eats 2,500 Calories a Night While Asleep," *The Telegraph*, April 24, 2013, http://www.telegraph.co.uk/news/newstopics/howaboutthat /10014769/Woman-eats-2500-calories-a-night-while-asleep.html.

53. Boodman, "Hungry in the Dark."

54. Chip Brown, "The Man Who Mistook His Wife for a Deer," *New York Times Magazine*, February 2, 2003, http://www.nytimes.com/2003/02/02 /magazine/the-man-who-mistook-his-wife-for-a-deer.html.

55. Ibid.

56. Winkelman, "Sleep-Related Eating Disorder," 205.

57. Randi Hutter Epstein, "Raiding the Refrigerator, but Still Asleep," *New York Times*, April 7, 2010, http://www.nytimes.com/2010/04/07/health /07eating.html.

58. Quoted in Boodman, "Hungry in the Dark."

59. Winkelman, "Sleep-Related Eating Disorder," 206–207.

60. Quoted in Chris Perez, "Confessions of a Sleep Eater," *New York Post*, September 22, 2014, http://nypost.com/2014/09/22/confessions-of-a-sleep -eater-2/.

61. Boodman, "Hungry in the Dark."

62. Schenck, *Sleep*, 193

63. Brown, "Man Who Mistook His Wife."

64. Schenck, *Sleep*, 201.

65. Lockley and Foster, *Sleep*, 86.

66. Schenck, *Sleep*, 198–199.

67. Ibid., 206.

68. Ibid., 208.

69. Quoted in Brown, "Man Who Mistook His Wife."

70. Tanya Lewis, "Acting Out Dreams Is Often Early Sign of Parkinson's Disease," Live Science, April 13, 2015, https://www.livescience.com/50468-dream -disorder-parkinsons.html.

71. Schenck, *Sleep*, 212–213.

72. Lewis, "Acting Out Dreams."

73. Schenck, *Sleep*, 215.

74. David Saul Rosenfeld and Antoine Jean Elhajjar, "Sleepsex: A Variant of Sleepwalking," *Archives of Sexual Behavior* 27, no. 3 (June 1998): 269–278.

75. Stephen Klinck, "I Have Sexsomnia—And Can't Be Cured," Motherboard, September 15, 2014, https://motherboard.vice.com/en_us /article/gvyjvw/i-have-sexsomniaand-cant-be-cured.

76. Lockley and Foster, *Sleep*, 10.

77. Nikola N. Trajanovic and Colin M. Shapiro, "Sexsomnias," in *The Parasomnias and Other Sleep-Related Movement Disorders* (New York: Cambridge University Press, 2010), 70.

78. John Cline, "Sexsomnia," *Psychology Today*, February 12, 2009, https://www .psychologytoday.com/blog/sleepless-in-america/200902/sexsomnia.

79. Michael Mangan, *Sleepsex: Uncovered* (Bloomington, IN: Xlibris, 2001), 89.

80. Klinck, "I Have Sexsomnia."

81. Mangan, *Sleepsex*, 91–92.

82. Trajanovic and Shapiro, "Sexsomnias," 72.

83. Mangan, *Sleepsex*, 83–84.

84. Trajanovic and Shapiro, "Sexsomnias," 72.

85. Quoted in Klinck, "I Have Sexsomnia."

86. Mangan, *Sleepsex*, 77–78.

87. Schenck, *Sleep*, 141.

88. Klinck, "I Have Sexsomnia."

89. Quoted in Mick Brown, "Stevie Nicks: A Survivor's Story," *The Telegraph*, September 8, 2007, http://www.telegraph.co.uk/culture/3667803/Stevie-Nicks-a-survivors-story.html.

90. Schenck, *Sleep*, 110–111.

91. Brown, "Stevie Nicks."

92. Schenck, *Sleep*, 222.

93. Ibid., 227.

94. Ibid., 224.

95. Christina J. Calamaro and Thornton B. A. Mason, "Sleep-Related Dissociative Disorder," in *The Parasomnias and Other Sleep-Related Movement Disorders* (New York: Cambridge University Press, 2010), 165–166.

96. Debbie Foulkes, "Dr. William Minor (1834–1920) Insane Doctor Who Contributed to the Oxford English Dictionary," Forgotten Newsmakers, November 8, 2010, https://forgottennewsmakers.com/2010/11/08/dr-william-minor-1834-1920-insane-doctor-who-contributed-to-the-oxford-english-dictionary.

97. Tijana Radeska, "The Sad Life of William Chester Minor," Vintage News, September 18, 2016, https://m.thevintagenews.com/2016/09/18/sad-life-william-chester-minor-one-largest-contributors-oxford-english-dictionary-held-lunatic-asylum-murder-time.

98. Simon Winchester, *The Professor and the Madman: A Tale of Murder, Insanity and the Making of the Oxford English Dictionary* (New York: HarperPerennial), 1999.

99. "Betty," "Confessions of a Fed-Up Flight Attendant: Attack of the Ambien Zombies," Yahoo Travel, April 26, 2014, https://www.yahoo.com/style/confessions-of-a-fed-up-flight-attendant-attack-of-the-83629894522.html.

100. Theresa Fisher, "How, Exactly, Does Ambien Work?," Van Winkle's, September 6, 2016, https://web.archive.org/web/20180703132611/http://vanwinkles.com/how-does-ambien-make-you-fall-asleep.

101. Christopher Daley, Dale E. McNiel, and Renée L. Binder, "'I Did What?' Zolpidem and the Courts," *Journal of the American Academy of Psychiatry and the Law* 39, no. 4 (2011): 535–542.

102. Oryx, "ITT: Crazy Behavior on Ambien Stories," Reddit, February 24, 2011, https://www.reddit.com/r/reddit.com/comments/frqz8/itt_crazy_behavior_on_ambien_stories/.

103. Jamal Stone, "Insane Stories of People on Ambien That'll Brighten Your Day," Milk.xyz, February 1, 2016, https://milk.xyz/articles/the-ambien-walrus-will-steal-your-memories/.

104. Little_bus, "TIFU by Taking Ambien and Having Sex with My New Boyfriend," Reddit, January 24, 2016, https://www.reddit.com/r/tifu/comments/42hwbt/tifu_by_taking_ambien_and_having_sex_with_my_new/.

105. Theresa Fisher, "What the 'Ambien Walrus' Really Is, According to the Person Who Made It Up," Van Winkle's, April 7, 2017, https://web.archive.org/web/20180603103813/http://vanwinkles.com/what-is-the-ambien-walrus.

106. Siobhan C., "What Is the Ambien Walrus?," Quora, March 25, 2014, https://www.quora.com/What-is-the-Ambien-Walrus.

107. Laurie Sandell, "Diary of a Sleeping Pill Junkie," Glamour, March 2, 2008, https://www.glamour.com/story/sleeping-pill-junkie.

108. Kai Falkenberg, "While You Were Sleeping," Marie Claire, September 27, 2012, http://www.marieclaire.com/culture/news/a7302/while-you-were-sleeping/.

109. Ibid.; Allison McCabe, "The Disturbing Effect of Ambien, the No. 1 Prescription Sleep Aid," Huffington Post, January 15, 2014, http://www.huffingtonpost.com/2014/01/15/ambien-side-effect-sleepwalking-sleep-aid_n_4589743.html.

110. Daley, McNiel, and Binder, "'I Did What?'"

111. Falkenberg, "While You Were Sleeping."

112. Genevra Pittman, "Sleep Aids Tied to Hip Fractures in the Elderly," Reuters, March 6, 2013, http://www.reuters.com/article/us-sleep-aids/sleep-aids-tied-to-hip-fractures-in-the-elderly-idUSBRE9251CY20130306.

CHAPTER THREE: SLEEPWALK MURDERS

1. Laura Smith-Spark, "How Sleepwalking Can Lead to Killing," BBC News, March 18, 2005, http://news.bbc.co.uk/2/hi/uk_news/4362081.stm.

2. Bridget B. Striker, "The Kiger Murders of 1943," Boone County Public Library, https://www.bcpl.org/cbc/doku.php/the_kiger_murders_of_1943.

3. Leslie Watkins, The Sleepwalk Killers (Graham Watkins: 2016), 2–5.

4. Bernie Spencer, "The Murder of Karl Kiger," Northern Kentucky Views, http://www.nkyviews.com/boone/text/kiger.html.

5. Quoted in Robert Schrage, Carl Kiger: The Man beyond the Murder (Covington, KY: Merlot Group, 2012).

6. Ibid.

7. Karen Abbott, "The Case of the Sleepwalking Killer," Smithsonian Magazine, April 30, 2012, https://www.smithsonianmag.com/history/the-case-of-the-sleepwalking-killer-77584095.

8. Meir H. Kryger, Thomas Roth, and William C. Dement, Principles and Practice of Sleep Medicine (Philadelphia: Elsevier, 2017), 654.

9. Abbott, "Case of the Sleepwalking Killer."

10. Berit Brogaard and Kristian Marlow, "Sleep Driving and Sleep Killing," Psychology Today, December 13, 2012, https://www.psychologytoday.com/blog/the-superhuman-mind/201212/sleep-driving-and-sleep-killing.

11. Abbott, "Case of the Sleepwalking Killer."

12. Henry Cockton, Sylvester Sound, the Somnambulist (London: Clark, 1844), 2.

13. "Chief Inspector Ledru, the Policeman Who Caught . . . Himself," *Look and Learn*, no. 897 (March 31, 1979), http://www.lookandlearn.com/blog/15523/chief-inspector-ledru-the-policeman-who-caught-himself/.

14. Ibid.

15. Watkins, *Sleepwalk Killers*, 18.

16. Matthew J. Wolf-Meyer, *The Slumbering Masses* (Minneapolis: University of Minnesota Press, 2012), 222.

17. Frederick Oughton, *The Two Lives of Robert Ledru—An Interpretative Biography of a Man Possessed* (London: Muller, 1963).

18. Carlos H. Schenck, "The Curious Case of Kenneth Parks," World Science Festival panel discussion, *The Mind after Midnight: Where Do You Go When You Go to Sleep?*, March 8, 2015, https://www.youtube.com/watch?v=AuWAkREjl6U.

19. David K. Randall, *Dreamland* (New York: Norton, 2012), 155.

20. Brogaard and Marlow, "Sleep Driving."

21. Schenck, "Curious Case."

22. Ibid.

23. Zachary Crockett, "What Happens If You Commit a Murder While Sleepwalking?," Priceonomics, August 7, 2014, https://priceonomics.com/what-happens-if-you-commit-a-murder-while.

24. Ibid.

25. Randall, *Dreamland*, 160.

26. Ibid., 163–164.

27. Rosalind D. Cartwright, *The Twenty-Four-Hour Mind* (Oxford, UK: Oxford University Press, 2010), 84.

28. Brogaard and Marlow, "Sleep Driving."

29. Randall, *Dreamland*, 165.

30. *American Justice*, "It's Not My Fault: Strange Defenses," season 7, episode 2, A&E, October 30, 1999.

31. *Forensic Files*, "Walking Terror," season 9, episode 30, truTV, March 2, 2005.

32. Paul Rubin, "Wake-Up Call," *Phoenix New Times*, July 1, 1999, http://www.phoenixnewtimes.com/news/wake-up-call-6421198.

33. Cartwright, *Twenty-Four-Hour Mind*, 78.

34. Paul Rubin, "A Killer Sleep Disorder," *Phoenix New Times*, November 19, 1998, http://www.phoenixnewtimes.com/news/a-killer-sleep-disorder-6432989.

35. *Forensic Files*, "Walking Terror."

36. Cartwright, *Twenty-Four-Hour Mind*, 81.

37. Quoted in Paul Rubin, "Wake-Up Call."

38. *Forensic Files*, "Walking Terror."

39. Ibid.

40. Cartwright, *Twenty-Four-Hour Mind*, 84–85.

41. Philip Jaekl, "Sleepwalking Is the Result of a Survival Mechanism Gone Awry," Aeon, March 3, 2017, https://aeon.co/ideas/sleepwalking-is-the-result-of-a-survival-mechanism-gone-awry.

42. "Dangerous Dreamers," *Fordham Law News*, September 23, 2013, https://news.law.fordham.edu/blog/2013/09/23/dangerous-dreamers/.

43. Quoted in Randall, *Dreamland*, 180.

CHAPTER FOUR: SLEEP DEPRIVATION

1. This story is a dramatic reconstruction, using information from notes 2, 3, and 4.

2. *Horizon*, "The Secrets of Sleep," season 10, episode 27, BBC Two, June 17, 1974, https://www.youtube.com/watch?v=4MT8ekBGyM4.

3. Esther Inglis-Arkell, "The Sleep Deprivation Stunt That Drove One Man Crazy," io9/Gizmodo, March 24, 2014, https://io9.gizmodo.com/the-sleep-deprivation -publicity-stunt-that-drove-one-ma-1550084876.

4. Thomas Bartlett, "The Stay-Awake Men," *New York Times*, April 22, 2010, https://opinionator.blogs.nytimes.com/2010/04/22/the-stay-awake-men.

5. Nick Ravo, "Peter Tripp, 73, Popular Disc Jockey" (obituary), *New York Times*, February 13, 2000, http://www.nytimes.com/2000/02/13/nyregion /peter-tripp-73-popular-disc-jockey.html.

6. Stanley Coren, "Sleep Deprivation, Psychosis, and Mental Efficiency," *Psychiatric Times*, March 1, 1998, http://www.psychiatrictimes.com/sleep -disorders/sleep-deprivation-psychosis-and-mental-efficiency.

7. Sarah Keating, "The Boy Who Stayed Awake for 11 Days," BBC Future, January 18, 2018, http://www.bbc.com/future/story/20180118-the-boy-who-stayed-awake -for-11-days.

8. Ibid.

9. Coren, "Sleep Deprivation."

10. Bartlett, "Stay-Awake Men."

11. BBC News, "How Man Pushed Sleepless Limits," May 25, 2007, http://news .bbc.co.uk/2/hi/uk_news/england/cornwall/6690485.stm.

12. Tony Wright and Graham Gynn, *Left in the Dark* (Cornwall, UK: Kaleidos Press: 2008), 21.

13. Ibid., 14.

14. Edward Richards, "What's It Like to Hallucinate from Sleep Deprivation?," Vice, June 30, 2015, https://www.vice.com/en_us/article /exqvzw/whats-it-like-to-hallucinate-from-sleep-deprivation.

15. Seth Maxon, "How Sleep Deprivation Decays the Mind and Body," *The Atlantic*, December 30, 2013, https://www.theatlantic.com/health/archive /2013/12/how-sleep-deprivation-decays-the-mind-and-body/282395/.

16. Lee Moran, "Chinese Football Fan, 26, Dies after Going Eleven Nights without Sleep as He Watched Every Single Euro 2012 Match," *Daily Mail*, June 22, 2012, http://www.dailymail.co.uk/news/article-2163057 /Jiang-Xiaoshan-dies-watching-Euro-2012-match-going-11-nights-sleep .html.

17. Maxon, "How Sleep Deprivation Decays."

18. Stanley Finger, *Origins of Neuroscience* (Oxford, UK: Oxford University Press: 2001), 245.

19. Brandon R. Peters, "Not Quite Enough: The Consequences of Sleep Deprivation," Stanford Center for Sleep Sciences and Medicine, July 11, 2013, https://www.huffingtonpost.com/stanford-center-for-sleep-and-medicine /sleep-deprivation_b_3536674.html.

20. Maxon, "How Sleep Deprivation Decays."

21. Sara G. Miller, "The Spooky Effects of Sleep Deprivation," Live Science, October 27, 2015, https://www.livescience.com/52592-spooky-effects-sleep -deprivation.html.

22. Joseph Cannell, "Trucking Story from the Road: The Black Dog," July 18, 2014, https://www.youtube.com/watch?v=vYLoc401fQo&t=3s.

23. Andy Wright, "Devil Dogs: The Mysterious Black Dogs of England," *Modern Farmer*, June 13, 2014, https://modernfarmer.com/2014/06/black-shuck/.

24. Finger, *Origins of Neuroscience*, 245.

25. Greg Emmanuel, *Extreme Encounters* (Philadelphia: Quirk Books, 2002), 103.

26. Jeff Mann, "A Brief History of Sleep Deprivation and Torture," Sleep Junkies, June 25, 2017, https://sleepjunkies.com/features/sleep-deprivation-and-torture -a-brief-history/.

27. Ebenezer Cobham Brewer, *Dictionary of Phrase and Fable* (London: Cassell, 1895), 1280.

28. Aleksandr Solzhenitsyn, *The Gulag Archipelago* (Harper and Row, 1974), 120–125.

29. Megan Lane and Brian Wheeler, "The Real Victims of Sleep Deprivation," *BBC News Online Magazine*, January 8, 2004, http://news.bbc.co.uk/2/hi /3376951.stm.

30. Dina Temple-Raston, "Interrogators Adapted to New Foe in Afghanistan," *Morning Edition*, NPR, June 3, 2009, https://www.npr.org/templates/story/story .php?storyId=104578582.

31. Steven J. Frenda, Lawrence Patihis, Elizabeth F. Loftus, Holly C. Lewis, and Kimberly M. Fenn, "Sleep Deprivation and False Memories," *Psychological Science* 25, no. 9 (September 2014): 1674–1681.

32. Gary Warth, "Kamikaze Pilots, Beats and Hells Angels All Part of Meth Crisis History," *San Diego Union-Tribune*, September 9, 2007, https://www .sandiegouniontribune.com/sdut-kamikaze-pilots-beats-and-hells-angels -all-part-2007sep09-story.html.

33. J. Christian Gillen, "How Long Can Humans Stay Awake," *Scientific American*, March 25, 2002, https://www.scientificamerican.com/article /how-long-can-humans-stay/.

34. William Saletan, "Modafinil and the Arms Race for Soldiers without Fatigue," *Slate*, May 29, 2013, http://www.slate.com/articles/health_and_science /superman/2013/05/sleep_deprivation_in_the_military_modafinil _and_the_arms_race_for_soldiers.html.

35. This story is a dramatic reconstruction, using information from notes 36, 37, 38, and 41.

36. D. T. Max, "Case Study: Fatal Familial Insomnia; Location: Venice, Italy; To Sleep No More," *New York Times Magazine*, May 6, 2001.

37. D. T. Max, "The Story of the Family That Couldn't Sleep," *Talk of the Nation— Science Friday with Ira Flatow*, NPR, November 17, 2006.

38. *My Shocking Story*, "Dying to Sleep," season 2, episode 16, Discovery Channel UK, September 12, 2009, https://www.youtube.com/watch?v =iPdgog3afTI

39. National Institute of Neurological Disorders and Stroke, "Kuru Information Page," https://www.ninds.nih.gov/Disorders/All-Disorders/Kuru-Information-Page.

40. Max, "Story of the Family."

41. David Robson, "The Tragic Fate of the People Who Stop Sleeping," BBC Future, January 19, 2016, http://www.bbc.com/future/story/20160118-the-tragic-fate-of-the-people-who-stop-sleeping.

42. Quoted in Dr. Arif Akhtar, "Dying to Sleep—The Waking Nightmare of Fatal Familial Insomnia," *Medium*, June 6, 2017, https://medium.com/@arifakhtar/dying-to-sleep-the-waking-nightmare-of-fatal-familial-insomnia-874126b43c3a.

43. J. Schenkein and P. Montagna, "Self-Management of Fatal Familial Insomnia. Part 2: Case Report," *Medscape General Medicine* 8, no. 3 (September 14, 2006): 66, https://www.ncbi.nlm.nih.gov/pubmed/17406189.

44. Quoted in Robson, "Tragic Fate."

45. Schenkein and Montagna, "Self-Management," 7.

46. Ibid., 9.

47. Ibid., 18.

48. Ibid.

49. Aimee Swartz, "Insomnia That Kills," *The Atlantic*, February 5, 2015, https://www.theatlantic.com/health/archive/2015/02/insomnia-that-kills/384841/.

50. Rae Ellen Bichell, "'Scientist-Patient' and Her Husband Race to Find a Cure for Her Rare Brain Disease," NPR, June 19, 2017, https://www.npr.org/section/health-shots/2017/06/19/527795512/a-couples-quest-to-stop-a-rare-disease-before-it-takes-one-of-them.

51. Ibid.

52. Antonio Regalado, "One Woman's Race to Defuse the Genetic Time Bomb in Her Genes," *MIT Technology Review*, July 23, 2018, https://www.technologyreview.com/s/611672/one-womans-race-to-defuse-the-genetic-time-bomb-in-her-genes/.

CHAPTER FIVE: THE NIGHTMARE REALM

1. Lafcadio Hearn, "Nightmare Touch," in *Shadowings* (Little, Brown: Boston, 1900), 235–246.

2. Theresa Fisher, "How Our Understanding of Nightmares Has Changed over the Last 3 Centuries," Van Winkle's, March 22, 2016, https://web.archive.org/web/20160327185001/http://vanwinkles.com/what-we-ve-learned-about-bad-dreams-over-time.

3. Robert Louis Stevenson, "A Chapter on Dreams," *Scribner's Magazine*, January 3, 1888.

4. Tore A. Nielson and Antonio Zadra, "Nightmares and Other Common Disturbances," in *Principles and Practice of Sleep Medicine*, 4th ed. (Philadelphia: Saunders, 2005), 927.

5. Michael Schredl, "Nightmare Disorder," in *The Parasomnias and Other Sleep-Related Movement Disorders* (Cambridge, UK: Cambridge University Press: 2010), 154.

6. Ernest Hartmann, *The Nightmare* (New York: Basic Books, 1984), 255–256.

7. Carlos H. Schenck and Mark W. Mahowald, "Parasomnias from a Woman's Health Perspective," in *Sleep Disorders in Women* (Totowa, NJ: Humana Press, 2006), 157.

8. Robert Macnish, *The Philosophy of Sleep* (New York: Appleton, 1834), 46–47.

9. Natalie Angier, "In the Dreamscape of Nightmares: Clues to Why We Dream at All," *New York Times*, October 23, 2007, https://www.nytimes.com/2007/10/23/science/23angi.html.

10. Michelle Carr, "The Upside of Nightmares: How Bad Dreams Are Also Good for You," *New Scientist*, April 27, 2016, https://www.newscientist.com/article/mg23030710-900-the-upside-of-nightmares-how-bad-dreams-are-also-good-for-you/.

11. John E. Mack, *Nightmares and Human Conflict* (Boston: Houghton Mifflin, 1970), 16.

12. J. A. Hadfield, *Dreams and Nightmares* (Baltimore: Penguin, 1954), 187–188.

13. Mack, *Nightmares*, 26.

14. Hadfield, *Dreams and Nightmares*, 178–179.

15. Mack, *Nightmares*, 12–13.

16. Ibid., 208.

17. Hartmann, *Nightmare*, 62.

18. Schredl, "Nightmare Disorder," 153.

19. Hartmann, *Nightmare*, 39, 166–167.

20. Robbie Gonzalez, "What Is the Most Common Nightmare?," io9/Gizmodo, November 8, 2013, https://io9.gizmodo.com/what-is-the-most-common-nightmare-1461032988.

21. Angier, "Dreamscape."

22. Beth Rochford, "The Upside of Nightmares: Why Bad Dreams May Be Our Best Friend," Van Winkle's, July 30, 2015, https://web.archive.org/web/20150926000725/http://vanwinkles.com/our-brutally-honest-best-friend-the-upside-of-nightmares.

23. Angier, "Dreamscape."

24. Hartmann, *Nightmare*, 174.

25. Angier, "Dreamscape."

26. Mack, *Nightmares*, 219.

27. Hartmann, *Nightmare*, 216.

28. Quoted in Seth Simons, "Why Some People Have Recurring Nightmares," Van Winkle's, March 7, 2016, https://web.archive.org/web/20160311154518/http://vanwinkles.com/why-some-people-have-recurring-nightmares.

29. Hartmann, *Nightmare*, 212.

30. Ibid., 191.

31. eboyer, "Weird Nightmares That I've Been Having All My Life," PsychCentral forum, December 10, 2009, https://forums.psychcentral.com/sleep-issues

-dream-interpretation/123596-weird-nightmares-ive-been-having
-all-my-life.html.

32. Victor I. Spoormaker, "A Cognitive Model of Recurrent Nightmares," *International Journal of Dream Research* 1, no. 1 (2008): 18, http://journals .ub.uni-heidelberg.de/index.php/IJoDR/article/viewFile/21/102.

33. Hartmann, *Nightmare*, 257.

34. Ibid.

35. J. Allan Hobson, *Dreaming as Delirium* (Cambridge, MA: MIT Press, 1999), 275.

36. Thomas De Quincey, *Confessions of an English Opium-Eater and Other Writings* (New York: Penguin, 2003), 76.

37. Ibid., 80.

38. Ibid., 82.

39. JustSoSick, "Thread: Geometric Night Terrors @ Fever Dreams," Dream Views forum, December 6, 2008, https://www.dreamviews.com/nightmares-recurring -dreams/29794-geometric-night-terrors-%40-fever-dreams-3.html.

40. Canterbury, "Thread: Geometric Night Terrors @ Fever Dreams," Dream Views forum, December 3, 2009, https://www.dreamviews.com/nightmares -recurring-dreams/29794-geometric-night-terrors-%40-fever-dreams-4.html.

41. Higgs2, "Thread: Geometric Night Terrors @ Fever Dreams," Dream Views forum, April 18, 2010, https://www.dreamviews.com/nightmares-recurring -dreams/29794-geometric-night-terrors-%40-fever-dreams-5.html.

42. Lenz82, "Thread: Geometric Night Terrors @ Fever Dreams," Dream Views forum, March 25, 2011, https://www.dreamviews.com/nightmares -recurring-dreams/29794-geometric-night-terrors-%40-fever-dreams-6.html.

43. Michael Schredl, Olivia Küster, Angelika Spohn, and Anne Victor, "Bizarreness in Fever Dreams: A Questionnaire Study," *International Journal of Dream Research* 9, no. 1 (2016): 86–88.

44. Quoted in Anna Hodgekiss, "Bizarre Dreams? That's Because They Get Weirder the Longer You Sleep For, Scientists Reveal," *Daily Mail*, September 19, 2014, http://www.dailymail.co.uk/health/article-2762316 /Bizarre-dreams-That-s-weirder-longer-sleep-scientists-reveal.html.

45. Quoted in Lex Lonehood, "America's Shaman Battles Brain Cancer," *Art Bell's After Dark* (October 1999), 4–5.

46. Oliver Sacks, *Awakenings* (New York: Vintage Books, 1999), 117–118.

47. Hartmann, *Nightmare*, 182–183.

48. Hobson, *Dreaming*, 94–95.

49. Tore A. Nielson, "Disturbed Dreaming in Medical Conditions," in *Principles and Practice of Sleep Medicine*, 6th ed. (Philadelphia: Elsevier, 2016), 939.

50. Mack, *Nightmares*, 163–164.

51. Elwood Worcester and Samuel McComb, *Body, Mind and Spirit* (New York: Scribner, 1932), 168–169.

52. Robert L. Van de Castle, *Our Dreaming Mind* (New York: Ballantine, 1994), 406–407.

53. Carlos H. Schenck, *Sleep: The Mysteries, the Problems, and the Solutions* (New York: Avery, 2007), 145.

54. Ibid., 153.

55. Rebecca Turner, "Night Terrors," World of Lucid Dreaming, http://www
.world-of-lucid-dreaming.com/night-terrors.html.

56. Schenck, *Sleep*, 153–159.

57. Edwin Kahn, Charles Fisher, and Adele Edwards, "Night Terrors and Anxiety
Dreams," in *The Mind in Sleep: Psychology and Psychophysiology* (New York:
Wiley: 1991), 446.

58. Ibid., 765.

59. Francesca Siclari, Benjamin Baird, Lampros Perogamvros, Giulio Bernardi,
Joshua J. LaRocque, Brady Riedner, Melanie Boly, Bradley R. Postle, and Giulio
Tononi, "The Neural Correlates of Dreaming," *Nature Neuroscience* 20, no. 6
(June 2017): 872.

60. Schenck, *Sleep*, 146–157.

61. Quoted in Jasbinder Garnermann, "Embracing the Shadow," *Network
Magazine*, April 3, 2014, https://networkmagazine.ie/articles/embracing
-shadow.

62. C. J. Jung, *On the Nature of the Psyche* (London: Routledge Classics, 1969), 40.

63. Alex Lukeman, *Nightmares: How to Make Sense of Your Darkest Dreams*
(New York: Evans, 2000), 11, 13.

64. Quoted in Matt Schneiderman, "How to Escape Any Nightmare Using This
One Simple Technique," Van Winkle's, April 14, 2016, https://web.archive.org
/web/20160429154344/http://vanwinkles.com/how-to-vanquish-any-nightmare.

65. Ibid.

66. Sarah Kershaw, "Following a Script to Escape a Nightmare," *New York Times*,
July 26, 2010, https://www.nytimes.com/2010/07/27/health/27night.html.

67. Quoted in ibid.

68. Carina Storrs, "Can Nightmares Be Good for You?," CNN, June 23, 2017,
https://www.cnn.com/2015/10/21/health/nightmares-health-benefits
/index.html.

69. Quoted in Schneiderman, "How to Escape."

70. Shelby F. Harris and Michael J. Thorpy, "Behavioral and Psychiatric
Treatments of Parasomnias," in *The Parasomnias and Other Sleep-Related
Movement Disorders* (Cambridge, UK: Cambridge University Press,
2010), 317.

71. Quoted in Jeremy Hsu, "Video Gamers Can Control Dreams, Study Suggests,"
Live Science, May 25, 2010, https://www.livescience.com/6521
-video-gamers-control-dreams-study-suggests.html.

72. Peter J. Hauri, Michael H. Silber, and Bradley F. Boeve, "The Treatment of
Parasomnias with Hypnosis: A 5-Year Follow-Up Study," *Journal of Clinical Sleep
Medicine* 3, no. 4 (June 15, 2007): 369–373.

73. Schenck, *Sleep*, 108–109.

74. Roc Morin, "Nine People Told Us Their Absolute Worst Nightmares," Vice,
October 23, 2017, https://www.vice.com/en_us/article/59dnv8/conan-obrien-and
-others-share-their-nightmares-from-around-the-world.

CHAPTER SIX: HYPNAGOGIA

1. Andreas Mavromatis, *Hypnagogia* (London: Thyrsos Press, 2010), 3.

2. Ibid., 15.

3. Havelock Ellis, *The World of Dreams* (Boston: Houghton Mifflin, 1911), 31.

4. Daniel L. Schacter, "The Hypnagogic State: A Critical Review of the Literature," *Psychological Bulletin* 83, no. 3 (1976): 461.

5. Edmund Gurney, F. W. H. Myers, and Frank Podmore, *Phantasms of the Living, Vol. 1* (London: Trübner, 1886), 474.

6. Elmer Green and Alyce Green, *Beyond Biofeedback* (New York: Dell, 1977), 131.

7. Peter McKellar, "Between Wakefulness and Sleep: Hypnagogic Fantasy," in *The Potential of Fantasy and Imagination* (New York: Brandon House, 1979), 190–191.

8. Peter McKellar and Lorna Simpson, "Between Wakefulness and Sleep: Hypnagogic Imagery," *British Journal of Psychology* (November 1954): 266.

9. Mavromatis, *Hypnagogia*, 28–29.

10. Kristin Leutwyler, "Tetris Dreams," *Scientific American*, October 16, 2000, https://www.scientificamerican.com/article/tetris-dreams/.

11. Ryan Hurd, "The Mystery of Hypnagogia," Dream Studies Portal, December 10, 2010, http://dreamstudies.org/2010/12/10/hypnagogic-dreams -and-imagery/.

12. Schacter, "The Hypnagogic State," 461.

13. Mavromatis, *Hypnagogia*, 34.

14. Paul Martin, *Counting Sheep: The Science and Pleasure of Sleep and Dreams* (New York: Macmillan, 2004), 93.

15. Peter McKellar, *Mindsplit: The Psychology of Multiple Personality and the Disassociated Self* (London: Dent, 1979), 105.

16. Gary Lachman, "Waking Sleep: The Hypnogogic State," *Fortean Times*, October 2002.

17. F. E. Leaning, "Introductory Study of Hypnagogic Phenomena," *Proceedings of the Society for Psychical Research*, Vol. 35 (Glasgow: Maclehose, 1926).

18. Mavromatis, *Hypnagogia*, 57, 59.

19. Lachman, "Waking Sleep."

20. Iamblichus, *Iamblichus on the Mysteries of the Egyptians, Chaldeans, and Assyrians*, trans. Thomas Taylor (Chiswick, UK: Whittingham, 1821), 115–116.

21. Lachman, "Waking Sleep."

22. Ellis, *World of Dreams*, 30.

23. Wilson Van Dusen, *The Presence of Other Worlds: The Findings of Emmanuel Swedenborg* (New York: Harper and Row, 1974), 35.

24. Ibid., 38.

25. Lachman, "Waking Sleep."

26. P. D. Ouspensky, *A New Model of the Universe*, 2nd ed. (New York: Knopf, 1931), 291.

27. Gary Lachman, *A Secret History of Consciousness* (Great Barrington, MA: Lindisfarne Books, 2003), 79.

28. Rudolf Steiner, "The Dead Are with Us," lecture given in Nüremberg, Germany, February 10, 1918, https://wn.rsarchive.org/Lectures /19180210p01.html.

29. Wilson Van Dusen, *The Natural Depth in Man* (West Chester, PA: Swedenborg Foundation, 1981), 86, 94.

30. Ibid., 93.

31. Mavromatis, *Hypnagogia*, 130, 126.

32. James H. Austin, *Zen and the Brain* (Cambridge, MA: MIT Press, 1998), 91–92.

33. Robert Moss, *Dreamgates: Exploring the Worlds of Soul, Imagination, and Life Beyond Death* (Novato, CA: New World Library, 1998), 27.

34. Oliver Fox, *Neometaphysical Education: Astral Projection* (n.p.: Society of Metaphysicians, n.d.), 46.

35. Robert Monroe, *Journeys Out of the Body* (Garden City, NY: Doubleday, 1971), 207–208.

36. Mavromatis, *Hypnagogia*, 131.

37. Paul Huson, *How to Test and Develop Your ESP* (New York: Stein and Day, 1975), 81–83.

38. Adrian Parker, "Ganzfeld," PSI Encyclopedia, March 7, 2017, https://psi -encyclopedia.spr.ac.uk/articles/ganzfeld.

39. W. E. Butler, *How to Read the Aura, and Practice Psychometry, Telepathy, and Clairvoyance* (New York: Warner Books, 1978), 138–139.

40. Raymond Moody, interview, *Coast to Coast AM*, August 7, 2007, https://www .coasttocoastam.com/show/2007/08/07.

41. Celia Elizabeth Green and Charles McCreery, *Apparitions* (London: Hamilton, 1975), 77.

42. Quoted in ibid., 449–450.

43. Quoted in Gurney, Myers, and Podmore, *Phantasms of the Living*, 390–391.

44. Charles Tart, *Altered States of Consciousness* (New York: Wiley, 1969), 174.

45. D. Scott Rogo, "Astral Projection, a Risky Practice?," *Fate* (May 1973): 74–80.

46. Mavromatis, *Hypnagogia*, 151.

47. Ibid., 293, 138.

48. Robert Moss, "Spend More Time in the Twilight Zone," http://www .mossdreams.com/Design%202009/Workshops%20and%20Training/Tools %20and%20Techniques/twilight%20zone.htm.

49. Maddie Stone, "Could You Charge an iPhone with the Electricity in Your Brain?," Gizmodo, https://gizmodo.com/could-you-charge-an-iphone-with -the-electricity-in-your-1722569935.

50. Richard A. Russo, "Hypnagogic Imagery," in *Encyclopedia of Sleep and Dreams, Vol. 1* (Santa Barbara, CA: Greenwood, 2012), 327–328.

51. Neel V. Patel, "Sleeping On, and Dreaming Up, a Solution," Science Line, June 27, 2014, http://scienceline.org/2014/06/sleeping-on-and-dreaming-up-a -solution/.

52. Lachman, "Waking Sleep."

53. Lachman, *Secret History*, 88.

54. American Academy of Sleep Medicine, "Sleep Starts," August 22, 2013, http://www.sleepeducation.org/news/2013/08/22/sleep-starts.

55. Tom Stafford, "Why Your Body Jerks before You Fall Asleep," BBC Future, May 22, 2012, http://www.bbc.com/future/story/20120522-suffer-from-sleep-shudders.

56. Frederick L. Coolidge and Thomas Wynn, *The Rise of Homo Sapiens: The Evolution of Modern Thinking* (New York: Oxford University Press, 2018), 142.

57. J. M. S. Pearce, "Exploding Head Syndrome," *Lancet* 332, no. 8605 (July 30, 1988): 270–271.

58. J. M. S. Pearce, "Clinical Features of the Exploding Head Syndrome," *Journal of Neurology, Neurosurgery, and Psychiatry* 52, no. 7 (1989): 909.

59. Brian Sharpless, "Exploding Head Syndrome Is Common in College Students," *Journal of Sleep Research*, August 24, 2015, https://www.ncbi.nlm.nih.gov/pubmed/25773787.

60. Sara G. Miller, "Hearing Crashes, Seeing Light: Life with Exploding Head Syndrome," Live Science, April 24, 2017, https://www.livescience.com/58800-exploding-head-syndrome.html; Helen Thomson, "I Have Exploding Head Syndrome," BBC Future, April 10, 2015, http://www.bbc.com/future/story/20150409-i-have-exploding-head-syndrome.

61. Quoted in Thomson, "I Have Exploding Head Syndrome."

62. Francis R. Japp, *Memorial Lectures Delivered Before the Chemical Society, Vol. 1* (London: Gurney and Jackson, 1901), 100.

63. Mavromatis, *Hypnagogia*, 193.

64. Quoted in Charles Panati, *Supersenses: Our Potential for Parasensory Experience* (Garden City, NY: Anchor Books, 1976), 162.

65. Mavromatis, *Hypnagogia*, 203–204.

66. Sirley Marques Bonham, "Consciousness and Hypnagogia," Institute for Neuroscience and Consciousness Studies, May 31, 2010, http://inacs.org/2010/05/31/sirley-marques-bonham-on-experiences-of-consciousness-beyond-hypnagogia/.

67. Patel, "Sleeping On."

68. Ibid.

69. "Salvador Dali Biography," Biography.com, https://www.biography.com/people/salvador-dal-40389.

70. Salvador Dali, *50 Secrets of Magic Craftsmanship* (Mineola, NY: Dover, 1992), 52–54.

71. Patel, "Sleeping On."

72. Robin Scher, "Why the State Between Sleep and Wakefulness Breeds Creativity," Van Winkle's, October 9, 2015, https://web.archive.org/web/20151011175641/http://vanwinkles.com/how-does-hypnagogia-state-between-sleep-and-wake-inspire-artists

73. McKellar, *Mindsplit*, 101.

74. Jeffrey Kluger, "The Spark of Invention," *Time*, November 14, 2013, http://techland.time.com/2013/11/14/the-spark-of-invention/.

75. Daniel Oberhaus, "MIT Researchers Have Developed a 'System for Dream Control,'" Motherboard, April 23, 2018, https://motherboard.vice

.com/en_us/article/ywxjvg/steel-ball-control-dreams-dormio-mit
-hypnagogia.
76. H. S. Porte, "Slow Horizontal Eye Movement at Human Sleep Onset," *Journal of Sleep Research* 13, no. 3 (September 2004): 239–249.
77. Mavromatis, *Hypnagogia*, 275–276.

CHAPTER SEVEN: PSYCHIC ATTACKS

1. Virginia Santore, "The Vengeful Succubus," *Fate* (September 1977): 43–46.
2. Brad Steiger, *Sex and the Supernatural* (New York: Lancer Books, 1968), 168–170.
3. Robert Bruce, *Practical Psychic Self-Defense* (Charlottesville, VA: Hampton Roads, 2002), 5.
4. Ibid., 6–22.
5. Ibid., 27.
6. Ibid., 10–11.
7. Robert Bruce, interview, *Coast to Coast AM*, July 6, 2011, https://www .coasttocoastam.com/show/2011/07/06.
8. James McClenon, "The Sociological Investigation of Haunting Cases," in *Hauntings and Poltergeists: Multidisciplinary Perspectives* (Jefferson, NC: McFarland, 2001), 67–70.
9. Steiger, *Sex and the Supernatural*, 29–30.
10. Rosemary Ellen Guiley, *The Encyclopedia of Ghosts and Spirits*, 2nd ed. (New York: Checkmark Books, 2000), 293.
11. Nandor Fodor, *The Haunted Mind* (New York: Garrett, 1959), 56–57.
12. Ibid., 59.
13. Guiley, *Encyclopedia*, 382.
14. Fodor, *Haunted Mind*, 62–63.
15. Dion Fortune, *Psychic Self-Defense* (York Beach, ME: Weiser, 2011), 67.
16. Ibid., 79–81.
17. Ibid., 221–227.
18. Michelle Belanger, *Psychic Dreamwalking* (San Francisco: Red Wheel/ Weiser, 2006), 25.
19. Ibid., 150.
20. Ibid., 175–180.
21. Father "X," "Reflections on Lucid Dreaming and Out-of-Body Experiences," *Lucidity Letter* 10, no. 1–2 (1991).
22. Bruce, *Practical Psychic Self-Defense*, 96–97.
23. Samuel Hatfield, "Dream Invasion," https://samuelhatfield.com/articles /dream-invasion.html.
24. Lady Warrior Ravynwynn, "Psychic Attack in Dreams?," Unexplained -Mysteries.com forum, November 10, 2005, https://www.unexplained-mysteries .com/forum/topic/54938-psychic-attack-in-dreams/.
25. Jenny Randles, *Mind Monsters: Invaders from Inner Space?* (London: Aquarian Press, 1990), 130–132.
26. Lon Milo DuQuette, "Terrors of the Threshold," *Fate* (October 2004): 48–55.

CHAPTER EIGHT: THE ALIEN IN QUESTION

1. Lex Lonehood, "Close Encounters of the Commercial Kind," Sfweekly .com, Web Extra, October 1998.

2. John Mack, *Abduction: Human Encounters with Aliens* (New York: Scribner, 1994), 98–99.

3. Jennifer Bayot, "Dr. John E. Mack, Psychiatrist, Dies at 74," *New York Times*, September 30, 2004, https://www.nytimes.com/2004/09/30/us /dr-john-e-mack-psychiatrist-dies-at-74.html.

4. Mack, *Abduction*, 404–406.

5. Thomas Eddie Bullard, "Abductions" in *The Encyclopedia of Extraterrestrial Encounters*, edited by Ronald D. Story (New York: New American Library, 2001), 7

6. John Fuller, *The Interrupted Journey* (New York: Dial, 1966), 263.

7. John Keel, *Operation Trojan Horse* (Lilburn, GA: Illuminet Press, 1996), 252.

8. Mack, *Abduction*, 398.

9. Bullard, *"Abductions,"* 8.

10. David Jacobs, *The Threat* (New York: Simon and Schuster, 1998), 45.

11. Karla Turner, *Into the Fringe* (New York: Berkley, 1992), 124.

12. Ibid., 172, 175.

13. Ibid., 166–169.

14. Keith Thompson, *Angels and Aliens* (New York: Fawcett Columbine, 1991), 146.

15. Ibid., 147.

16. Patrick Harpur, "Daimonic Reality," lecture from FortFest 2003, March 20, 2008, https://www.youtube.com/watch?v=AutmgJJcvV4.

17. Jacques Vallée, *Passport to Magonia* (Chicago: Regnery, 1969), 102.

18. Thomas Eddie Bullard, "Fairy Lore and UFO Encounters" in *The Encyclopedia of Extraterrestrial Encounters*, edited by Ronald D. Story (New York: New American Library, 2001), 186-187

19. Jacques Vallée, *UFOs: The Psychic Solution* (London: Granada, 1977), 38.

20. Bill Chalker, "Peter Khoury and the 'Hair of the Alien'—20 Years On," *The Oz Files*, July 29, 2012, https://theozfiles.blogspot.com/2012/07 /peter-khoury-and-hair-of-alien-20-years.html.

21. Bill Chalker, *Hair of the Alien* (New York: Paraview Pocket Books, 2005), 25–33.

22. Michael Shermer, "Abducted!," *Scientific American*, February 2005.

23. Susan Blackmore, "Abduction by Aliens or Sleep Paralysis?," *Skeptical Inquirer* 22, no. 3 (May–June 1998), https://www.csicop.org/si/show /abduction_by_aliens_or_sleep_paralysis.

24. Ibid.

25. Colm Kelleher and George Knapp, *Hunt for the Skinwalker* (New York: Paraview Pocket Books, 2005), 253.

26. Lex Lonehood, "America's Shaman Battles Brain Cancer," *Art Bell's After Dark* (October 1999): 4–5.

27. Susan Blackmore, "Alien Abduction," *New Scientist* (November 19, 1994), 29-31.
28. Susan A. Clancy, *Abducted* (Cambridge, MA: Harvard University Press, 2005), 138-140.
29. Budd Hopkins, "The Faith-Based Science of Susan Clancy," Unknown Country, December 22, 2005, http:// http://www.unknowncountry.com /insight/faith-based-science-susan-clancy-budd-hopkins.
30. Timothy Good, *Alien Contact* (New York: Morrow, 1993), 65.
31. Emmanuel Dehlinger, "A Colorado Case Study," trans. George Hoskins, 2003, https://www.ovnis-armee.org/prologue_ufos_book.htm.
32. Good, *Alien Contact*, 67–68.
33. Kelleher and Knapp, *Hunt for the Skinwalker*, 183–184.
34. Brent Swancer, "High Strangeness at the Mysterious Bradshaw Ranch," *Mysterious Universe*, July 30, 2018, https://mysteriousuniverse.org/2018 /07/high-strangeness-at-the-mysterious-bradshaw-ranch.
35. Linda Bradshaw and Tom Dongo, *Merging Dimensions: The Opening Portals of Sedona* (Flagstaff, AZ: Light Technology, 1995), 11–12.
36. Swancer, "High Strangeness."
37. Kelleher and Knapp, *Hunt for the Skinwalker*, 208.
38. George Knapp, interview, *Coast to Coast AM*, September 11, 2018, https:// www.coasttocoastam.com/show/2018/09/11.
39. Kelleher and Knapp, *Hunt for the Skinwalker*, 208.
40. Ibid., 250.
41. George Knapp, *Coast to Coast AM Insider Chat*, July 18, 2018.
42. Keel, *Operation Trojan Horse*, 45.
43. Vallée, *UFOs*, 199–200, 209.
44. Mack, *Abduction*, 397, 399, 407–409, 415.
45. Kathleen Marden, "Psychological Studies on Abduction Experiencers," http:// www.kathleen-marden.com/psychological-studies.php.
46. Jenny Randles, "Position Statement" in *The Encyclopedia of Extraterrestrial Encounters*, edited by Ronald D. Story (New York: New American Library, 2001), 459.
47. Robert Monroe, *Journeys Out of the Body* (New York: Doubleday, 1971), 202–203.
48. Jon Klimo, *Channeling* (Los Angeles: Tarcher, 1987), 53.
49. Lex Lonehood, "Spotlight On: Dr. George King," *Coast to Coast AM*, January 23, 2003, https://www.coasttocoastam.com/show/2003/01/23.
50. Klimo, *Channeling*, 56; Lynn Picknett and Clive Prince, "Behind the Mask: Aliens or Cosmic Jokers," *New Dawn Magazine*, special issue no. 17 (2011).
51. Klimo, *Channeling*, 66.
52. J. J. Hurtak, "Keys of Enoch Overview," https://keysofenoch.org /teachings/overview.
53. James J. Hurtak, *The Book of Knowledge: The Keys of Enoch* (Los Gatos, CA: Academy for Future Science, 1977), 116.
54. Laura Knight-Jadczyk, *High Strangeness: Hyperdimensions and the Process of Alien Abduction* (Otto, NC: Red Pill Press, 2008), 140, 152, 155–156.

55. Ibid., 144.

56. Michael Harner, *The Way of the Shaman*, 3rd ed. (San Francisco: HarperCollins, 1990), 27–29.

CHAPTER NINE: LUCID DREAMING

1. Andrew Holecek, *Dream Yoga* (Boulder, CO: Sounds True, 2016), 6.

2. Frederik van Eeden, "A Study of Dreams," *Proceedings of the Society for Psychical Research* 26 (1913).

3. Stephen LaBerge, *Lucid Dreaming* (New York: Ballantine, 1985), 73.

4. Keith Hearne, *The Dream Machine: Lucid Dreams and How to Control Them* (London: Aquarian Press, 1990), 11.

5. Benjamin Svetkey, "Some People Are Using Lucid Dreams to Be More Productive While They Sleep," Details.com, August 18, 2014, https://www .businessinsider.com.au/inside-lucid-dreaming-2014-8.

6. David Jay Brown, *Dreaming Wide Awake* (Rochester, VT: Park Street Press, 2016), 92.

7. Kelly Bulkeley, "Lucid Dreaming by the Numbers," in *Lucid Dreaming: New Perspectives on Consciousness in Sleep*, Vol. 1 (Santa Barbara, CA: Praeger, 2014), 1–22.

8. Jeff Warren, *Head Trip* (Oxford, UK: Oneworld, 2008), 143, 149.

9. LaBerge, *Lucid Dreaming*, 172.

10. Kenneth Kelzer, *The Sun and the Shadow* (Virginia Beach, VA: A.R.E. Press: 1987), 145.

11. Holecek, *Dream Yoga*, 19–22.

12. Charles Q. Choi, "Am I Asleep? A Jolt to the Brain Can Trigger Lucid Dreams," *Popular Mechanics*, May 12, 2014, https://www.popularmechanics .com/science/health/a10481/a-jolt-to-the-brain-can-trigger-lucid-dreams -16785550/.

13. Marc Kaufman, "Meditation Gives Brain a Charge, Study Finds," *Washington Post*, January 3, 2005, http://www.washingtonpost.com /wp-dyn/articles/A43006-2005Jan2.html.

14. Laura Sanders, "Brain Waves May Focus Attention and Keep Information Flowing," *Science News*, March 13, 2018, https://www.sciencenews.org/article /brain-waves-may-focus-attention-and-keep-information-flowing.

15. Susannah Locke, "Scientists Find Switch for People to Control Their Dreams," Vox, May 11, 2014, https://www.vox.com/2014/5/11/5707204 /scientists-switch-on-lucid-dreaming.

16. SpaceTimeBadass (James S. Bray), "LucidCatcher Review," July 8, 2017, https://www.youtube.com/watch?v=HDvu6_Q7Kus&feature=youtu.be&t=1m47s; "InstaDreamer: This Year's Lucid Dreaming Kickstarter Device," August 6, 2018, https://www.facebook.com/notes/spacetimebadass-james-s -bray/instadreamer-this-years-lucid-dreaming-kickstarter-device /1025695164275686/.

17. Lucid Dreamer website: https://www.luciddreamer.com.

18. Pete Dockrill, "A New Method for Having Lucid Dreams Has Been Discovered by Scientists," Science Alert, August 21, 2018, https://www .sciencealert.com/scientists-figured-out-new-technique-having-lucid -dreams-acetylcholine-galantamine-alzheimer-s-drug.

19. LaBerge, *Lucid Dreaming*, 155–156.

20. A. Roger Ekirch, *At Day's Close, Night in Times Past* (London: Norton, 2005), 300–301.

21. Stephen LaBerge and Howard Rheingold, *Exploring the World of Lucid Dreaming* (New York: Ballantine, 1990), 41.

22. Paul Tholey, "Overview of the Development of Lucid Dream Research in Germany," *Lucidity Letter*, 10th anniversary issue (1991): 9–10.

23. Robert Waggoner, *Lucid Dreaming: Gateway to the Inner Self* (New York: Chartwell Books, 2016), 12.

24. Warren, *Head Trip*, 123.

25. Waggoner, *Lucid Dreaming*, 276.

26. Stephen LaBerge, "Prolonging Lucid Dreams," *NightLight* 7, no. 3–4 (1995), http://www.lucidity.com/NL7.34.RU.SpinFlowRub.html.

27. Waggoner, *Lucid Dreaming*, 36–37.

28. Patricia Garfield, *Pathway to Ecstasy: The Way of the Dream Mandala* (n.p.: Prentice Hall, 1990), 44–45.

29. Beverly D'Urso, "The Ethics of Dream Sex," paper presented at the conference of the International Association for the Study of Dreams (IASD), Berkeley, CA, June 2005, http://durso.org/beverly/IASD05_The_Ethics_of_Dream_Sex .html.

30. LaBerge and Rheingold, *Exploring the World*, 177–178.

31. LaBerge, *Lucid Dreaming*, 173.

32. Waggoner, *Lucid Dreaming*, 156.

33. Quoted in Svetkey, "Some People."

34. Patricia Garfield, *The Healing Power of Dreams* (New York: Fireside, 1992), 256.

35. Ed Kellogg, "Lucid Dream Healing Experiences: Firsthand Accounts," Reality Sandwich, 2013, http://realitysandwich.com/175481/lucid_dream _healing_accounts/.

36. Waggoner, *Lucid Dreaming*, 126–127.

37. Deirdre Barrett, "The Dream Character as Prototype for the Multiple Personality Alter," *Dissociation* 8, no. 1 (March 1995): 61.

38. Jeremy Taylor, *Dream Work* (New York: Paulist Press, 1983), 215.

39. *The Lucid Dream Exchange* (December 1992): 18 (cited by Waggoner, *Lucid Dreaming*, 47).

40. Brown, *Dreaming Wide Awake*, 218, 224.

41. Waggoner, *Lucid Dreaming*, 222, 257.

42. Ibid., 56.

43. Kelzer, *The Sun and the Shadow*, 212–213.

44. Waggoner, *Lucid Dreaming*, 17.

45. Ibid., 52–54.

46. Brown, *Dreaming Wide Awake*, 331.

47. Lynne Levitan and Stephen LaBerge, "Other Worlds: Out-of-Body Experiences and Lucid Dreams," *NightLight* 3, no. 2–3 (1991), http://www.lucidity.com/NL32.OBEandLD.html.

48. LaBerge, *Lucid Dreaming*, 235.

49. Brown, *Dreaming Wide Awake*, 282.

50. Lucy Gillis, "Simultaneous Dreaming and the Lucidity Advantage," 2012, http://www.dreaminglucid.com/wp-content/uploads/2015/05/Simultaneous-Dreaming-and-the-Lucidity-Advantage.pdf.

51. Kelzer, *The Sun and the Shadow*, 118–124.

52. Holecek, *Dream Yoga*, 154.

53. Garfield, *Healing Power*, 162.

54. Holecek, *Dream Yoga*, 260.

55. La Berge, *Lucid Dreaming*, 176–178.

56. Kelzer, *The Sun and the Shadow*, xxiv, 245–246.

57. Ryan Hurd, "Unearthing the Paleolithic Mind in Lucid Dreams," in *Lucid Dreaming: New Perspectives on Consciousness in Sleep*, Vol. 1 (Santa Barbara, CA: Praeger, 2014), 300.

58. Jayne Gackenbach and Jane Bosveld, *Control Your Dreams* (New York: HarperCollins, 1990), 129–134.

59. Ibid., 124.

60. Ryan Hurd, "Lucid Nightmares: The Dark Side of Self-Awareness," presentation at the annual conference of the International Association for the Study of Dreams, Chicago, IL, June 27, 2009, https://www.academia.edu/34277759/Lucid_Nightmares_the_Dark_Side_of_Self-Awareness_in_Dreams.

61. Frederik van Eeden, *The Bride of Dreams*, trans. Mellie von Auw (Fairfield, IA: 1st World Library, 2007), 143.

62. Waggoner, *Lucid Dreaming*, 62–63.

63. Mark Barroso, letter to the editor, *Lucidity Letter* 6, no. 2 (December 1987).

64. Nick Baumann, "Loughner Friend Explains Alleged Gunman's Grudge against Giffords," *Mother Jones*, January 10, 2011, https://www.motherjones.com/politics/2011/01/jared-lee-loughner-friend-voicemail-phone-message/.

65. Christopher Beam, "Logic Puzzle," *Slate*, January 10, 2011, https://slate.com/news-and-politics/2011/01/kent-slinker-jared-lee-loughner-s-philosophy-professor-on-the-shooting-in-arizona.html.

66. A. J. Daulerio, "Lucid Dreams Deferred: Jared Loughner's Extraordinary Email Madness," Gawker, November 9, 2012, http://gawker.com/5959006/lucid-dreams-deferred-jared-loughners-extraordinary-email-madness.

67. "Jared Lee Loughner Biography," Biography.com, https://www.biography.com/people/jared-lee-loughner.

68. Bruce G. Marcot, "A Journal of Attempts to Induce and Work with Lucid Dreams," http://www.sawka.com/spiritwatch/ajournal.htm.

69. Vincent MacTiernan, letter to the editor, *Lucidity Letter* 6, no. 2 (December 1987).

70. Ed Kellogg, "Alien Encounters, Lucid Dreams, and OBEs," *Lucid Dreaming Experience* 3, no. 4 (March 2015): 8–12, https://www.academia .edu/35871738/Alien_Encounters_Lucid_Dreams_and_OBEs.
71. Carlos Castaneda, *The Art of Dreaming* (New York: HarperCollins, 1993), 88–89.

Recommended Reading

Abduction: Human Encounters with Aliens by John Mack. New York: Scribner, 1994.

Angels and Aliens by Keith Thompson. New York: Fawcett Columbine, 1991.

The Art of Dreaming by Carlos Castaneda. New York: HarperCollins, 1993.

Channeling by Jon Klimo. Los Angeles: Tarcher, 1987.

Confessions of an English Opium-Eater and Other Writings by Thomas De Quincey. New York: Penguin, 2003.

Control Your Dreams by Jayne Gackenbach and Jane Bosveld. New York: HarperCollins, 1990.

Creative Dreaming by Patricia Garfield. New York: Simon and Schuster, 1975.

Dark Intrusions by Louis Proud. San Antonio: Anomalist Books, 2009.

Dream Worlds by Stuart Holroyd. Garden City, NY: Doubleday, 1976.

Dream Yoga by Andrew Holecek. Boulder, CO: Sounds True, 2016.

Dreamgates: Exploring the Worlds of Soul, Imagination, and Life Beyond Death by Robert Moss. Novato, CA: New World Library, 1998.

Dreaming as Delirium by J. Allan Hobson. Cambridge, MA: MIT Press, 1999.

Dreaming Wide Awake by David Jay Brown. Rochester, VT: Park Street Press, 2016.

Dreamland by David K. Randall. New York: Norton, 2012.

The Encyclopedia of Extraterrestrial Encounters edited by Ronald D. Story. New York: New American Library, 2001.

Exploring the World of Lucid Dreaming by Stephen LaBerge, and Howard Rheingold. New York: Ballantine, 1990.

The Family That Couldn't Sleep by D. T. Max. New York: Random House, 2006.

Hair of the Alien by Bill Chalker. New York: Paraview Pocket Books, 2005.

Hallucinations by Oliver Sacks. New York: Knopf, 2012.

The Haunted Mind by Nandor Fodor. New York: Garrett, 1959.

Head Trip by Jeff Warren. Oxford, UK: Oneworld, 2008.

High Strangeness: Hyperdimensions and the Process of Alien Abduction by Laura Knight-Jadczyk. Otto, NC: Red Pill Press, 2008.

Hunt for the Skinwalker by Colm Kelleher and George Knapp. New York: Paraview Pocket Books, 2005.

Hypnagogia by Andreas Mavromatis. London: Thyrsos Press, 2010.

Into the Fringe by Karla Turner. New York: Berkley, 1992.

Journeys Out of the Body by Robert Monroe. Garden City, NY: Doubleday, 1971.

Kellogg, Ed. Published papers: http://duke.academia.edu/EdKellogg.

Left in the Dark by Tony Wright and Graham Gynn. Cornwall, UK: Kaleidos Press: 2008.

Lucid Dreaming by Stephen LaBerge. New York: Ballantine, 1985.

Lucid Dreaming: Gateway to the Inner Self by Robert Waggoner. New York: Chartwell Books, 2016.

Mind Monsters: Invaders from Inner Space? by Jenny Randles. London: Aquarian Press, 1990.

The Nightmare by Ernest Hartmann. New York: Basic Books, 1984.

Nightmares: How to Make Sense of Your Darkest Dreams by Alex Lukeman. New York: M. Evans and Company, Inc., 2000.

Operation Trojan Horse by John Keel. Lilburn, GA: Illuminet Press, 1996.

Passport to Magonia by Jacques Vallée. Chicago: Regnery, 1969.

Phantasms of the Living, Vol. 1 & 2 by Edmund Gurney, F. W. H. Myers, and Frank Podmore. London: Trübner, 1886.

Practical Psychic Self-Defense by Robert Bruce. Charlottesville, VA: Hampton Roads, 2002.

The Presence of Other Worlds: The Findings of Emmanuel Swedenborg by Wilson Van Dusen. New York: Harper and Row, 1974.

Psychic Dreamwalking by Michelle Belanger. San Francisco: Red Wheel/ Weiser, 2006.

Psychic Self-Defense by Dion Fortune. York Beach, ME: Weiser, 2001.

A Secret History of Consciousness by Gary Lachman. Great Barrington, MA: Lindisfarne Books, 2003.

The Secret Life of Sleep by Kat Duff. New York: Atria Books, 2014.

Sleep: The Mysteries, the Problems, and the Solutions by Carlos H. Schenck. New York: Avery, 2007.

Sleep Demons: An Insomniac's Memoir by Bill Hayes. New York: Pocket Books, 2001.

Sleep Paralysis by Shelley R. Adler. New Brunswick, NJ: Rutgers University Press, 2011.

Sleep Paralysis by Ryan Hurd. Los Altos, CA: Hyena Press, 2011.

Sleepsex: Uncovered by Michael Mangan. Bloomington, IN: Xlibris, 2001.

The Sun and the Shadow by Kenneth Kelzer. Virginia Beach, VA: A.R.E. Press, 1987.

The Terror That Comes in the Night by David J. Hufford. Philadelphia: University of Pennsylvania Press, 1982.

The Twenty-Four-Hour Mind by Rosalind D. Cartwright. Oxford University Press, 2010.

Van Winkle's. Website articles archived at https://web.archive.org /web/20180224020505/http://vanwinkles.com/news.

INDEX